M000218285

# ANCIENT GREECE, MODERN PSYCHE

Between Ancient Greece and modern psyche lies a divide of not only three thousand years, but of two cultures that are worlds apart in art, technology, economics, and the accelerating flood of historical events. This unique collection of essays from an international selection of contributors offers compelling evidence for the natural connection and relevance of ancient myth to contemporary psyche, and emerges from the second *Ancient Greece, Modern Psyche* conference held in Santorini, Greece, in 2012.

This volume is a powerful homecoming for those seeking a living connection between the psyche of the ancients and our modern psyche. The book looks at eternal themes such as love, beauty, death, suicide, dreams, ancient Greek myths, the Homeric heroes, and the stories of Demeter, Persephone, Apollo, and Hermes as they connect with themes of the modern psyche. The contributors propose that the link between them lies in the underlying archetypal patterns of human behavior, emotion, image, thought, and memory.

*Ancient Greece, Modern Psyche: Archetypes Evolving* makes clear that an essential part of deciphering our dilemmas resides in a familiarity with Western civilization's oldest stories about our origins, our suffering, and the meaning or meaninglessness in life. It will be of great interest to Jungian psychotherapists, academics, and students as well as scholars of classics and mythology.

**Virginia Beane Rutter**, MA, MS, and **Thomas Singer**, MD, are both Jungian psychoanalysts affiliated with the C. G. Jung Institute in San Francisco who have life-long connections to Greek culture. They are co-authors and editors of a previous volume of *Ancient Greece, Modern Psyche* which originated from the first Nomikos Conference in Santorini. Beane Rutter studies ancient myths and rites of passage through art, archaeology, and psychology and writes about the archetype of initiation as it appears in the clinical work of individuals today. Singer has produced and written multiple publications that focus on "the cultural complex." He currently serves as President of the National Board of ARAS (the Archive for Research in Archetypal Symbolism).

# ANCIENT GREECE, MODERN PSYCHE

## Archetypes Evolving

*Edited by Virginia Beane Rutter and Thomas Singer*

For Peggy —
With love
and admiration —
Virginia Beane Rutter
5/23/15

**R Routledge**
Taylor & Francis Group

LONDON AND NEW YORK

First published 2015 by Routledge
27 Church Road, Hove, East Sussex, BN3 2FA

and by Routledge
711 Third Avenue, New York, NY 10017

*Routledge is an imprint of the Taylor & Francis Group, an informa business*

© 2015 Virginia Beane Rutter and Thomas Singer

The right of the editors to be identified as the authors of the editorial
material, and of the authors for their individual chapters, has been asserted
in accordance with sections 77 and 78 of the Copyright, Designs and
Patents Act 1988.

All rights reserved. No part of this book may be reprinted or reproduced or
utilised in any form or by any electronic, mechanical, or other means, now
known or hereafter invented, including photocopying and recording, or in
any information storage or retrieval system, without permission in writing
from the publishers.

*Trademark notice*: Product or corporate names may be trademarks or
registered trademarks, and are used only for identification and explanation
without intent to infringe.

*British Library Cataloguing in Publication Data*
A catalogue record for this book is available from the British Library

*Library of Congress Cataloging in Publication Data*
Ancient Greece, modern psyche : archetypes evolving / edited by Virginia
Beane Rutter and Thomas Singer.
pages cm
1. Social psychology—Greece—History. 2. Civilization, Modern.
3. Archetypes in civilization. I. Rutter, Virginia Beane. II. Singer, Thomas,
1942-
HM1027.G8A53 2015
302.09495—dc23
2014040269

ISBN: 978-0-415-71431-0 (hbk)
ISBN: 978-0-415-71432-7 (pbk)
ISBN: 978-1-315-73119-3 (ebk)

Typeset in Times New Roman
by Swales & Willis, Exeter, Devon, UK

Printed and bound in the United States of America by
Edwards Brothers Malloy on sustainably sourced paper

FOR PETER, NAFTALI, AND MELINA
WITH ALL MY HEART . . .
Virginia Beane Rutter

FOR JANE WHO IS THE LOVE OF MY LIFE . . .
Thomas Singer

# CONTENTS

# CONTENTS

# FIGURES

# EDITORS

**Virginia Beane Rutter, MA, MS,** is a Jungian analyst who trained at the C. G. Jung Institutes of Zurich and San Francisco. Her first master's degree in art history (University of California, Berkeley) and an early sustaining love of Greece developed into a passion for studying ancient myths and rites of passage through art, archaeology, and psychology. These studies grew out of her clinical practice and coalesced around archetypal themes of initiation as they manifest in the unconscious material of women and men today. She is the author of three books, including *Woman Changing Woman: Restoring the Mother–Daughter Relationship* (HarperCollins, 1993, and Spring, 2009); *Celebrating Girls: Nurturing and Empowering Our Daughters* (Conari Press, 1996); and *Embracing Persephone: How to Be the Mother You Want for the Daughter You Cherish* (Kodansha, 2000, Conari Press, 2001). Her article, "The Archetypal Paradox of Feminine Initiation in Analytic Work," is a chapter in *Initiation: The Living Reality of an Archetype* (Routledge, 2007), which she co-edited with Thomas Kirsch and Thomas Singer; and her article "Saffron Offering and Blood Sacrifice: Transformation Mysteries in Jungian Analysis," is a chapter in the first volume of *Ancient Greece, Modern Psyche: Archetypes in the Making* (Spring, 2011), which she co-edited with Thomas Singer.

**Thomas Singer, MD,** is a Jungian analyst and psychiatrist. After studying religion and European literature at Princeton University, he graduated from Yale Medical School and later trained at Dartmouth Medical Center and the C. G. Jung Institute of San Francisco. His writing includes articles on Jungian theory, politics, and psychology, and he has written and/or edited the following books: *Who's the Patient Here? Portraits of the Young Psychotherapist* (Oxford University Press, 1978, with Stuart Copans); *A Fan's Guide to Baseball Fever: The Official Medical Reference* (Elijim Publications, 1991, with Stuart Copans and Mitchell Rose); *The Vision Thing: Myth, Politics and Psyche in the World* (Routledge, 2000); *The Cultural Complex: Contemporary Jungian Perspectives on Psyche and Society* (Routledge, 2004, with Samuel L. Kimbles); *Initiation: The Living Reality of an Archetype* (Routledge, 2007, with Thomas Kirsch and

Virginia Beane Rutter); *Psyche and the City: A Soul's Guide to the Modern Metropolis* (Spring, 2010); *Ancient Greece, Modern Psyche: Archetypes in the Making* (Spring, 2011, with Virginia Beane Rutter), *Placing Psyche: Exploring Cultural Complexes in Australia* (Spring, 2011); and *Listening to Latin America: Exploring Cultural Complexes in Brazil, Chile, Colombia, Mexico, Uruguay, and Venezuela* (Spring, 2012).

# CONTRIBUTORS

**Jules Cashford, MA,** is a Jungian analyst from the Association of Jungian Analysts in London. She studied philosophy at St. Andrews University and post-graduate literature at Cambridge, where she was a Supervisor in Tragedy for some years. She has translated *The Homeric Hymns* from the Greek for Penguin Classics and is the author of *Gaia: From Goddess to Symbol* (The Gaia Foundation, 2011), *The Mysteries of Osiris* (Atalanta, 2010), *The Moon: Myth and Image* (Cassell Illustrated, 2003), and co-author of *The Myth of the Goddess: Evolution of an Image* (Penguin, 1993). She has made two films on the paintings of the Early Northern Renaissance Painter, Jan van Eyck. Originally a student of ancient Greek, she has a great love of Greece and of the wisdom of Greek mythopoeic thought.

**Ben Ferris** is a writer and director who was born in Sydney, Australia. He studied Latin and Classical Greek at the University of Sydney. In 1998, he graduated with First Class Honors in Classical Greek, after reconstructing the surviving fragments of the *Alexandros,* a play by the Athenian tragedian, Euripides. In 2000, Ben established the UBS Film School at the University of Sydney, which he ran from 2000 to 2004, and in 2004, he founded the Sydney Film School where he is currently Executive Director. Two of Ben's short films – *The Kitchen* and *Ascension* – have won awards, and in 2006, he was present as an international juror at the One Take Film Festival in Zagreb. *The Kitchen* attracted international critical acclaim by winning the Grand Prix at the inaugural Akira Kurosawa Memorial Short Film Festival held in Tokyo in 2005. He wrote and directed the film *Penelopa.*

**Donald Kalsched, PhD,** is a clinical psychologist and Jungian psychoanalyst in private practice in Albuquerque, New Mexico. He is a training analyst with the Inter-Regional Society of Jungian Analysts and lectures widely on the subject of his first book, *The Inner World of Trauma: Archetypal Defenses of the Personal Spirit* (Routledge, 1996). His second book, *Trauma and the Soul: Spiritual Aspects of Human Development and its Interruption* (Routledge, 2013), continues to explore the effects of trauma on the inner world. He and his wife, Robin, migrate yearly between Albuquerque and their home in Newfoundland,

Canada, where they spend the warmer six months of the year, surrounded by the luminous beauties of the northern Atlantic coastline.

**Melina Centomani Rutter, MFA,** is a writer, artist, teacher, and traveler. She earned a BA in Drama and Theatre Arts from Columbia University and an MFA in Creative Writing from the Inland Northwest Center for Writers in Spokane, Washington. An excerpt from her novel in progress, *These Girls Run After Darkness All the Days,* was recently published in chapbook form by The Head and the Hand Press. She writes for thebarking.com, works at Kala Art Institute in Berkeley, California, and is co-founder of the art collective MYTHS. She lives in the San Francisco Bay Area.

**Craig San Roque, PhD,** trained as an analyst in London with the SAP and has, since 1986, worked in Sydney and then in Central Australia as a psychologist for Health Services and for diverse Aboriginal organizations. His current focus is on projects specializing in European and indigenous interface and consulting and supervising professionals involved in mental health, drug and alcohol dependence, indigenous governance, intercultural communications, and Aboriginal land-development projects. He lives in Alice Springs, Australia. His publications and intercultural communication projects include *Brain Story, The Sugarman/Dionysos* – Alcohol Intoxication Project; *Trouble Story* – Diagnosis and Treatment of Young People; *Thinking about Young People* projects with Andrew Spence Japaljarri; *Arresting Orestes* on bicultural law issues in Central Australia; "Coming to Terms with the Country" in *The Geography of Meanings: Psychological Perspectives on Place, Space, Land, and Dislocation* (Karnac Books, 2007); and "On Tjukurrpa and Building Thought" in *Explorations in Psychoanalysis and Ethnography* (Berghahn Books, 2007). He has contributed to four books edited by Tom Singer et al., on complex psychocultural themes, including *The Vision Thing* (Routledge, 2000), *The Cultural Complex* (Routledge, 2004), *Psyche and the City* (Spring, 2010), and *Placing Psyche* (Spring, 2011). *The Long Weekend,* his chapter from *The Cultural Complex,* was adapted into the first Jungian graphic novel by Joshua Santospirito.

**Richard Trousdell, DFA,** is a Jungian analyst in Northampton, Massachusetts, and Professor Emeritus of Theater at the University of Massachusetts-Amherst. He holds the Doctor of Fine Arts from the Yale School of Drama, where his dissertation was on the ethical role of women in Euripidean tragedy. He has lectured widely, including presentations at the 2009 Santorini Conference and at the 2010 Annual Conference of the National Association for the Advancement of Psychoanalysis in New York. His writings have appeared in *Yale Theater, The Drama Review,* the *Massachusetts Review,* and *Jung Journal: Culture & Psyche,* among others. His work on hero and victim complexes appeared in the first volume of *Ancient Greece, Modern Psyche* (Spring, 2011), also edited by Virginia Beane Rutter and Thomas Singer.

**Robin van Löben Sels, PhD,** is a Jungian analyst who trained at the C. G. Jung Institutes of Zurich and New York. Her early degrees were in literature and the arts, but she completed her doctoral work at Union Theological Seminary where she graduated with a MPhil and a PhD in psychiatry and religion. She is the author of *A Dream in the World: Poetics of Soul in Two Women, Modern and Medieval* (Brunner Routledge, 2003), *Wanting a Country for This Weather and Other Poems* (Mellen Press, 2003), and *Dreamwork(ing): A Primer* (Trout & Mountain Press, 2010).

# ACKNOWLEDGMENTS

Once again, the Peter Nomikos family made the *Ancient Greece, Modern Psyche* Conference possible by extending their wonderful generosity and hospitality to us in September 2012. The spectacular beauty of the Nomikos Conference Center in Santorini, Greece, inspired the participants to enter a liminal space where ancient myth and modern psyche could come alive.

The speakers and authors – Jules Cashford, Ben Ferris, Donald Kalsched, Melina Centomani Rutter, Robin van Löben Sels, Craig San Roque, and Richard Trousdell – unsparingly contributed their time and energy to bring imaginative creations to this project.

Baruch Gould applied his own unique eros to every aspect of planning and coordinating the event. And LeeAnn Pickrell gave the manuscript the care and attention to detail that good copy editing requires if a book is going to come together.

## Academic acknowledgments

### Chapter 2, Kalsched

Material in Chapter 2 from "The Importance of Beauty in the Psychoanalytic Experience" by Susan Reid, originally published in the *Journal of Child Psychotherapy* (1990, vol. 16, no. 1, 29–52) is reprinted by permission of Taylor & Francis.

### Chapter 4, Trousdell

Figures 4.1 and 4.2 © Soprintendenza per i Beni Archeologici dell'Etruria Meridionale.
Figure 4.3, the cover of Elizabeth Smith's dream manuscript © Estate of Elizabeth B. Smith, by permission.
Figure 4.4, Photograph of Sophie Scholl © 2014 Manuel Aicher, Dietikon (Switzerland).

## *Chapter 5, Cashford*

Figures 5.7, Hermes between sphinxes, and 5.10, Hermes flying ©The Trustees of the British Museum.

Figure 5.8, Hermes leading the Horai © Acropolis Museum, photo: Socrates Mavrommatis.

Figure 5.9, Hermes in his cradle, Hydrie de Caeré à figures noires / Peintre de l'aigle (6e siècle av. J.-C.) © RMN – Grand Palais (musée du Louvre) © Hervé Lewandowski.

# INTRODUCTION

*Dawn in her saffron robe rose from the*
*River of Ocean*
*To bring daylight to the immortals and to*
*men*
(Homer, *The Iliad*, 19.9)

Dawn blessed the second *Ancient Greece, Modern Psyche: Archetypes Evolving* Conference in both her symbolic and literal forms as we convened again in 2012 on the island of Santorini, ancient Thera. The Petros M. Nomikos Conference Center sits on the edge of a caldera, a huge crater that drops into the sea, formed by the volcanic eruption of ca.1627 BCE. The island shimmers with ancient Greek mythology. Thera was fabled by the ancient Greeks as Plato's lost kingdom of Atlantis. Thus appointed, the island offered us a unique opportunity to concentrate our studies.

Santorini's Bronze Age site of Akrotiri was first excavated in 1967 by the late Professor Spiro Marinatos.[1] Archaeologists found, preserved in the volcanic ash, beautiful frescoes, pots, and other objects that tell the stories and rituals of the people who thrived on the island before 1500 BCE. The frescoes show crocus-gathering festivals, men's and women's initiation rites, seafaring dramas, and fantastical landscapes. The Cycladic-Minoan style of painting in vivid ochres and Egyptian blues emanates a joyous life energy and emotional depth. Psyche, mana, and life-force fuse in depictions of plants, seas, mountains, and skies inhabited with animals, people, birds, and mythical creatures, with a goddess presiding over all. In this prehistoric unity, the deities were alive both inside and outside their human worshippers.[2]

As Jung said of classical Greek culture:

Everything had its demon, was animated by a human being, or like his brothers the animals. Everything was conceived anthropomorphically or theriomorphically, in the likeness of man or beast . . . Thus there arose a picture of the universe which was completely removed from reality, but which corresponded exactly to man's subjective fantasies.[3]

This vibrant, integrated inner and outer world phenomenon was even more fundamental in Greek Bronze Age culture.

Against this backdrop of spectacular natural beauty and Neolithic painted mysteries, participants and presenters gathered to discuss the influence of ancient Greek thought on the modern psyche. In an atmosphere designed to promote intimacy and dialogue, we delved into analytical psychology and its connection to the psychology of the ancient Greeks. The papers from the conference, collected and edited in this volume, reveal a psychological interpenetration of ancient myth, modern psyche and modern myth, ancient psyche. For the participants, Greek mythology came to life in the moment; they were intellectually and emotionally engaged. Each paper demonstrates in a different way how mythological motifs well up from the psyches of modern men and women undergoing psychotherapy with healing intent for the individual or the culture.

The root of the ancient Greek word *myth*/μυθος (μυθαρευομαι) means to speak or to relate fabulously; the word *mythistoria*/μυθιστορια means fabulous history; the word *mythographeo*/μυθογραφεω, to write fabulous accounts; the word *mythologeo*/μυθολογεω, to tell word for word or to tell mythic tales such as those of Homer, which came out of an oral tradition. *Mythology*/μυθολογια then becomes the tales in which the heroic stories of men and women and the gods and goddesses as well as the origin myths of ancient Greek civilization were told. *Mythos*/μυθος also meant word or speech, tale, story, or narrative.[4]

For the Greeks, mythology mapped out their entire cosmos; human behavior was mirrored in that of the gods and goddesses and vice versa. Human motivations and intentions were attributable to the god or goddess who tended that arena of life. Human beings also were at the mercy of the whims of the gods and goddesses and were constantly attempting to win favor by making sacrifices and offering suitable prayers. For Jung, mythology reveals the archetypes of the collective unconscious. Jung speaks of

> the tremendous richness and vitality of Greek mythology. All the creative power that modern man pours into science and technics [technology], the man of antiquity devoted to his myths. This creative urge explains the bewildering confusion, the kaleidoscopic changes and syncretistic regroupings, the continual rejuvenation, of myths in Greek culture.[5]

Jung's description of the plastic nature of Greek mythology applies to the evolution of the archeype over time, which the papers in this book address. The mythological archetypes that arise "are read for their symbolic value . . . putting the personal problem in the wider context of the archetypal world which is mediated by the symbol[6] . . . and lifts the individual out of himself and connects him with humanity."[7]

The soul creates symbols out of the inner world grounded in the unconscious archetype, but the symbols manifest in images familiar to our conscious mind. Jung says:

The archetypes are the numinous structural elements of the psyche and possess a certain autonomy and specific energy which enables them to attract, out of the conscious mind, those contents which are best suited to themselves. The symbols act as *transformers,* their function being to convert libido from a "lower" to a "higher" form . . . The symbol works by suggestion; that is to say, it carries conviction. It is able to do this because of the numen, the specific energy stored up in the archetype. Experience of the archetype is not only impressive, it seizes and possesses the whole personality.[8]

The conscious mind of the ancient Greek man or woman was oriented according to his or her upbringing and cultural exposure to the community. Yet, the archetypes that animated Greek mythology and the Greek unconscious continue to appear today in modern guises, changed to suit modern needs. Mythology abides, carrying the archetypes forward.

The drastic change in culture that has occurred over the last 2,000 years through science and technology is opposite to the Neolithic Minoan-Cycladic life of the interconnectedness of all beings. Jung says:

. . . our world has become dehumanized. Man feels himself isolated in the cosmos. He is no longer involved in nature and has lost his emotional participation in natural events which hitherto had symbolic meaning for him. Thunder is no longer the voice of a god, nor is lightning his avenging missile. No river contains a spirit, no tree means a man's life, no snake is the embodiment of wisdom, and no mountain still harbors a great demon. Neither do things speak to him nor can he seek to speak to things, like stones, springs, plants, and animals. He no longer has a bush-soul identifying him with a wild animal. His immediate communication with nature is gone for ever, and the emotional energy it generated has sunk into the unconscious.[9]

This vast loss is compensated by the work done in deep psychotherapy as the symbols arising from the unconscious are illuminated in the analytic relationship – images that appear either in dreams or other unconscious material. An archetype manifests when feeling and image collide. As Jung indicates, "if the image is charged with numinosity, that is, with psychic energy then it becomes dynamic, and will produce consequences."[10] As the psychological truth of the symbol is unmasked, the archetype serves a purpose in the individuation of the person or the culture.

Each of the papers in this volume addresses the value of specific ancient Greek myths and their archetype or archetypes as they arise in a modern context. In "The hero who would not die: warrior and goddess in ancient Greek and modern men," I examine elements of the heroic archetype and the archetype of death, dramatized in the epics of *The Iliad* and *The Odyssey,* as they were activated in the psyches of three men – one man in World War I and two men in World War II. In the Trojan War, the heroes Achilles, Odysseus, and Herakles, and their patron goddesses,

Athena, Hera, and Artemis, are archetypes that energized the actions and traumas of the modern men, both in war and in their families. The paper demonstrates the changing myth of the hero and points the way to the post-heroic archetype as described by Joseph Henderson in *Thresholds of Initiation*.[11]

In "Death and necessity at the threshold of new life," Richard Trousdell draws upon the dramatic images of *Thanatos* and *Ananke* in the *Alcestis* of Euripides, tracing how Death and Necessity enter life to end one sense of being and to open new ones. Whether in physical life or the life of the spirit, the death of a person or the death of an attitude, the necessity of death initiates a deepening of life experience that is central to tragic action and to psychological individuation. Trousdell layers these archetypes within the context of a mythical marriage and that of the coniunctio of analysis in a dream sequence of a modern woman approaching her literal death and its symbolic promise of renewal.

In "Dreaming in place: Santorini, Greece," Robin van Löben Sels offers a model of how the dream psyche embodies what Jung described as being lost to modern men and women: a connection to nature. Through dreams van Löben Sels activates the mythopoetic imagination as it might have been alive in the Akrotirian Greeks on Thera 3,000 years ago. As she explores the liminal space between conscious and unconscious psyche, she unearths the archetype of Hestia, the Greek goddess of hearth and fire.

Ancient Greek mythology begets mysteries, and mysteries endure and beget meaning. One inscription at Eleusis, site of the Demeter-Kore mysteries for 2,000 years, reads: "There are holy things that are not communicated all at once: Eleusis always keeps something back to show those who come again."

*Virginia Beane Rutter*

## JOURNEY TO SANTORINI

### A homecoming to the mythic vision

In September 2012, I traveled to the second *Ancient Greece, Modern Psyche* Conference on Santorini, Greece, under considerable personal duress. There was a serious illness in my family, and it was not clear whether I would be able to attend, although I wanted to be there as one of the conference conveners. As a compromise with wanting to be in two places at once, I arranged for a five-day trip to Greece, a ridiculously fast turnaround, and I had little expectation that I would enjoy it. Surprisingly, from the moment I arrived in Santorini, I felt myself transported to a liminal place of feeling, as though I was participating in the moment of creation, the sensation that Henry Miller wondrously, even outrageously, describes on visiting Phaestos in Crete in the *Colossus of Maroussi*:

> I sent out a benediction in every direction – to old and young, to the neglected savages in the forgotten places of the earth, to wild as well as domesticated

animals, to the birds of the air, to creeping things, to trees and plants and flowers, to rocks and lakes and mountains. This is the first day of my life, said I to myself, that I have included everybody and everything on this earth in one thought. I bless the world, every inch of it, every living atom, and it is all alive, breathing like myself, and conscious through and through . . . At the very gates of Paradise the descendents of Zeus halted here (Phaestos) on their way to eternity to cast a last look earthward and saw with the eyes of innocents that the earth is indeed what they had always dreamed it to be: a place of beauty and joy and peace. In his heart man is angelic; in his heart man is united with the whole world. Phaestos contains all the elements of the heart; it is feminine through and through. Everything that man has achieved would be lost were it not for this final stage of contrition which is here incarnated in the abode of the heavenly queens.[12]

Almost invariably, something inside me opens to a timeless feeling of well being when I am in Greece. And, thrilling to me, those who attended the meeting at the Nomikos Conference Center in Santorini seemed to open to something numinous and creative. The conference papers and participants were exceptional; I was privileged to serve as the moderator. For me, to be present at the inaugural delivery of these papers was, again, to participate in mythic creation. Myth and psyche held court together. This volume of essays offers compelling evidence for the natural connection and relevance of ancient myth to contemporary psyche. It is my hope that this book will make clear that an essential part of deciphering our dilemmas resides in a familiarity with Western civilization's oldest stories about our origins, our suffering, and the meaning or meaninglessness in life.

## Archetypes evolving

Our editors at Routledge charged us with the job of making clear to the reader why we think that the study of myth is relevant to contemporary psyche. Virginia Beane Rutter has addressed the Greek origin of the word *myth* and Jung's attitude toward mythology in the earlier part of the Introduction. I want to add to her comments a few thoughts about archetypes as evolving, rather than fixed, realities.

The notion of archetypes, like any idea, is susceptible to reification or reduction. But, along with Jung, Virginia Beane Rutter and I take the view that archetypes are elastic and shape shifting, that they are unknowable potentials in themselves that have a home in the brain's circuitry as well as psyche's thread. Archetypes evolve as culture evolves, an idea that to some will seem new and exciting and to others unacceptable, either because the whole notion of archetypes is suspect or because they are viewed as being fixed and eternal. But in *Answer to Job,* Jung himself affirmed the heretical notion that God is not a fixed being but, indeed, evolves with the evolution of humankind and the creation.[13] The second *Ancient Greece, Modern Psyche* Conference was a living example of "archetypes evolving."

## Recombinant visionary mythology

I like to think of the modern world and its multicultural psyche as being engaged in a process similar to the biology of recombinant genetics in which parts of DNA strands exchange genetic information to create new DNA sequences. I have called this phenomenon "recombinant visionary mythology" in which bits and pieces of archetypal material from different cultures are reshuffled to create new mythologies. We can see this, for example, when Jewish Americans embrace Buddhism with the resultant recombinant faith/person at times humorously referred to as the *BuJew*. A similar syncretism or hybridization can be observed when nonindigenous people adopt the dream time (*Alchuringa*) of Aborigines or when Aboriginals mix the faith of evangelical Christianity with shamanistic excursions into the Alchuringa.

Let's take a closer look at how the notion of "archetypes evolving" contributes to recombinant visionary mythology as a motif of the *Ancient Greece, Modern Psyche* papers. Between Ancient Greece and modern psyche lies a divide of not only 3,000 years but two cultures that are worlds apart in art, technology, economics, and the accelerating flood of historical events. Presumably, they are worlds apart in terms of psyche, so much so that we must ask, "What links them?" Our proposed answer is that the link lies in the underlying archetypal patterns of human behavior, emotion, image, thought, and memory.

Paradoxically, these patterns can be thought of as both fixed and changing over time. Fixedness resides in the common human situations that are unchanging over time, such as birth and death. The dynamic of change addresses the evolving human culture and environment that is in a state of perpetual movement. In response to dynamic movement, the archetypes themselves are capable of changing and of being recombined into new patterns in keeping with the exchange of genetic information in recombinant DNA that governs the basic patterns of living systems. Myths are capable of being revisioned and restructured over time to incorporate new modes of believing, thinking, and being. Jules Cashford's remarkable chapter, "How Hermes and Apollo came to love each other in the *Homeric Hymn to Hermes:* Imagination and Form in Ancient Greece and modern psyche," demonstrates how the myth of Hermes has undergone dramatic change within the history of Ancient Greece itself and then in subsequent historical evolution, especially in the Romantic poets. And Craig san Roque's retelling of the Kore/Persephone myth, *The Kore Story/Persephone's Dog* is an extraordinary example of recombinant visionary mythology in which the central myth of Ancient Greece has been adapted for the purpose of helping contemporary indigenous and nonindigenous peoples understand and undertake the Aborigines' transition from being a hunter-gatherer society to an agricultural society. His bold undertaking is stunningly creative.

## Homecoming: an example of an archetypal pattern evolving

A primary goal of the human journey is to complete the cycle of life, often by returning to one's origins. T. S. Eliot memorably wrote that we will know the place from which we started for the first time only at the end of our journey.[14]

Several papers in this volume show how prevalent the homecoming theme is and how it serves as a perfect example of both "archetypes evolving" and "recombinant visionary mythology."

In his hauntingly beautiful film, *Penelopa,* Ben Ferris, a young Australian filmmaker, borrows elements of the Bosnian war, draws out the feeling of the archetype of "waiting," and then transforms Homer's version of Odysseus' homecoming with a surprise ending. Melina Centomani Rutter reviews and interprets this film in her insightful chapter, "Penelope scapes." Both Penelope and Odysseus emerge as modern characters who are not entirely in keeping with their traditional identities or the original story's conventional, narrative trajectory. The homecoming that Virginia Beane Rutter narrates in "The hero who would not die: warrior and goddess in ancient Greek and modern men," is the deeply moving, personal story of her father's homecoming from World War II, a hero's return that echoes in the stories of many veterans who have returned from Korea, Vietnam, Iraq, and Afghanistan. Donald Kalsched's "Beauty and the psychoanalytic enterprise: reflections on a rarely acknowledged dimension of the healing process" describes vignettes from his analytic practice showing the experience of beauty with reference to the early Greek understanding of beauty's *daimonic* nature and its intimate relationship to the human soul. Here, the exquisite intimacy and beauty of psychic reality led to the patient's coming home to the Self, to wholeness.

In our first volume of *Ancient Greece, Modern Psyche,* Ronald Schenk hilariously retells the tale of Odysseus' homecoming in a chapter titled, "Bed, bath and beyond: the journey that is not a journey/the home that is not a home: psyche between home and homelessness in the *Odyssey.*"[15] Schenk's postmodern riff takes us on an escapade that turns Homer upside down, ruthlessly debunking the ancient vision of homecoming and reunited love between Odysseus and Penelope.

Homecoming echoes from Homer's Odysseus to modern American homecomings, whether they be from wars in the past century to touching home plate in baseball – the national pastime. Years ago I tried a bit of my own recombinant visionary mythologizing by designing a cartoon for *A Fan's Guide to Baseball Fever*[16] based on Odysseus' roundtrip journey to Ithaca and Bart Giamatti's journey "home" via his love of baseball. Giamatti, a former President of Yale University, turned in his cap and gown for a baseball cap when he became Commissioner of Major League Baseball. Baseball was a lifelong passion of Giamatti's, as was the study of romance literature, his academic field of expertise. Ironically, Giamatti's own journey "home" ended with a heart attack in the midst of an epic battle with Pete Rose, a great baseball player caught in a gambling scandal that is well documented in a perfectly named book, *Collision at Home Plate.*[17]

Giamatti summed up the archetype of homecoming in this comment:

So home is the goal – rarely glimpsed, almost never attained – of all the heroes descended from Odysseus – if baseball is a narrative, an epic of exile

xxiv

and return, a vast communal poem about separation, loss, and the hope for reunion – if baseball is a Romance epic – it is finally told by the audience. It is the Romance Epic of homecoming America sings to herself.[18]

Such new interpretations and recombinant visions of ancient myths can be provocative and controversial. The reunion of Penelope and Odysseus on his return to Ithaca after her long, patient waiting for him has been the story par excellence of love overcoming separation in a war-torn world. To see or hear this story transformed or reinterpreted to express a contemporary truth is challenging for those who are attached to the ancient vision. These chapters may seem a far cry from Henry Miller's ecstatic "homecoming" to Phaestos, yet each one emanates a conscious aliveness that parallels Miller's experience. And this volume is a powerful homecoming for those seeking a living connection between the psyche of the ancients and our modern psyche.

*Thomas Singer*

## Notes

1 When Marinatos died in 1976, Professor Christos Doumas took over the direction of the ongoing work.
2 Virginia Beane Rutter and Thomas Singer (eds) *Ancient Greece, Modern Psyche: Archetypes in the Making,* New Orleans, Spring Journal Books, 2011, chapters 1 and 2.
3 C. G. Jung, *Symbols of Transformation: The Collected Works of C. G. Jung,* Vol. 5, trans. R. F. C. Hull, Princeton, Princeton University Press, 1967, para. 24. Hereafter references to Jung's *Collected Works* will be indicated by CW followed by volume number.
4 Henry George Liddell and Robert Scott, *Liddell and Scott's Greek-English Lexicon,* Revised Ed., Oxford, Oxford University Press, 1940, pp. 1150–1.
5 Jung, *Symbols of Transformation,* CW 5, para. 24.
6 Jung, "The Tavistock Lectures," *The Symbolic Life,* CW 18, 1935/1976, para. 231.
7 Ibid., para. 232.
8 Jung, *Symbols of Transformation,* CW 5, para. 344.
9 Jung, "Symbols and the interpretation of dreams," *The Symbolic Life,* CW 18, 1961/1976, para 585.
10 Ibid., para 589.
11 Joseph Henderson, *Thresholds of Initiation,* Ashville, NC, Chiron Publications, 2005.
12 Henry Miller, *The Colossus of Maroussi,* San Francisco, Colt Press, 1941, pp. 140–1.
13 Jung, "Answer to Job," *Psychology and Religion: West and East,* CW 11, 1952/1969.
14 T. S. Eliot, "Little Gidding, V," *Four Quartets,* London, Faber and Faber Ltd., 2001, p. 43.
15 Rutter and Singer, *Ancient Greece, Modern Psyche,* 2011.
16 Thomas Singer and Stuart Copans, *A Fan's Guide to Baseball Fever: The Official Medical Reference,* Mill Valley, CA, Elijims Publications, 1991.
17 James Reston, *Collision at Home Plate: The Lives of Pete Rose and Bart Giamatti,* Lincoln, University of Nebraska Press, 1997.
18 Bart Giamatti, *Take Time for Paradise,* New York, Bloomsbury USA, 2011.

# INVOCATION
# DIONYSOS
# HOW IT ALL BEGAN

## A ritual invocation for the 2012
## *Ancient Greece, Modern Psyche* Conference

### *Craig San Roque*

*This is a retelling of the mythic origins of the Greek God Dionysos, relocated to the modern setting of Central Australia and presented as the invocation to the 2012* Ancient Greece, Modern Psyche *Conference at the Nomikos Conference Center in Santorini, Greece. For additional information about the creation and context of this invocation, please see the note.*[1]

### The first mother

A woman is sitting by a fire, the grandmother is sitting, the first mother, she does not move, the rivers move, the mountains move, she does not move. She is sitting where everything begins, she is sitting where everything comes out, everything comes out from her; smoke, mosquito, lizard, fish, snake, bird, kangaroo, dog, people; they all move but she does not move.

She laughs, she smiles, she cries, but she does not move; everything moves in and out of her but *she* does not move; she breathes, she sucks things in; they pass through her; stars, motor cars, me.

### Euronome

In the beginning night was dancing, she was dancing, you feel her in your blood dancing;

Who is that coming, dancing? that is my blood dancing on the water, before I was born.

1

Who is that coming? that is the wind dancing on the water before I was born; night on the water, snake on the water, dancing; before I was born;

What is that coming, shining on the water? an egg before I was born; before I was born, my father, a snake, my mother dancing, an egg burning on the water, shining and broken; all things dancing, coming out, coming out; my mother dancing on my own country.

## Kronos crow

Crow was the first one through, her first baby, her first son, her second husband too.
Who was her first husband? *Ouranos,* that big old snake in the beginning, he was the first father for all of us; where did he come from? he came out of the sky, he rolled the sky around, he came out of nothing, he rolled the sky around around, he took a shape, he took a name – *Ouranos* – father from the sky; *Ouranos* is father to crow, father to all crow's wild brothers, gigantic bellies beginning all our time; crow was the first little baby to fall out of mother, the first one through, the biggest shit of all; watch carefully, crow is grandfather to sugarboy, (*Dioniso*) know about crow, understand about sugarboy; know about crow; understand *Dioniso.*

(What shall we call him, crow said? call him *Dioniso,* the grandmother said, that sweet little juice out of crow's black belly.)

## Family violence

Crow is watching his father, crow is watching his mother; they explode like rocks, they fight; the mother and father fight, his father is killing the children, he throws them like rocks, they explode like stars, he digs holes, he buries them.

Crow's mother and father fight, they explode like fire, they make mountains, they make rivers, they make caves in the ground, they make fire, the water comes rushing, steam and smoke, the children rumble, the world is covered in mud and blood.

Crow sits watching the rolling trouble (his mother and father fighting and fucking), crow's head tucked under his wing, watching the rolling trouble, the mud and blood; this is how my mother and father do it, he says when I am big, I'll do it too.

Crow's mother calls him, she gives him a knife, a stone knife, white as crystal; here she says, I am sick of this, do something; crow watches his father, crow watches a snake, he takes the knife, his eye is sharp; his father comes down like a pile of mud.

Crow cries out; the old man's coming again, he rears up, he slides, rolling and coiling the father slops on the mother's belly; he rises, a snake hard to strike; the mother cries; the old man's coming again, do it, she says, do it now.

Crow is fast, fast as an eye, he comes between them, he cuts the snake, he slices the father, the world is covered in blood, his mother heaves like a river in flood; good she says, enough of him, now we can start again.

Crow looks at the knife, he looks at the mud boiling, he thinks about love.

## Crow incest babies

Crow is dancing with his mother, he dances the loverboy dance, the loverboy dance; am I big enough yet, he says, yes she says now you can be the father, now you make the babies, crow looks at the knife, he thinks about love.

Crow's mother squats on the ground, what's that coming, says crow; that's your baby; nice says crow, I'll look after him, I'll keep him warm, look says crow, I'll swallow him like this . . .

What's that coming; that's another baby, your little girl . . . nice, says crow, and swallows her; one two three four five crow swallows the babies all alive, just like that; nice says crow, I'll keep them safe and warm.

Swallowing his children, that's when crow's brain began – "split brain crow" they call him – he can think two different things at the same time and keep smiling at you; what juicy babies I have, he said, gobbling them up, they're nice and safe in my belly.

That's how the whitefeller mob began, crow's kids, that's us, that's how we began; true story, split brain, everything whitefellers do you got to watch the two sides; they swallow you all up, just like that; they keep smiling at you; this'll be good for you they say; yum yum.

## The one who got away

The mother was getting sick of it, she looks at the knife, she looks at crow; crow said, I love you let's have some more . . .

Another baby came, number six; the mother turned her back, crow's missus turned her back, she picked up a rock, she wrapped it in mud and blood,

3

she gave it to crow; here she said look after this one; crow did it nicely; he swallowed it . . . oh he said that was a big one, I'm full now; the mother turned her back; she hid the baby, the little lightning one, she hid him; she gave him to her sisters, here, she said, you look after him; the sisters looked after him in secret, they didn't let crow know where he was; crow didn't get to swallow that baby little lightning; oh no, he got away.

Crow swallowed the other five, he swallowed the cooking fire; he swallowed the seeds and fruit; he swallowed the power of order, he gobbled up women's affairs; he swallowed the power of water; he swallowed the powers underground, he swallowed the power of death; he did not swallow lightning; lightning makes life and life came back . . .

## Lightning and crow

The lightning baby grew up, he came back, he came travelling across the plain, rain and clouds travelling across the plain, the lightning boy, he came travelling, looking for his father, looking for crow; looking for his brothers and sisters, he was carrying something for crow, it was a trick.

Crow was sitting in a tree, he opened up his brain, he was looking inside, he was trying to dream himself some food; he was hungry.

The young man said, hello old man what you doing; I'm thinking said crow; the young man said, ok I brought you something; what's that, said crow; something good, something to drink, said lightning; what stuff, what stuff you got there, said crow; good stuff said the young man, really sweet; what . . . ? baby blood, really sweet; give me that, said crow; crow sipped it, hmmm . . . he said, really sweet.

He drank the lot, he drank it all at one go; it hit his belly like a bomb; he fell out of his tree, he hit the ground, he started vomiting, he vomited everywhere; those babies started jumping about, lightning boy was clever, he knew the right thing to do; he sang out to his brothers and sisters; jump he said, let's get out of here.

The brothers and sisters heard him, they were kicking around inside crow's belly, let's get out of here, they said; they chucked the rock out first; crow kept vomiting, the five of them jumped out covered with mud and blood; crow was rolling around on the ground; they looked at their father rolling, he was a mess; that must be our father, they said, ohh nooo, what a mess; you should give up drinking baby blood; they said.

4

Crow's children got back together, they grew up fast, they picked up rocks, they threw rocks at crow, they threw rocks at their father, we are sick of you, they said; piss off, they said, piss off; we'll be boss now.

Crow flew off, he flew north west, he flew vomiting all the way, his vomit hit the ground; he ended up in England; he settled down there; his vomit hit the ground all the way to England; where his vomit hit the ground; you know what happened? cities started up, Darwin Singapore Tokyo Bombay London . . . . crow stayed there a long time, he came back one day; he came back with captain cook.

that's it.

# Note

1 This retelling of the mythic origins of the Greek God Dionysos is part of a series of performance events developed experimentally within Australian Aboriginal settings from 1996 to 2000. Intoxication and dismemberment are central to the myth of Dionysos. Intoxication and dismemberment have also been a catastrophic consequence for the Aboriginal people of Australia as a result of the British colonization of that continent. These performance events were created as part of a bicultural project to address the problems of intoxication/dismemberment in a mythopoetic form that might speak to local Aboriginal people and to those of European descent.

The opening story "sung" by Craig San Roque as the "invocation" to the *Ancient Greece, Modern Psyche* Conference recounts the ancestry of Dionysos. The ancestral origin actions narrated in the invocation prefigure later actions of violence and sexual derangement that emerge in varied drunken states. These become repetitive acts of violence and derangement that are all too familiar to those who live in the proximity of breakdown.

In the adaptation of the Dionysos cycle for the Australian performance, Dionysos' name is tentatively translated as "Sugarman." This is because local indigenous language terms, such as *Wama, Nkwerle,* and *Parma,* are now used to refer to the European-produced substances of wine, beer, and alcohol. Originally such words referred to natural sweet substances found in flowers, plants, and insects. An Australian alias for Dionysos emerged as *Wati Wama* – man of sweetness – man of sugar – Sugarman.

Historically, the hunter-gatherer, desert-dwelling, indigenous Australians did not distill and manufacture alcohol except in a very mild form. More potent alcoholic intoxicants were introduced to the Australian Aborigines by the European colonization of the continent. In ancient Mediterranean/European cultures, the origin of wine and beers is attributed to mythic beings such as Dionysos, Zagreus, and Bakkos. In Australian indigenous culture, the origin of plants, animals, and cultural law are also attributed to the activities of mythic beings. In that sense, European and Aboriginal ancestral psychocultural mentalities are similar. In the narrative cycle of Dionysos adapted for the Aboriginal audience, the birth, life, and intoxication-carrying ventures of Dionysos are retold, as well as his travels and those of his later associates, including Ariadne. Composed as a poetic narrative accompanying the performance, the text is best recited aloud, enabling the reader to more fully enter the actual lyrical breath and emotional content of the story line. The rhythm and style is reminiscent of the patterns of Aboriginal-English local storytelling of Central Australia. The original text had no punctuation, being composed in short line phrases. For publication, the lines have been condensed into paragraph-like verse forms. Commas or semicolons, as an aid to recitation, mark the end of each significant phrase line.

# 1

# THE HERO WHO WOULD NOT DIE

## Warrior and goddess in Ancient Greek and modern men

*Virginia Beane Rutter*

My father was the hero who would not die, who during World War II flew a B-24 Liberator plane on so-called suicide missions to bomb the oil fields of Ploieşti, Romania. On 5 April 1944,[1] his plane was shot down, and he, along with his co-pilot, spent five months as prisoners of war, along with other Allied men, in two prisons, the last a converted schoolhouse in the town of Timisul del Sus.[2] As the squadron commander and the highest-ranking officer, a Major, my father was in charge of the other men in the prison. On the day he was shot down, beaten, and interrogated before being incarcerated, he wrote:[3]

> That night, as I lay on the bed waiting for the morrow, some half-remembered lines from John Milton's *Paradise Lost* ran through my mind and served to toughen my soul for the trying days ahead. After the war, I looked these lines up again to refresh my memory, and here they are:
>
>> What though the field be lost?
>> All is not lost; th' unconquerable will,
>> And study of revenge, immortal hate,
>> And courage never to submit or yield.
>>
>> (*Paradise Lost,* Book i, Lines 105–8)
>
> I kept those half-remembered lines in my mind all through my prison stay.

Four and a half months later, King Michael of Romania ordered the German commander, Colonel Alfred Gerstenberg (who had occupied Romania for four years), to remove the German Wehrmacht from Romanian soil. This set off days of murder and terror on the part of the Germans and prepared the way for the Russians, who proved to be even more brutal. Amid this chaos, the guards abandoned the

Allied prisoners. Emaciated and disoriented, the Allied men were 200 miles from the Yugoslavian border and 80 miles from the main prison at Bucharest to the south. An Army man from the camp appropriated some trucks, evacuated the prisoners, and deposited them in the village of Pietroşiţa, which was nine miles away from the main road along which the Germans were fleeing. Germans, Russians, and Romanians all shot at each other while the Germans tried to recapture the American POWs to use them as hostages during their retreat from Romania.

My father and one of his fellow prisoners who spoke German[4] forced a sentry at gunpoint to stop the first passing car that looked Romanian. This proved to be a limousine driven by Dr. Dimitrie Gerota. Fortuitously, Dr. Gerota was an esteemed doctor in the country, renowned for his humanitarian deeds.[5] Dr. Gerota, who was on his way to visit his wife and children at his summer house, took the two prisoners along, hiding them until he could get them to his Bucharest home. Then he arranged with the Minister of War to supply them with transportation to return to get the troops left at the schoolhouse. As their commanding officer, my father felt responsible for guiding them out of the bedlam. He and his buddy drove to pick up the remaining prisoners and then made their dangerous way back to the main prison in Bucharest.

All the Allied prisoners were eventually evacuated by a squadron of B-17s sent by the 15th Army Air Corps in Bari, Italy. There, after being stripped of the uniforms they had been wearing for months, deloused with DDT and debriefed, the bombing groups received a presidential citation from Franklin D. Roosevelt for their heroic bombing of the Ploieşti Oil Fields.

This was only one of the myriad stories – of harrowing flights, narrow escapes, and heroic actions – that my father told about his wartime experiences, which included "liberating" a B-17 from the US as a mercenary in the Arab–Israeli War in 1947/48 and serving in the Korean War until 1953, as I was growing up. He was proud of having been "a gold and glory boy," along with other men of his ilk who would do anything for the honor, fame, or money. After WWII, he requested to attend Commanding General Staff School and eventually retired from the service with the rank of Lieutenant Colonel.

Embedded in these stories was the code of honor that my father lived by as a war pilot – integrity and respect for the responsibilities and the rules in so far as they served the mission. Listening to each story over and over, I took in the subliminal awareness that war and flying had been the zenith of his life, that he had not feared dying, and that something in him regretted that he had not.

The other side of this heroic storytelling was the trauma my father exhibited in the years when he was home – the startle reflex and defensive position he assumed when hearing a loud noise, the nightmares during which he cried out, his aggressiveness toward any perceived slight from colleagues or authority figures, and periods of depression that increased as he grew older.

For years, questions floated around in the back of my mind: What had it all meant, my father's heroism and reveling in his service experience? Why did a hero then become an embittered man? What would it have been like if the diagnosis of post-traumatic stress disorder had existed when he finally left the service, "his nerves shot" after the Korean War? If he had gone into treatment with a good psychiatrist, instead of taking the increasing dosages of barbiturates the VA hospital doled out, could he have adjusted to civilian life and found fulfillment there?

Later, when reading Homer's *Iliad* and *Odyssey,* other questions arose. What does it mean to be a hero? Achilles died a heroic death whereas Odysseus, despite his valorous wanderings, died a decidedly unheroic one. To be a Greek hero, the warrior had to die fighting and thereby transcend his mortality. My father, although identified with the ancient archetypal ideal of the hero, did not die in combat and felt conflicted and incomplete. Some of the ancient Greek concepts of honor, glory, integrity, and duty to the polis or country resonated with my father's experience of war. I wondered why the goddesses and the feminine were such an important part of the action in the epics. I became intrigued with the goddess Fate/*Nemesis* and her counterpart Shame/*Aidos.* What role does the feminine play in heroism? And might that be a useful question for soldiers in treatment today as they return from active duty?

This essay is a meditation on these questions in the form of addressing the ancient Greek heroes – Herakles, Achilles, and Odysseus – and three modern men – two heroes of WWII and one of WWI.

***********

Beginning with the Bronze Age, heroes in Ancient Greece were "great men of a past age."[6] They were believed to have power over the living and, as a consequence, were worshipped alongside gods at shrines all over Greece. Each hero had a cult, and these cults developed independently of Homer and other early epic poets out of a social need. The worship of heroes allowed communities and groups to lay claim to the past.[7] The name of the prototypical Greek hero, Herakles, whose myths were rooted in Mycenae, means "the glory of Hera."[8]

The "gold and glory boys" of WWII, who volunteered for the most dangerous missions, pursued both "gold," which can be seen as money or treasure, as well as glory. The treasures or spoils of war, the geras/γερας that reflect the warrior's honor in wartime, lie at the heart of *The Iliad* and also are central to *The Odyssey* and its hero Odysseus, "the man of profit" who brings goods home from his 20-year journey that he wants to store as treasure. The Greek warrior's code of ethics and the laws and rules of his culture determined the treasure that was due.

Homeric morality originated from the idea that any individual's act only had meaning in relation to what he did to others. The Greek quality aidos/αιδως, shame or modesty, inhibited a person from violating this principle.[9] There were high standards of justice based on a soldier's sense of *dignity*. The heroic code praised the virtues of courage, allegiance, and magnanimity, and abhorred cowardice, treachery, and stinginess. This sense of dignity and decency belonged to the aristocratic virtue of the time.[10] In *The Iliad,* the first turning point in the narrative happens when the girl Brisēís, Achilles' war prize, is taken from him by Agamemnon,

9

insulting the younger man, "the best of the Achaeans." The commander's action is a breach of warrior etiquette.

One of my father's morality tales, tinged with humor, described an incident that occurred when he was evacuated from Bucharest to Italy. Before he boarded the plane, the Romanians gave him two suitcases of cash that had been taken from soldiers' "escape kits" while they were imprisoned in Romania. He felt honor-bound to turn it in during the debriefing. But, as with all irregular happenings in the service, no one knew who to give it to or what to do with it. After much red tape, a Colonel relieved my father of the cash and officially took charge of it. My father remarked that the Colonel told him he should have just chucked it into the ocean and saved them all a lot of trouble! My father privately thought that he himself could have used the $50,000 that the suitcases contained but felt he would still be answering questions if he had appropriated it. I believe those would have been questions to himself about the fairness of his action. He had a commitment to his own integrity as it related to the honor of flying for the Army Air Corps.

************

Herakles is less concerned with morality; his excellence/αρετε is his great strength. The Homeric heroes saw Herakles as an ancestor who executed astounding deeds that utterly transcended their own lives and skills. "Herakles' tremendous strength is even credited with the actual transformation of the landscape. He changed the course of rivers, drained swamps, and flooded plains. Some of these efforts seem to be related to Bronze Age hydraulics works."[11]

Herakles' 12 famous labors redound to the glory/κλεος of the goddess Hera, whose pre-Homeric identity was larger than that of her role as Zeus' jealous wife. The earlier Hera was an aspect of the Aegean great goddess potnia/ποτνια.[12] In Homer, two of Hera's epithets are white-armed/λευκωλενος and ox-eyed/βοωπις.

Herakles, a hero god, is the son of Zeus and a mortal woman Alkmene. Motivated by jealousy and spite, Hera tricks Zeus and manipulates Herakles' birth to change his destiny. Herakles has to serve his cousin King Eurystheus and, therefore, Hera.

Hera persecutes Herakles relentlessly from birth; she sends two huge snakes to kill him (and his twin brother, Iphikles) when he is eight months old, but Herakles wakes and squeezes the serpents to death. Through this mythic achievement, he becomes known as Alexikakos/Αλεχικακος, the averter of evil and the guardian of the household. Worshippers owned jewelry with Herakles' image and wrote verses over their doors invoking him to protect their homes from both material and meta-physical dangers, including disease and misfortunes caused by malevolent spirits.[13]

In addition to engineering Herakles' 12 labors for King Eurystheus, Hera inter-mittently drives the hero mad. The first time that he loses his mind, he kills his wife Megara and his own children, conduct usually associated with women such as Medea in Greek myth. In the ancient Greek male view, "masculinity consists of power and self-control while submission and physical or mental loss of con-trol are attributes of the feminine."[14] The berserk episodes that Herakles endures, instigated by Hera, are similar to the episodes that veterans with post-traumatic stress experience when they return home with their psyches fractured.

One of Herakles' tasks is to obtain the war belt/ζοστερ of an Amazon queen. This motif enacts male physical dominance over the female and affirms the primacy of the cultured Hellenic way of life over what were seen as primitive customs.[15] But Herakles bridges this dichotomy in Greek thought because his hypermasculinity is neutralized not only by his episodes of madness, but also by two periods of cross-dressing in which women force him to dress as a woman and to do women's work.[16] "Herakles transcends all the conceptual boundaries in Greek thought for he is at once king and slave; beast, man, and god; lawless transgressor and vanquisher of the uncivilized."[17]

Hera's manipulation of his birth sets a pattern, a fate/μοιρα that Herakles continues to live out in his life. Critically, he makes a moral choice to rise to the challenge of each task or punishment assigned him,[18] therefore fulfilling both his great gift of strength and his heroic fate.

In his labors, Herakles uses his bare hands, a club, or bow and arrows, and wears a lion skin, all references to the mastery of animals that confirm his origin in the Bronze Age "when the iconography and ideology of kingship was tied to the hunt."[19] During the Bronze Age, the Greek Mistress of Animals, partially of Syrian origin, was the patroness of warriors and hunters. By the sixth century BCE, she was called Artemis, when she became the goddess of the wild and the mistress of sacrifices who patronized young males and prepared them to be warriors.[20] The Mistress of Animals was a sexual woman, often shown nude, untamed, even violent;[21] the later classical Artemis is a maiden and a hunter with bow and arrow. Yet she retains her alliance with the heroes.

The Syrian goddess came to Greece and Crete at a time when the social order was changing and the focus was no longer the king. The Greek Mistress of Animals exercised power over animals; she was not a nurturing goddess.[22] She championed the aristocratic institution of the warrior in the polis and its incarnation in the hero. Many goddesses assume the function of this goddess in the Homeric epics, including Hera, Athena, and especially Artemis.

In one of Herakles' labors, Artemis demonstrates uncharacteristic leniency when the hero captures the Ceryneian Hind/ελαφος κερυνιτις, a golden-horned deer sacred to her. Instead of punishing him, Artemis allows Herakles to keep the deer in order to complete his labor.

Artemis is the initiatrix for the stages of initiation in the hero's life.[23] The male youth's marriage was one sign of maturity. His departure for a war or mission was another stage. And last, for adult status, he had to brutally murder a child, woman, or innocent. The climax of a warrior's self-realization was acting in a madness or rage that involved brutality. It was "the ultimate shedding of all inhibitions; the warrior had to do this to qualify as a soldier. The winged Mistress of Animals . . . legitimized the extreme violence."[24]

One of the most famous demands of the bloodthirsty goddess was at Aulis when Artemis demands the sacrifice of Agamemnon's daughter Iphigenia, in order to release the winds that will allow the Greeks to sail to Troy. This demand tests Agamemnon's allegiance to the polis and to his identity as a warrior. "In the practice of her cult, a goat was sacrificed to Artemis Agrotera before a battle, an analogy to the sacrifice of the maiden.[25] Instigated and inflamed by the goddess, the warrior's aggression serves to protect the city."[26]

\*\*\*\*\*\*\*\*\*\*

During battle, a man has to cut off his feeling to continue fighting and be a warrior. I quote from my father's memoir:

> The confidence or morale of the commander was magnified by his subordinates, and therefore the commanding officer had to be very careful as to what he said or how he acted about combat losses. Losses were always a blow to us, but you could not let your men know that it affected you. One night my senior officers gathered in my room discussing the mission of the day and there was much talk about the two crews that we had lost, and my reply was that "they were good men, I hate to have lost them, but there's not a damn thing we can do about it. So drink up and let's hit the sack because we've got another mission coming tomorrow."

For me, the intensity of the early Aegean goddess of wild beasts, the Mistress of Animals who initiated young men into warriorhood, raises the question of what happens when the savage feminine shadow falls into the unconscious? What happens when a man whose feeling is paralyzed is forced to resume his "normal life" with minimal transition and comes home from war to a loving wife and perhaps children? In that context, he cannot examine the dark side of his experience and how it has impacted and changed him. How can he resume a life that he has outgrown?

In his memoir, my father speaks of the leave the Army gave the prisoners after they were debriefed in 1944:

> they made a bad psychological error in sending us home for one month with nothing to do, after a long period of internment. Most of us really did not need – except those who were quite ill – a period of rest and recuperation at home. What we needed was to be put back to work immediately, to get our minds off of what we had just come out of.

Artemis prepares men to be hunters as well as warriors. My father had already undergone an initiation into hunting because he grew up in the deep southern United States, where boys were taught to hunt as well as to dance. As a hunter of animals, he adhered to ethical codes. Ortega y Gasset's book *Meditations on Hunting* was one of his bibles. In his treatise on the essence and ethics of hunting, the philosopher Ortega y Gasset says "one does not hunt in order to kill; on the contrary, one kills in order to have hunted."[27] My father hunted dove and deer in season and killed only as many birds or animals as we, as a family or with friends, could eat. He condemned the random slaughtering of wildlife. His personal honor reigned in hunting as it did in flying for the Air Corps.

My father could also be an audacious trickster on behalf of his values. During his incarceration in Romania, he was interrogated by a group of German officers and took great delight in giving bogus answers to their questions to avoid giving them ammunition for propaganda. At one point he said to them:

> I don't care who I'm fighting as long as I have good pay, good food, plenty of women to kiss and a good airplane to fly . . . I like war . . . it's just like a big game hunt, except that we use guns against one another rather than fangs or horns. You shoot at me, I shoot at you – if one of us gets killed, why hell, we're dead; we don't know a thing about it. If we get shot down, we're treated like officers and gentlemen. I don't care who I fight, it's a game hunt.

Stalking animals, identifying with them in order to know their ways, and shooting them gives the hunter an experience of mastery, control over the environment, and a self-sufficiency in being able to feed himself. If conscious, hunting allows him to examine the edge between life and death in a structured, ongoing way. Hunting also, if properly engaged, gives the hunter a connection to the life, death, rebirth cycle of the great mother. The death of the animal, respected by the hunter, then nourishes the man who knows that one day he will die.

**************

Herakles' bow and arrow places him firmly in the hero lineage of the hunter. Rituals for gods and for heroes involved animal sacrifice in Greece, but "the hero cult was adapted from rites for the dead and had a different convention for the handling of the victim's blood and meat."[28] The cult activity emphasized the sacred rite of killing animals.

Herakles' last three labors take him to lands associated with the afterlife, that is, the far west and the underworld of Hades. First, he must capture the red cattle of Geryon, a three-bodied red monster on a red island, Erytheia; second, he must fetch the apples of the Hesperides. His third labor is to bring back the multiheaded dog Kerberos who guards the River Styx in Hades. In order not to offend the gods of the underworld by violating the sacred realm, Herakles first undergoes his initiation into the Eleusinian Mysteries. He then travels to Hades as an initiate.[29] Moving into the afterlife prefigures his move toward immortality. He is a hero who is forced by his cursed fate/μοιρα or portion to move back and forth from the land of the dead to the land of the living.

Herakles dies a mortal death at the hands of a woman, his wife Deianeira, who gives him a robe soaked with what she thinks is a love potion. The blood is tainted with that of the Lernaean Hydra, however, which Herakles had earlier slain. Herakles had killed Nessus with the Hydra's venom while saving his bride

13

from being raped by the centaur. Before he died, Nessus had tricked Deianeira, whispering to her that if she ever worried that her husband was being unfaithful, she should put some of Nessus' blood on a garment and give it to him. When Herakles wears the cloak, it burns him with such excruciating pain that he has a funeral pyre built, climbs onto it, and has it lit by a passing shepherd, Philoktetes, to whom he gives his bow and arrows. Herakles dies and goes to Olympus where Hera finally relents and gives him her daughter Hebe in marriage.[30] In *The Odyssey* (II. 601–26), however, an image/εἰδολον of Herakles is said to reside in Hades while he himself feasts on Olympus.

\*\*\*\*\*\*\*\*\*\*\*\*

In any prolonged experience of war, the soldier moves back and forth between life and death every hour of every day. Psychologically, he must develop a capacity to endure that liminal space. If he returns home without a rite of passage that moves him firmly into life, he is stuck in that liminal traumatic field. His psyche cannot comprehend quotidian needs where everyone is concerned with seeming trivia. He has often been decorated for his rage-filled actions, that glorified state of murderous power, and yet the ghost of himself now finds itself in an ordinary family – an ordinariness that no longer touches him in the deep emotional way that living on the edge of life and death did. In ordinary life ambiguities prevail and decisions must be based on individual judgment, not military code, which has a clear objective. Boredom often prevails by contrast to the elevated high of life or death risk with buddies around to bolster him. These considerations must be taken up seriously and openly in a post-combat psychotherapeutic situation to help a soldier integrate the terrible initiation ordeal he has endured.

Although my father never talked about the shadow side of his experience during the war, or the tortured feelings he had afterward, he acted it out, not only in his nightmares, but also in his excessive anxiety and aggression in the face of commonplace life problems, and in an attachment to his role of commanding-officer-in-charge, both within the family and in his job. Even in civilian life, he was known as the Colonel. These inner conflicts between civilian life and service life were never resolved in him.

\*\*\*\*\*\*\*\*\*\*\*\*

John had a different experience of his father's post-traumatic stress following his fighting in the army infantry in WWI – called "the war to end all wars." As a boy with an older sister, John remembered his family as warm and loving. His parents ran a dairy farm.

> All my parents talked about were their childhoods and early days in farming; they had a good relationship. But my father's war experience in WWI was a taboo subject, even during WWII. He had put away his gas mask and helmet and never said a word about it. My mother told us not to bring up the topic of war.

In 1949, when John was 16, he had a group of high school friends over with their girlfriends.

> That evening, my father came out of the dairy in a frenzied state muttering things like, "that son-of-a-bitch captain . . . " and stayed up all night raving and playing the piano. I was mortified. After a few days, my mother had to hospitalize him. I remember asking her at some point, "Why don't you leave him?" She said, "You have no idea what he went through and you can leave if you feel that way!"

With no avenue for discussion, John felt alienated from his father and turned away from him. Disappointed and embarrassed, he became afraid of his father. To add to his alienation, John was skinny and sickly in high school and didn't feel he fit in with his peers, most of whom were better off financially than his family. His sister also refused to talk about what had happened to their father. John felt isolated within the family.

After high school, John left home and struck out on his own. In 1951, at 18 and a half, he enlisted in the Navy and was immediately sent to Korea. He spent his time on a Navy Heavy Cruiser that periodically shelled targets on the shore from the ship. The ship had two turrets, each with three eight-inch guns.[31] The men were locked into the turrets so if one of the turrets blew up – although all the sailors in it would die – the whole ship wouldn't sink. There was a radio spotter on land who would report Korean and Chinese tank convoys traveling within range of the ship's shells. The ship also carried 20-mm anti-aircraft machine guns on board.

His Navy service proved to be an initiation into manhood for John:

> My buddies and I talked about girls, about how to get laid on land. We fished out the body of one of the Army pilots who had been shot down and died in the cold sea. But it was a romantic adventure to me. I was now 172 lbs., girls were hitting on me, and I was accepted as I had never been in high school.

The bonding with other young men and his naval training helped John develop a sense of competence and self-esteem based on a strong body image and his identity within the group.

After two years, John returned from Korea and spent nine months on an airbase. Then, in 1955, John enrolled at UCLA on the GI Bill. There, he walked into the University clinic to see a therapist, saying, "I do not want to end up like my father." He went on to law school and drove a cab to support himself. He married, fathered three children, and practiced law as a public prosecutor and defense attorney.

In his early 30s, John happened into a Jungian analysis with an older male analyst and had the following dream: *I was 18 months old and my hair was on fire. My father was standing next to me and had dropped me or thrown me to the ground* . . . The analyst told John that the dream was showing him the original traumatic event in his psyche, the key to his father problem. The fire signaled the eruption of the trauma that had been buried deep in John's psyche. The analyst told him, "You have to go to the hospital and look up the records of your father's hospitalization, and you must tell at least two male friends about that experience with your father." It was testament to the power of the family's vow of secrecy that John had never spoken to anyone about the incident when he was 16 except the University therapist.

En route to the hospital where his father had been treated, John stopped to get coffee in a café. Suddenly, a Vietnam vet came in ranting and raving and the proprietor had to have him forcibly removed. John was shaken by the synchronicity, clearly constellated with the intensity of the dream that had created an opening in John's psyche.

From his father's hospital records, John discovered that in 1917 his father, at the age of 25, was drafted into the US Army Infantry. A year later, during the Meuse-Argonne Offensive, the last battle of WWI, he was wounded, picked up for dead, and awoke on a cartload of dead bodies. This battle had had the highest number of US casualties in any war to date – 27,000 dead and 96,000 wounded.

Honorably discharged in 1919, his father had returned, married, and started the dairy farm in the depth of the Great Depression. The records showed that when John was a year and half old and his elder sister five, his father went "berserk," as many veterans do, staying up all night, talking incoherently, and generally decompensating. At that time, he was hospitalized for a year, treated for shell shock or a nervous breakdown. During his hospitalization, his wife had to run the farm alone and take care of her two children. John's understanding of the dream of himself as an 18-month-old being dropped on the ground with his hair on fire clarified itself with this information. John said, "I could see it all in the photos . . . Until eighteen months I was a plump healthy baby . . . then I became skinny, sickly, and came down with pneumonia." By recovering this piece of history, meaning clicked for John about his upbringing and his father. The focus remained on his father during the rest of that analysis, which lasted several years.

Then, 40 years later, John, at the age of 78, was having a routine physical. When the woman doctor gently probed the right side of his abdomen, John burst into tears as a vision of one of the shellings he had done in Korea filled his mind. "In 1952, we were watching a tunnel on the shore from the ship and saw a train coming. We bombed both ends of the tunnel, then all us sailors rejoiced with cries of 'we got them fucking gooks and such.'" In the doctor's office, John was overwhelmed by shame, guilt, and grief, and spilled out the story and his feelings to the doctor.

Through a series of synchronicities, John found a PTSD program for successful veterans of the Korean War at a Veterans' Hospital. He said, "I was afraid to go at first, afraid they were going to lock me up and I'd never get out." But he found not only a sympathetic woman therapist, but also a therapeutic container of men who had been in combat, all of whom suffered from nightmares that replayed the scenes of war carnage. The therapy group was a mix of Chinese, black, and white men who were all in long-term marriages and financially stable. Some were taking care of ill wives; some had physical injuries. They talked about their nightmares and flashbacks in which they woke up thrashing and terrified, facing the men they killed.

John said:

> I find I can relate to this group of men very well because we have this experience of war in common. Sometimes I get really scared, brought to the edge of tears. One man was in a Korean prisoner of war camp with 2000 guys; 1100 died. He told me, "I was 22, one of the oldest and I had to go be with the dying men . . . every single one of them cried out for mama."

The Korean War was called the Forgotten War, even with 54,000 dead and 8,700 missing. Given the cultural ignoring of this war and his familial history, it was easy for John to repress his personal experience in the overriding trauma of his father. In the context of this Veterans' group, he has found another layer of purification and healing.

John already had a healthy connection to the feminine through his early positive relationship with his mother, which persisted through his Korean War masculine initiation. As a lawyer, he became successful in an environmentally oriented business startup and also participated in several nonprofit art programs. In his Jungian analysis, through his attention to the unconscious, he managed to integrate the traumatic splits in himself.

In Homeric Greek thought, the hero has a choice about fulfilling the fate he is dealt in relation to the gods. John's choices in the context of his fate furthered his individuation. The designation of post-traumatic stress disorder since 1980, when it was first included in the DSM, has helped to raise the collective consciousness. My father, on the contrary, in 1947, as a recovering prisoner of war and after years of combat missions, had three children and was on his own with no psychiatric support. He made the choice, wrongfully in my opinion, to not return to school, finish his degree, and become a college professor. The Veterans Administration did nothing but send him limitless supplies of tranquillizers for his nightmares, which only deepened his depression over the years.

\*\*\*\*\*\*\*\*\*\*\*\*\*

Like Herakles, Achilles is a demi-god, the son of an immortal sea creature, Thetis, and Peleus, a mortal man, and his fate is bound to his skill in battle. His excellence or *arête* is martial art. His mother, Thetis, initially tries to protect him from his destiny by disguising him as a girl in the court of a forgotten king on a faraway island. But Odysseus flushes him out of hiding with an irresistible call to action. Achilles' choices during the Trojan War affect not only him but also the Greek Army and the war itself. When Achilles' sense of superiority is insulted by his commander Agamemnon, who seizes his war prize, the girl Brisēís, from him, Achilles withdraws from battle and takes his men, the Myrmidons, with him. The Trojans then gain the upper hand.

Later, Agamemnon comes to Achilles, offering both to return the girl and give him other treasure so that he will return to the fight. The commander claims that he himself was the victim of Zeus' elder daughter Ate/ατη, the goddess of delusion, when he unfairly seized the girl Briseís. Although originally the wronged party in the quarrel, Achilles holds on to his resentment and pridefully refuses to accept the peace offering.[32]

Aias and Odysseus intervene, appealing to Achilles' "love of his comrades." They accuse him of being a "pitiless one"[33] and try to persuade him to change his feelings. Aias claims, "As for you, the gods have put in your breast a heart or spirit [thymos/θυμος] that is obdurate and evil because of one girl only"[34] and he entreats "make gracious the heart/spirit [θυμος] within you."[35] The thymos is the heart or spirit of the warrior's manhood. Achilles replies:

> . . . all this you seem to speak almost after my own heart but my heart [thymos/θυμος] swells with wrath when I think of this, how the son of Atreus has worked an indignity on me among the Argives, as though I were some refugee who had no rights.[36]

Achilles is emotionally wounded and insulted, but he seems to accept his feeling as his own; he does not blame a god or goddess for it. He is aware of the inner struggle that prevents him from making the heroic choice of compromise for the good of the Greek Army and his comrades.[37] The conflict between personal morality and the good of the group on behalf of the country is intrinsic to a warrior in any army.

On a deeper level, Achilles struggles with a larger question, the choice he must make about his fate. His glory, in ancient Greek called his Timi/τιμη, eos/εος, or kleos/κλεος, will be determined by his choice.

> . . . for my mother, the goddess, silver footed Thetis, tells me that twofold fates are bearing me toward the doom of death: if I remain here and fight about the city of Trojans, then lost is my return home, but my renown will be imperishable; but if I return home to my native land, lost then is my glorious renown, yet will my life long endure, and the doom of death will not come soon on me.[38]

While his judgment is clouded by anger, Achilles makes the tragic error of allowing his dear friend – and perhaps lover – Petraklos to take his armor and join the battle in his place. He violates his relationship with his friend out of his own pride. When glorious Hektor/Φαιδιμος Εκτωρ [39] kills Petraklos, Achilles' pain and fury of another kind are aroused, and he makes his choice: to pursue and kill Hektor, knowing that his own death will soon follow.

After Achilles dispatches Hektor with clear-eyed Athena's help, he dishonors the body by dragging it around the battlefield behind his chariot each day. Only when King Priam comes to Achilles' tent and evokes the hero's compassion by speaking of Achilles' father does he take the grief-stricken old king by the hand, relent, and give Priam the body for burial.[40] This empathic response shows a more subtle change of heart/θυμος in which Achilles shifts from revenge to submission to his fate. And eventually Apollo accomplishes Achilles' death by means of Paris' arrow.

********

My father, too, was allied with what he saw as his fate. He went out to face death over and over but did not find it. My father's enthusiasm, a word of Greek origin, from "en theos" meaning "with god," permeates his WWII memoir and every letter he wrote my mother during both that war and the Korean War. Only after he was grounded from flying due to "combat fatigue" in 1953 did the depressive shadow of his wartime experiences begin to creep in. The enthusiasm he exhibited was different from battle rage; it was an identification with the liberating experience of flying, with the fight that he was fighting, and with the challenge of each moment in the service of his country. The threat of death was fuel for exercising his wit, taking risks, and fulfilling a mission.

That enthusiasm fired my father's heroic tales and lived in my imagination as a girl. The story came true in the mid-1950s when a princess of Romania came to dinner at our home in California. I remember the elaborate preparations and the setting of a grand table for the occasion.

Princess Catherine Caradje (1893–1993) was a humanitarian who opposed the Nazi occupation of Romania. In 1943–44, when the Allied forces bombed the Ploieşti oilfields, she took custody of some of the surviving crews, saw that they were cared for in hospitals, and facilitated their escape to Italy. These men began to call her the "Angel of Ploieşti." Princess Catherine finally escaped the subsequent tyranny of the Russians in Romania and came to the United States where she traveled and lectured about freedom, especially anti-communism. Along the way, she saw some of the airmen she had met in the prisons. I did not understand the politics of this visit to our home, but experienced awe at having one of the characters from my father's odyssey come to life.

An energetic field of goddesses moves around the Greek heroes, guiding, blessing, cajoling, and orchestrating their actions. Hera both persecutes Herakles and incites him to greater glory. Achilles' mother Thetis intervenes in his life and Athena is his patroness. In addition to the individual goddesses by the sides of the heroes during the Trojan War, the semi-divine woman Helen, the cause of Troy's destruction at the hands of the Greeks, hovers in the background. Some have seen her as the instrument of Nemesis, the goddess of revenge and balance, the source of Troy's ruin by the Greeks.[41]

In this version of the myth, Nemesis is Helen's mother who is ashamed of her own father, Zeus, for raping her. Nemesis becomes companion to shame/Αιδος, the emotion a warrior feels when he does not do the honorable thing on the battlefield. Helen is infantilized by the Greek mind just as her beauty is idealized. She is the

19

treasure whom Menelaos owns and also the source and object of deep shame. And with subsequent authors, she transcends even the multiple contradictory characterizations of her that the earlier stories promulgated.[42]

************

The third modern hero, Fred's father, died at the age of 39 testing a fighter plane, a Bell Air Cobra, for Bell Aircraft in March 1944 before WWII ended. He was revered by his wife who set him up as an example to her sons. She became the center of the family and never remarried because she said she never met anyone to compare with her wonderful husband. Psychologically, the absent father was enshrined in the psyches of his sons.

Fred was almost five years old, on the verge of entering kindergarten, when his father died. He was the second of three brothers, and his mother was pregnant with a fourth boy. Fred's mother had been criticized by family members and friends for not stopping her husband from testing planes. But she told Fred, "It was all he ever wanted to do. He loved flying and I wouldn't interfere with what he loved."

In Fred's family, post-traumatic stress was lived out in the sons. The two eldest sons failed in their initiations into manhood. The eldest resented the fact that his father had died, hated his younger brothers, and defied his mother. He dropped out of college and became obese and dysfunctional. Fred said, "My older brother was like an abusive father who not only hit me but also never missed an opportunity to put me down." The second son took after the father he barely knew in risk-taking for thrills, including flying small planes, and was killed at age 27 when his small plane crashed into a mountain. The baby born after his father's death fared well and became a high school Spanish teacher.

Fred found refuge from his bullying older brother in the workshop basement where his father had spent much of his time. Gifted with his hands and with artistic vision, Fred seemed to have inherited the essence of the father he lost at an early age: his father had not only been a pilot but also an inventor and mechanical engineer. Fred found male role models in camp counselors, school teachers, and eventually professors in college. He took up fine arts at the Art Institute of Chicago in 1960. After he finished his MFA in sculpture, he was offered a job at the Institute. Throughout graduate school and his five-year teaching career, Fred also avoided the Vietnam War through deferments for both studying and teaching. War held no attraction for him.

Another formative influence in Fred's life was a paternal aunt who ran a girls' camp in Arizona. She introduced her nephew to the Southwest, where he developed a deep affinity with both the cowboy and Indian culture. He found his masculine initiation in riding horses, blacksmithing, and making sculptures in the desert. Eventually, he moved from Chicago and settled in Tucson.

In 2002, Fred completed a stone and forged-steel sculpture in honor of his father that he named *Ploughshares into Swords.* The name of the sculpture is taken from a biblical description exhorting farmhands to turn their implements of cultivation into weapons for war. Fred decided to formally enshrine his father's life as a civilian test pilot by donating this sculpture to the Pima Air and Space Museum in Tucson, Arizona. Along with the elegant piece, which looks as if it is taking flight, he gave the museum photos of his father, his pilot logs, and other paraphernalia associated with testing planes.

Fred created a shrine for his father just as the ancient Greeks did for their heroes. This enactment continued his mother's tradition of prominently displaying photos of her handsome husband in his flight jacket in order to keep his memory sacred.

Fred's sensitivity and artistic genius allied him with his mother and with the feminine in himself. Even his father had called him "my heart" because Fred's character, even as a little boy, touched him. Fred, now in his 70s, reflected, "I would like to have known my father and talked to him, but not having a father made me closer to my mother. I appreciated her and sadly, she died at age 63 of ovarian cancer."

Fred's mother's devotion to her husband resonates with that of Penelope who becomes an archetype of womanly patience in *The Odyssey*. As the story goes, she remains faithful to her husband during his 20-year absence. Odysseus exhibits a different form of excellence/αρετε and has been dealt a different fate than either Herakles or Achilles. He is cunning/μετις, ever-ready/πολυμετις, and inventive/πολυμεχανος – qualities also highly praised by Greeks. And he is able to achieve two things that were mutually exclusive to Achilles: both fame/κλεος and homecoming/νοστος.

\*\*\*\*\*\*\*\*\*\*

Homer calls Odysseus the long-suffering/πολυτλας hero whose journey home includes shipwrecks and wanderings as a seafarer to the limit of human civilization. His convoluted path takes him, for example, to the cave of the one-eyed giant Polyphemos, to the cannibalistic Laestrygones, to Circe the enchantress, to the sirens whose songs bewitch sailors, and through the straits of Scylla and Charybdis, where he loses men. Athena is by his side as his patron goddess through all of these trials. But Odysseus makes the mistake of blinding and mocking Poseidon's son, Polyphemos and then boasting about it. The act of boasting incurs Poseidon's wrath and that enmity both delays Odysseus' journey home and incurs a debt to the god of the sea, which the warrior will have to pay later in his life. Faced with these hurdles and seductions, he nevertheless remains attached to his wife and his homeland.

Unlike Odysseus, Achilles abandons his attachment to life when Petraklos dies and chooses the glorious death fated for him. Our third hero, Herakles, risks his life over and over during his labors but only dies at the misguided hand of his wife Deianira.

Both John's and Fred's fathers, as well as mine, had devoted wives who respected them in life and in death. John's mother remained loving and loyal to her husband despite his long hospitalizations for what was then called "shell shock" or a "nervous breakdown." Fred's mother championed her husband in flying planes and in his commitment to serving his country, and never remarried after his death; my mother loved and supported my father through his combat and his post-traumatic behavior. Recognizing the depth of the wounds he carried, she attempted to facilitate my father seeing a psychiatrist, but sadly, his primary care physician, whom my father looked up to, told him he was too smart to see a psychiatrist.

***********

After a year with the goddess Circe, Odysseus persuades her to let him and his men leave. She instructs him to go down to Hades to speak with Tiresias who will give him instructions for the next stage of his journey. In order to enter the under-world, Odysseus performs a ritual to the dead[43] that requires the sacrifice of a ram and a black ewe; the dead spirits will drink the blood and speak, animating them for a few minutes. Looking for Tiresias, he crosses paths with both Achilles' and Herakles' shades.

When Achilles comes forward, Odysseus expresses his hope that Tiresias has a plan for the hero's return to Ithaca:

> For not yet have I come near to the land of Achaea, nor have I as yet set foot on my own country, but am forever suffering woes; whereas no man before this was more blessed than you, Achilles, nor shall ever be hereafter. For before, when you were alive we Argives honored you equally with the gods, and now that you are here, you rule mightily among the dead. Therefore, grieve not at all that you are dead, Achilles.[44]

And Achilles replies scornfully:

> Never try to reconcile me to death, glorious Odysseus. I should choose, so I might live on earth, to serve as the hireling of another, some landless man with hardly enough to live on, rather than be lord of all the dead that have perished.[45]

Although Achilles embraced his fate to die a hero, here he envies Odysseus' life. Only when he hears that his son Neoptolemus excelled as a warrior in Troy after his father's death is he joyful that his heroism lives on in his son. Odysseus later speaks with Herakles' phantom, who compares his labors with those faced by Odysseus on his journey and commiserates with the god-inflicted suffering they have both endured.[46]

Finally, after seven years on the island of Ogygia with the nymph Calypso, Odysseus pulls himself out of his trance:

I know very well myself that wise Penelope is less impressive to look upon than you . . . for she is a mortal, while you are immortal and ageless. But even so I wish and long day in and day out to reach my home, and to see the day of my return.[47]

He chooses mortality instead of staying with Calypso, who could make him immortal.

Calypso helps him build a raft on which the hero departs. Capsized by Poseidon 18 days later, Athena, who has been negotiating with Poseidon, arranges for Odysseus to wash up on the island of a friendly Phaeacian people who take him in and resocialize him. The interim time with the Phaeacians provides a liminal space between the warrior and his family when he returns.

But more fighting awaits Odysseus at home, where the men of Ithaca have been plaguing Penelope. With the help of Athena and his son Telemachus, he murders the suitors and the maids who have been cavorting with them.

Tiresias had told Odysseus that once he put his home in order, he would have to set out again on a journey and find a land where people do not know of the sea or the use of an oar, and there make generous sacrifices to Poseidon in order to be assured of a peaceful life and seaborne death. Odysseus' death finally comes about indirectly through a woman. His son with Circe, Telegonus, comes to Ithaca seeking his father but, not recognizing him, kills Odysseus with a spear tipped with the poison of a stingray.

**\*\*\*\*\*\*\*\*\*\***

When he returned from WWII, my father negotiated the tension between his unresolved war trauma and civilian life by growing orchids and supplying them to local florists. He had majored in tropical horticulture at the University of California Berkeley before he enlisted. We had a large greenhouse in our backyard where he grew the exotic flowers from seed to bloom, a process that takes seven years. Watching him fill a glass flask with seeds in jelly and patiently extract the tiny plants with tweezers to plant them in beds, it was difficult to imagine this was the same man who had flown bombers with such passion. His cultivation and love of the beautiful flowers brought the healing feminine into his psyche. It was a safe zone, a self-therapy sealed off from the wild pilot he had been and the ordeal of the war, and it was my first experience of alchemy.

After we three children were grown, my father grew his orchids and worked at his day job until age 55, when he took early retirement and began to write his WWII memoirs. The night before he died in October 1972, I dreamed *that a tall quiet man was walking through the gate of a chain-link fence while hordes of children were clambering over the fence and shouting . . . . the tall man just walked on quietly, calmly into a firing squad.*

The next day my father shot himself and died at the age of 57. When I received the call from my mother, I was shocked, yet unsurprised. In my heart I knew that it was the completion of his story; he had always said that he wanted to die like Hemingway, with his boots on. Mourning him came later for me. In one of his eloquent suicide notes, he said that he had expected to die in WWII but fate had deemed otherwise.

\*\*\*\*\*\*\*\*\*\*\*\*

Homer immortalized the heroes of the Trojan War by singing the story of their deeds. My father's storytelling was a catharsis for him, and writing his war memoir was an attempt to immortalize his heroic experience as a young man. Having fulfilled his roles as husband, father, and provider, he ended his life as befit a classical hero, archetypally identified with his warriorhood. In that sense, he finally fulfilled the ancient Greek ideal of the warrior becoming a hero in death.

In ancient Greek culture, there was a warrior class whose behavior was clearly delineated in war and in peace. In our culture, there is no respected class of civilian warrior. When soldiers return home, they are expected to adapt to civilian culture without a plan or procedure. The diagnosis of post-traumatic stress disorder did not exist for the men and the families that I have discussed here. Today, PTSD treatment attempts to address veterans' hypervigilance, traumatic nightmares, and, at times, murderous acting out. But my sense of the internal battleground of a soldier who has gone to war tells me that desensitization to trauma is only a small part of a soldier's reentry to civilian life.

I think all veterans need to come to grips with the archetype of initiation that they have just lived in order for their war experience to take shape in a meaningful pattern. The initiatory pattern consists of their separation from the community; mental and physical hardship training; the undergoing of ordeals in which physical privation, emotional stress, and bloody carnage play a part, along with transcendent experiences. The successful completion of the initiation must culminate with a reintegration into the life of the community.

Reintegration falls short in our culture. This stage requires self-reflection in a relational field of welcome and ritual. In such a container, I believe the ancient Greek values – such as Fate/μοιρα versus individual choices, a warrior's painful feelings of shame and revenge/νεμεσις, and the tension between his loving wife or mother and the bloody goddess from the battlefield still raging inside him – would help veterans find meaning in a dynamic, healing way.

As the warrior scrutinizes his initiatory experience, he would examine the heroic ideal, the values of integrity and loyalty to self or country that he was serving, whether he felt glory or only gore and loss. He would name his skill, his excellence as a soldier, and his failings. He would consider his bonding with the other men. He would mourn both friends who were lost and his own sacrifice of the intensity of living on the edge between life and death. And he would find absolution. Through such scrutiny the modern warrior would begin to integrate his dark initiation with his continuing individuation as a man in a civilian world.

# Notes

1 V-E Day was May 8 1945, and V-J Day was August 15 1945. V-J day followed the bombing of Hiroshima on August 6 and the bombing of Nagasaki on August 9.

2 Timusul del Sus is variously spelled Timişu de Sus and Timisul de Sus.

3 From an unpublished memoir dictated by Lt. Colonel James Bishop Beane II on reel-to-reel tapes in 1970, transcribed by Justine Beane Bradford in 2000. "I was commanding officer of the 724th bomb squadron, 451st bomb group, stationed at San Pancrazio; I had left the States on Thanksgiving day in November of 1943."

4 Ibid. The name of the other prisoner was Robert Johnson.

5 For example, according to "Solidarity and rescue: Romanian righteous among the nations," Yad Vashem, Dr. Gerota had a foundation that donated money to Jewish children interred in camps by the Germans. His work was documented in his letters published in Emil Dorian, *Jurnal din vremuri de prigoană, 1937–1944*, ed. Marguerite Dorian, Bucharest: Hasefer, 1996, available: http://www.yadvashem.org/yv/en/about/events/pdf/report/english/1.11_Solidarity_and_Rescue.pdf (accessed September 17 2013).

6 Jorge J. Bravo, III, "Recovering the past: The origin of Greek heroes and hero cult," in Sabine Albersmeier (ed.) *Heroes: Mortals and Myths in Ancient Greece*, Baltimore, Walters Art Museum, 2009, p. 25.

7 Ibid.

8 Jennifer Larson, "The singularity of Herakles," in Albersmeier, *Heroes: Mortals and Myths in Ancient Greece*, p. 32.

9 David Konstan, *The Emotions of the Ancient Greeks: Studies in Aristotle and Classical Literature*, Toronto, University of Toronto Press, 2007, chapter 4. Another word *aisk-hune/αισχυνε* refers to shame about a past action.

10 C. M. Bowra, "C. M. Bowra on the heroic in Homer" in Harold Bloom (ed.), *Homer's The Iliad*, New York, Chelsea House Publisher, 2005, p. 45.

11 Larson, "The singularity of Herakles," p. 32.

12 Simon Price and Emily Kearns (eds), *The Oxford Dictionary of Classical Myth and Religion*, New York, Oxford University Press, 2003, p. 250.

13 Larson, "The singularity of Herakles," p. 36.

14 Ibid., p. 32.

15 Ibid., p. 34.

16 During one Hera-induced madness, Herakles threw Iphitos, a king's son, off the castle wall, thereby violating the host–guest relationship. As punishment, he was sold into slavery to Omphale, the Queen of Lydia; the gold went to the king who refused to use it. Herakles took Iphitos' sister, Iole, as a concubine, and she, too, demanded his disgrace and shame in payment for her brother's death. Aaron Atsma, The Theoi project: Guide to Greek mythology, 2000–7, available: http://www.theoi.com/greek-mythology/heracles.html (accessed September 17 2013).

17 Larson, "The singularity of Herakles," p. 32.

18 Michael J. Anderson, "Heroes as moral agents and moral examples," in Albersmeier, *Heroes: Mortals and Myths in Ancient Greece*, pp. 145–73.

19 Larson, "The singularity of Herakles," p. 34.

20 Nanno Marinatos, *The Goddess and the Warrior*, London and New York, Routledge, 2000, p. 92.

21  Ibid., pp. 7–12.
22  Ibid., p. 128.
23  Ibid., p. 98, note 26.
24  Ibid., p. 105.
25  Ibid., p. 108.
26  Ibid., p. 109.
27  Jose Ortega y Gasset, *Meditations on Hunting,* New York, Charles Scribner's Sons, 1972, p. 45.
28  Larson, "The singularity of Herakles," p. 36.
29  Carl Kerenyi, *The Heroes of the Greeks,* London, Thames and Hudson, 1974, 1997, pp. 163–82.
30  Ibid., pp. 199–206.
31  Each shell cost $3000; only one was shot at a time.
32  Homer, *The Iliad,* Vol. I, Books 1–12, The Loeb Classical Library, trans. A. T. Murray, ed. William F. Wyatt, Cambridge, MA, and London, Harvard University Press, 1999, Book 9, pp. 373–85.
33  Ibid., 9.631–32
34  Ibid., 9.635–7.
35  Ibid., 9.639.
36  Ibid., 9.645–8.
37  One examination of the scholarly controversy over Homer's intention with regard to Achilles' inner awareness of his emotions versus their origin in an external authority, Ate, the goddess of illusion, is found in "The honey and the smoke: Achilles and Ate in the *Iliad,*" in John M. Lundquist and Stephen D. Ricks (eds), *By Study and also By Faith,* Vol. 1, Maxwell Institute, available: http://mimobile.byu.edu/?m=5&table=book s&bookid=108&id=1251 (accessed September 17 2013).
38  Homer, *The Iliad,* I, 9.410–17
39  Ibid., 6.466.
40  Homer, *The Iliad,* Vol. II, Books 13–24, The Loeb Classical Library, trans. A. T. Murray, ed. William F. Wyatt, Cambridge, MA, and London, Harvard University Press, 1999, Book 24, pp. 468–595.
41  H. A. Shapiro, "Helen: Heroine of cult, heroine in art" in Albersmeier, *Heroes: Mortals and Myths in Ancient Greece,* pp. 49–55.
42  Norman Austin surveys the varying views of Helen beginning with the Homeric epic and Sappho and moves on to Stesichorus, Herodotus, and Euripides in *Helen of Troy and Her Shameless Phantom,* Ithaca, Cornell University Press, 1994.
43  Homer, *The Odyssey,* Books 1–12, The Loeb Classical Library, trans. A. T. Murray, ed. George E. Dimock, Cambridge, MA, and London, Harvard University Press, 1995, Book 10, pp. 516–29.
44  Ibid., 11.481–6.
45  Ibid., 11.488–92.
46  Ibid., 11.617–24.
47  Ibid., 5.215–20.

# 2

# BEAUTY AND THE PSYCHOANALYTIC ENTERPRISE

Reflections on a rarely acknowledged dimension of the healing process

*Donald Kalsched*

In this chapter, I want to relate a series of clinical stories about beauty as encountered by three patients who entered the healing process of depth psychotherapy. The first of these is from my own practice and the second and third from the work of other analysts. These stories illustrate three facets of the subject I want to explore. The first vignette illustrates how encounters with the elemental beauty of the world can break through a traumatic childhood and sustain a child's hope, even in the face of unspeakable violence perpetrated by the people on whom the child depends. The second illustrates how the capacity for apprehending beauty in the world may have its beginnings in our earliest attachment relationships and specifically in certain experiences of mutuality and love between infant and caretaker. These experiences supply a beautiful and mysterious "unity-in-separateness," a paradoxical "between-space" that seems to be essential for healthy human development, and *perhaps* for later experiences of beauty as well. The third vignette illustrates the sometimes astonishing beauty of the analytic process itself, as it emerges from the combination of interpersonal intimacy on the one hand and the symbolic intrapsychic process of the mythopoetic imagination on the other. I suggest that the beauty of the psychoanalytic process itself is an underappreciated aspect of the work we do as depth psychotherapists.

Throughout these accounts, I will weave in the perspectives of various philosophers, poets, and psychologists on the subject of beauty. We will see that beauty opens us to a space "between the worlds" of matter and spirit – a space that Plato, among others, thought was uniquely the soul's domain. According to Plato, experiences of beauty awaken an echo of the soul's earlier life in the eternal world. When we glimpse the beautiful, we are "seeing through" the manifest content of our time- and space-bound vision to the *eternal* or *heavenly* beauty with which the soul once communed – in that early blessed time when the soul lived with the gods and had wings. Hence, a conscious experience of beauty here and now, gives us a chance to regrow those wings and restore wholeness to the soul.[1]

Restoring wholeness to the human soul was also uniquely Jung's healing pro- ject, as he came to understand it. Hence, a consideration of beauty as a crucial element in the healing process in the three cases described here may help bridge a dialogue between Jungian thought and contemporary psychoanalysis.

## Jennifer and her angel

My first case report demonstrates how the experience of the world's beauty – in a life otherwise oppressed by trauma and abuse – can inspire a desire to live – especially a desire to live creatively – even in the face of a desperately painful childhood.

A little girl named "Jennifer," who later became my patient, remembered with great grief the place where she was sitting on the school playground, separated from the other children, when she realized that she was "broken." She was only 7 years old. But for two years she had been sexually violated on a regular basis by her older stepbrother who threatened to injure her if she told anyone about it. Jennifer knew she was different now – somehow damaged . . . no longer able to play . . . robbed of her innocence . . . *broken*. Whereas before she had been "at- one" with herself, playing and growing like a normal child, after the sexual abuse started she was a divided self, split in two – "beside" herself: one part observ- ing, finding fault with herself, criticizing, and comparing; one part feeling lost and forsaken, full of shame, anxiously trying to fit in. The essential self that Jennifer previously knew herself to be – the very heart of her personality – had gone into hiding – so deep into hiding that she herself had lost contact with it. She soldiered on with great courage through her half-lived life, but something essential was miss- ing. Nothing was beautiful anymore.

When Jennifer grew up and entered therapy with me, she would tell me that she had lost her soul. There were fleeting moments, she reported, when her soul might return to her – moments when she felt more "open" and safe, painting alone in her studio, or isolated times in nature when she felt "moved" by a beautiful land- scape, or a flower, or a tree. But most of the time she felt empty inside, frightened, alienated, removed from the world, and convinced somehow of her own innate "badness." As the years went by, she felt increasingly defeated, an abject "failure" compared to others – and more and more bitter and victimized by her circum- stances. She was surviving, but she was not living.

Therapy was a place where Jennifer could begin to find and tell her true story – not the false, self-blaming victim/perpetrator story whispered to her in the background by her inner "voices." And yet, there was great resistance to this true story because of the grief that came up as she began to allow herself to feel compassion for the small and helpless, confused little person she was when the sexual abuse began. One of the memories she told me – one that helped her feel some compassion for herself – was a "visitation" she had at age seven from a "presence of light" – a presence she interpreted as an angel, an angel in whose presence she had an experience of beauty that prompted her to claim her own true life . . . at least for a while.

She was near death, lying in a busy emergency room on a gurney with a ruptured bowel caused by the repeated rape perpetrated by her violent, juvenile-delinquent stepbrother, when she heard one of the ER nurses remark "don't take much trouble with her; she's not going to make it anyway." She remembered fighting the sweet smell of the ether as she lost consciousness – vowing that she would live to spite them and prove them wrong. Later, she found herself in a narrow hospital corridor with the familiar pain that had companioned her for so long now replaced by the dull ache of tight bandages. She wondered if they knew she was there and that she was still alive, despite their prediction.

At last, she was moved into a room with another child. As she watched from her bed, she saw this other, beautiful blonde child drawing in a coloring book, using crayons from a box like she used at school. It was then that she formed the thought that there could be some reason to continue fighting. Though she had closed her eyes, the image of the large brightly colored crayons stayed with her and the need to draw a picture arose. "Can I color?" she asked. "I want to color." Her tenacity impressed the nurses, and they let her try. She became their "little wonder," the "miraculous recovery." But her recovery didn't last.

Months later – it was a bitter cold winter afternoon. She was at home alone in a cocoon of fever and pain from a recurrence of peritonitis. She was lying in bed, moving in and out of sleep, aware that things were not right, that she was getting worse not better, despite assurances to the contrary. She was alone with this secret. At her side lay the remnant of a Christmas that had occurred without her – a large tin box of watercolors. While she barely had the strength to hold her treasure, she had spent the weary afternoon examining each color. Each one was a beautiful jewel full of possibility and yet now, as her vital signs began to flag, she thought, What good is this to me now?

The angel came to her in the midst of a soft white-yellow light, beside her and to her right. Neither male nor female, it was at once terrible and cool – unsurprisingly familiar. Calmly and caringly, the ethereal messenger declared without preamble, "You don't have to continue; it's all right to let go now." The presence paused and then continued, "If you decide to stay, it will be very difficult."

Jennifer remembered that it was so tempting to let go at this moment and so easy not to call out for help. But in her agonizing deliberation, her eyes fell on the box of watercolors again and went to the color Rose Madder. A sense of longing came over her. She was overcome with the beauty of this color – Rose Madder. "I need to use this color," she thought. "How can I leave without using this color? I must stay to paint – to make something beautiful with this beautiful color." Without daring to look directly into the light, she told the angel that she knew that she must stay in life.

In the quiet stillness of this moment of grace, Jennifer had the experience of being found and held by a serene intelligence from beyond herself. With her angel's visit came a quiet sense of belonging, a realization that she was a part of something greater than herself – that she was companioned, and that she had work to do – a kind of calling. In the angel's presence, her love of color – and especially Rose Madder – called her out of the darkening despair of looming death and into life. And although she didn't know it then, the passion for color that helped her make this choice, stayed with her throughout her life and led to her vocation as an artist.

My patient felt very shy – almost embarrassed – as she tearfully related her secret encounter . . . a story she had told no one for more than 50 years. She remembered making the decision for life, and it impressed her that she had been able to do this . . . inspired by the *beauty* of a color. Her shy recounting of this story in our session moved *me* profoundly. A kind of poignant tenderness and soulful depth of which we were both aware entered the room. It was a beautiful moment. We sat together in the presence of this mystery, aware that beauty had given her something to live for when living had become almost impossible.

Our mutual discovery of this moment in Jennifer's early history opened up other stories in which beauty figured prominently. Over the course of Jennifer's troubled life, the experience of beauty was like a thread that continued to sustain her at different moments in her life. For example, she told me about a special place near her home – an abandoned farm, where the beauty of the natural world supplied a refuge from the violence and chaos at home that grew worse in her adolescence. From age 11 onward, she would go to this special place every March as the sunshine began to warm the fields. There, with the chill springtime winds nipping at her fingers, she would lie in the grass and look at the clouds moving across the deep blue sky. Surrounded by the songs of meadowlarks and other birds, she offered her tears to the earth-mother who would comfort her with sunshine and silence. It was in this special place that she also made a promise to God that if he would let her live, she would devote her life to helping other children who hurt like she did. She kept this promise and later became a therapist as well as an artist.

\*\*\*\*\*\*\*

This story illustrates how the experience of the world's objective, natural beauty can connect us, or reconnect us, with the desire to live, making life possible even in the face of impossible suffering in the interpersonal world. Having lost altogether any effective support from her personal mother, Jennifer found support from the earth-mother – the "Great Mother," what we Jungians call the archetypal mother – with all her radiant colors, her warm sunshine, spring winds, and secret beautiful places. Rose Madder is the color (and the flower) of Aphrodite, the goddess of love and beauty itself. Aphrodite gave a rose to her son, Eros, the god of love, so the rose became the flower of love and desire – an apt symbol for Jennifer's newfound desire to live. The deep red-purple of Rose Madder was her favorite among a whole palette of colors in her watercolor box. "I want to color" she said, and every artist in the world knows this passion. Paul Klee wrote in 1914: "Colour possesses me. I don't have to pursue it. It will possess me always, I know it. That is the meaning of this happy hour. Colour and I are one. I am a painter."[2]

The elemental beauty of color has always been numinous to those who are open to the transitional space between the worlds of matter and spirit. The late John O'Donohue reminds us that "color is the language of light,"[3] and we know from Jung that light is often a symbol of the Spirit. The beauty of color, therefore, becomes a way of accessing the spiritual reality of the world . . . a reality we can never access directly, as Moses discovered on Mt. Sinai.[4] The overwhelming radiance of the Spirit requires mediation, and color supplies this through refraction of the white light of pure Spirit through a medium. According to Percy Bysshe Shelley, "Life, like a dome of many-colour'd glass / Stains the white radiance of Eternity."[5] Thus is the unbearable "face of God" transmuted into the extraordinary beauty that adorns the earth with all the colors of the rainbow. Color made life worth living for Jennifer and gave her something to live for when life had become dark and gray. It supplied a world for her creativity and a palette for her imagination. In this redemptive moment, Jennifer remembered (or rediscovered) that she was a child of God, not just the child of her parents – that she had a soul as well as an ego. As Plato notes, beauty provides "food" for the soul. It awakens it and strengthens it.

As a very young infant, Jennifer undoubtedly had beautiful experiences with her mother and participated in the blissful playful union that is the birthright of every child beloved by its mother. When, at age seven, she rediscovered the beauty of the world through the color Rose Madder, there may have been an echo of those earlier times in her infancy. Or, in Plato's more spiritual idiom, there may have been an echo of those earlier blessed times when "her soul lived with the Gods and had wings." We cannot rule this out. The presence of her angel at the moment of her apprehension of beauty and her choice to go on living would seem to support a "spiritual" interpretation. In any case, Jennifer now saw her life in a different light. Her angel and Rose Madder had given her something that no one could take away from her – something sacred at the core of her experience that she would never forget.

Jennifer taught me that there is no healing of trauma without the soul's involvement, and probably no experience of the soul without an opening to the beauty of the world. Trauma eclipses beauty, even though we've seen it early, and trauma's defenses require us to close down instead of opening to the world. When trauma is healed, beauty comes back. Experiences of beauty seem to be "markers" of the returning health and soulful integration of a person.

How often, we might ask, in the psychoanalytic literature, do we hear about how important the natural world and its astonishing beauty can be to the developing child's psyche? Rarely. Certainly we do in Jung, which may be part of why we seekers after beauty were drawn to him in the first place. Jung spent much of his childhood in what he called "God's world" – the world of his No 2 personality – and he often felt a deep and intimate connection with nature, which he found unbearably beautiful. Jung's first memory was one of exquisite beauty while lying in his pram, watching the dappled sunlight filtered through the leaves above as he awoke with a sense of "indescribable well-being."[6] Later, in the darkest period of his life after the break with Freud, Jung had a dream of a dismal, dark, and foggy world – images expressing how depressed he felt at the time. The setting was Liverpool, England, and in the center of the darkened town square, on an island in a circular pool of sunlight, there was a beautiful magnolia tree bursting into bloom. The tree stood in the light but also seemed to be the source of light. Jung found this dream so powerful that he later painted a picture of it and called it *Window on Eternity*. Reflecting on the dream later, Jung said "[this was] a vision of *unearthly beauty,* and that is why I was able to live at all."[7] Beauty was why Jung "was able to live at all." That's quite a statement.

Among psychoanalysts, Harold Searles echoes Jung's deep appreciation for the beauty of nature and its importance in an individual's surviving otherwise unbearable suffering. In his book *The Nonhuman Environment in Healthy Development and in Schizophrenia*,[8] he points out how lacking in appreciation for nature psychoanalytic theory tends to be. By "non-human environment," Searles means the whole natural world order, including animals and plants, butterflies and birds, the wind and stars, and the great cosmos beyond. Our relationship to these realities is, he says, "one of the transcendentally important facts of human living"[9] and one we psychoanalysts don't seem to consider adequately in most of our theorizing about what makes us truly human. Emphasizing this point, Searles says:

> It is rare to find a great novel which so skeletally limits itself to a portrayal of human beings alone [i.e., relating only among themselves] as does psychoanalytic theory. Much more often, great literature embeds its studies of human beings in a portrayal of them as being collectively an integral part of larger, nonhuman Nature itself. Much great art, to the best of my limited knowledge, does likewise.[10]

I think Jung felt the same lack in Freud's theory. By adding a "collective" layer to the unconscious in his model of the psyche, he echoes Searles' concern to include our relatedness to Nature as an important part of our basic humanity. "The collective unconscious simply *is* Nature," Jung proclaimed.[11] For him, it was this non-personal or pre-personal layer of the unconscious that mediates transpersonal experience, including mystical experiences of great beauty like Jennifer's. We are held, in other words, by Nature without and Nature within – by the psyche and its collective depths, as well as by each other. When we are "broken" by traumatic injuries within the interpersonal world, Jungian theory would say we are also broken open to an implicate order that lies in the collective reality within – and our experiences of beauty may involve this deeper sustaining order and its harmonies.

Of course, not all experiences of beauty come through the nonhuman environment of Nature or via the collective unconscious. There are beautiful moments between people as well – moments of intense connection and love – and the psychotherapeutic relationship is a special case in point. My next case, taken from the published report of psychotherapy with a little boy named Georgie – only 18 months old – illustrates this relational field.

## Georgie and the experience of beauty

This case was reported by London analyst Susan Reid, in a paper titled "The Importance of Beauty in the Psychoanalytic Experience," which was published in the *Journal of Child Psychotherapy* in 1990.[12]

Georgie was born to a highly disturbed, episodically paranoid mother who became pregnant after a brief affair with an Afro-Caribbean man whom she never saw again after Georgie's birth. An earlier child had died at eight weeks – a crib death. Georgie was delivered at home without prenatal or obstetric care and was hospitalized shortly after birth with breathing difficulties. His mother, a woman named Ann, was briefly hospitalized with postpartum hallucinations, and after being discharged, Ann and her baby lived in isolation with social workers and health visitors gaining only occasional access.

Georgie's early life was bleak. His disturbed mother carried him around in a sack and fed him with bottles of lemonade and water. Reportedly, she loved to tease and torment Georgie, leaping out from behind him and yelling "boo!" until he screamed in terror. At 15 months, a social worker on an unscheduled visit found Ann in an agitated state claiming that she had been bugged and that voices were telling her that they did not like Georgie, that he was evil, and that she should hurt him. Examination revealed extensive injuries over his head and body. Ann admitted having caused his injuries by biting him.

Both mother and baby were admitted to hospital where Ann would allow none of the nursing staff to touch the baby, shouting at them if they approached. She mostly ignored her baby. Things went from bad to worse with Georgie in serious danger of death. Finally Georgie was placed with a noisy, busy, and caring working-class foster family with three other children of their own. In this rich environment, Georgie was completely withdrawn. He ate but did not grow. He suffered numerous infections and generally failed to thrive. A psychologist found him to be a strange, disturbed, and disturbing boy, and thought he might be autistic. Finally, psychotherapy with Susan Reid was arranged three times a week – despite Georgie's extremely young age of only 18 months.

Georgie was in a desperate situation when his therapy finally began. He had stopped walking and was losing weight. He had taken to bashing his head hard against the radiator until he would cry. His hair was falling out in clumps. He seemed ill, although medical examination revealed nothing. He was completely withdrawn.

Susan Reid's description of her little patient on first contact is almost unbelievable. Georgie was a

> small creature hunched in a chair, next to a harassed looking lady escort. His head looked like a chessboard – parts bald, parts with straggly matted dark curls that hung down in his eyes . . . A green trail left his nose and ran unheeded across his mouth to drop off his chin into oblivion . . . As I sat down next to him the stench hit my nostrils and raced into my stomach, inwardly sending me reeling with disgust. It was not a human smell, but an animal smell of fear and attack . . . This dreadful smell filled my room and pervaded my clothing, lasting long after he had gone, for the first and into the second week of therapy, when I suddenly became aware of its absence.[13]

Georgie was frozen in fear. He clung to Susan Reid like a little chimp as she walked him around the room. He made no eye contact, however, and remained rigid, but as she spoke reassuringly to him and tried to describe what she understood of his feelings, he began to relax a bit, and then at one point he broke apart in complete and utter panic. His mouth opened wide and he erupted with a terrified scream, tears spilling fast from his eyes until he had completely drenched himself.

At this point, Mrs. Reid reached for some tissues and began to dry his eyes and absorb some of the water from his soaked front, putting her arm around him to comfort him. The effect was magical and disconcerting – the crying stopped as abruptly as it had started. Georgie stood silently but clearly with some measure of relief, having allowed actual emotional contact with another human being. Susan Reid comments:

> The tissues from this first session continued to have great importance for Georgie. They represented in concrete form the soft, gentle, absorbing good mummy, and often in his first term of therapy, when in terror or great distress, he would reach for the tissues, or I would [and] this would calm him. The presence of the tissue-mummy would signify the disappearance of the monster-mummy.[14]

But the "monster-mummy" was a constant threat to Georgie. In the very next session, he was frozen in terror again. His body was hard and stiff – his eyes stared rigidly ahead, his breath came in short hard pants. The smallest movements from his therapist caused him to scream in agony. Mrs. Reid found herself paralyzed and helpless:

I know I have a terrified baby in my arms but this is of no use to me in knowing how to help him. I know he is frightened, I feel his terror and my body responds, my arms trying to hold him firmly but gently, but it has no effect on Georgie. I notice then my reluctance to really allow this degree of primitive terror inside me. I struggle with my counter-transference and then am able to give up, briefly, the boundaries between us. My suffocated sweat starts to drip down the back of my neck and my heart bangs so loudly in my chest I feel that I can also hear it. I have briefly had his terror and can withdraw from such intimacy with it. . . . I have no words. . . . I manage to stand almost perfectly still and respond by humming to him. Over minutes his body relaxes its grip and when the time feels right, I add words to the hum. It becomes a lullaby in which I use his name and sing of his fear. After a time, he gets down and moves around the room and to his box.[15]

From the second week on, Georgie took to therapy like a duck to water. His terror states continued but now assumed the form of dramatic acted-out communications to Mrs. Reid. When Georgie was frustrated or misunderstood, he would hurl himself to the floor, striking his head with a sickening blow and crying, but then he would turn to Mrs. Reid as the tissue-mommy for comfort and reassurance. By the third week, he was making longer and longer eye contact with his therapist and now depended on it for comfort. At times, he would join Mrs. Reid in a task. His upsets began to subside quickly. Still there were no words – mostly sympathetic actions and singing to which words were added.

I think at this point my actions could be described as demonstrations of my understanding of what Georgie brought to the transference via my counter-transference responses. Thus initially I dealt with Georgie's head banging by slipping my hand between his head and the floor, and then, when he looked at me, holding him with my eyes; gradually adding words. The time came when he threw himself to the floor [but] no longer cracked his head, holding it as though cupped by invisible hands . . . and eventually when about to throw himself on the floor he would bend his knees . . . look me in the eyes, and when I held his look, he would straighten his legs [and the tantrum was over].[16]

As the therapy progressed, Mrs. Reid began to hear from Georgie's foster mother who said she was dying to know what his therapist had been doing with Georgie. She had noticed such remarkable changes at home, including cuddling back when she hugged him, coming to her when she called . . . And, strangely, Georgie had started singing to himself.

*******

35

It was now two months into the therapy and nothing had prepared Mrs. Reid for how fast Georgie was progressing in the therapy nor for the remarkable breakthrough of beauty that was about to occur. They were two months in when the most important session in the whole course of Georgie's therapy occurred and formed the bedrock for his continuing development.

During the time preceding the breakthrough session, Mrs. Reid had been carefully following Georgie's play in an effort to understand its meaning. She could not find any. A piece of play would be repeated ritually but without any apparent meaning or pattern. One day Georgie was playing with water, filling cups from a plastic jug until the jug was empty. He then carried the filled cups to a table across the room where the doll's house was kept. But he needed Mrs. Reid's help. Each cup had to be delivered and placed in a certain order along the edge of the table. Mrs. Reid dutifully followed in Georgie's footsteps until all the cups had been transferred to the table.

Then Georgie raised his arms for her to lift him into the chair in front of the table and after emptying the doll's house and stuffing its contents into a top-floor room, Georgie began to move the cups in front of the house, placing them in a certain order and then passing them back to his partner. Here is Susan Reid's description of what happened then:

> . . . I pass the cups to him in some slow, thoughtful ritual. He peers into each one; nothing more. He then passes one of the cups back to me, I place it carefully in the order and position it was in before, he looks swiftly at me, and passes me another. I do the same again and he looks swiftly at me and passes me a third, his look stirs a tender response in me and I smile at him.
>
> Georgie scans my face, conveying the impression that he is reading it. Suddenly his face lights up, his eyes light up as though switched on from inside, and he smiles tenderly at me and reaches out his hand allowing his fingers to brush against my cheek. Georgie then points to the light switch and lifts his arms up to me and I carry him there. He struggles with the switch and switches the light on and off. As it goes on, I make an involuntary "aah!" and Georgie's mouth rounds into an O, and his eyes grow round too. He looks around the room, now transformed by the light, turns the light off and surveys the room again. He looks into my face sweeping, searching. I smile involuntarily and say "Oh, lovely light" and then "beautiful room with lights on," my arms sweeping around the room in the way his gaze had done. When it's off, he checks my face and I say, solemnly, "not so lovely now, not all lit up."
>
> With the light on, through Georgie's eyes, my scruffy room looks beautiful just as on other occasions it has also seemed dirtier than it really is, and full of monsters. He needs to play, for the first time in a joyful way, light on, light off, and he waits each time for me to say something about it. I verbalize everything, "beautiful – lovely light, beautiful room, beautiful Mrs. Reid with light in her eyes."

Georgie suddenly wriggles to get down and goes straight to his box and rummages inside it. This is very unusual. He is looking for something and I wait full of curiosity. Georgie takes out his Perspex ball which has a colorful butterfly inside which rotates as the ball is moved. He holds it up for me to see, and smiling full at me, places it with exquisite care onto the floor and gently rolls it, sucking in and holding his breath as he does so. I find it impossible to convey in words the beauty of the moment, of the sense of us both being in the presence of real beauty close to a religious experience of faith. The delicacy of it conveyed by Georgie's sucked in and held breath. I am reminded of an early childhood experience of my own at shimmering early morning in a wood full of bluebells. I am too full to speak, so nod at him to convey my feelings of sharing the experience. He plays with the ball, rolling it, watching the butterfly rotate inside. It seems to me, at this moment exquisite, beautiful beyond its actual self.

I try to verbalize his pleasure. I say "Beautiful ball, beautiful bally-breast, good mummy. Georgie has found her, you feel good inside, the good bally-breast inside fills you up and you feel warm like the light." He looks at me and nods, he wants me to play with him; he wants to play losing the ball and cannot do it on his own. [Later he loses and finds the ball again and again on his own].

. . . After the session, on the way to the waiting room, his eyes seem wide drinking in everything around him; the freshness of his vision was infectious making all seem new and beautiful to me. He pointed to each of the lights on the way back to the waiting room. . . . Journeys to [and from] the therapy room now took a long time as new and beautiful discoveries were made [each time] within the otherwise drab Tavistock building. This sense of beauty and goodness spread to people in the building whom he began to find fascinating. People we passed on the stairs had to be studied and often admired. He frequently smiled warmly, eliciting the same response. Georgie was not only becoming human, he was becoming an attractive little human "baby," for baby was the only way I could think of him.[17]

In the week following this session, Georgie started to speak for the first time, using single words but clearly and with pleasure. [And from this time forward], he never lost his sense of beauty, no matter how disastrous events turned out to be on the outside. And there were plenty of disasters in the later months and years.

********

What is captured in Susan Reid's paper is one of those mysterious empathic "meetings" when the baby's spontaneous smile of delight meets the mother's or caretaker's equally spontaneous smile and the darkened world "lights up" both from within and without. This beautiful moment seems to involve both a discovery of *ourselves* (in and through the eyes of the other) and a discovery of *the world* and its awesome beauty (suddenly seen for the first time consciously).

I think of Georgie's remarkable moment with Mrs. Reid as the prototype for all later experiences of being deeply met and understood by another person. The terrors of raw experience are mediated for the first time interpersonally, and the result is the apprehension of beauty. Such a moment represents a welcoming into the world that "lights us up" from inside and simultaneously releases us into a unity of self-other *being* that can only be described as love. When it happens in a child's early life, it's a *cause for coming into being,* feeling beautiful inside and seeing beauty in a friendly world at the same time. Attachment theory teaches us that these sacred wordless moments occur in the shared gaze, voice-play, and embodied emotional exchange of the mother/infant pair and form the basis of all later secure attachments.

How, we might ask, do we describe such a beautiful moment with our stilted scientific language of good and bad inner objects, milk- or shit-filled breasts, libidinal cathexis, Id, Ego, Superego, projection and identification? Susan Reid, Georgie's therapist, struggles to do this within a Kleinian metaphor, namely that the child's experience of inner goodness comes from the infant's experience of unity with the mother and her good breast such that the good breast is taken in and becomes part of the ego, warding off persecution and giving the infant hope and enthusiasm for life. She employs Wilfred Bion's more sympathetic ideas about reverie, expanding this metaphor to include the loving mother who sees her child as beautiful and who has space in her mind for beautiful thoughts about her baby. Such a mother reveals by the light and expression in her eyes and expression on her face the nature of the baby in her mind, which is there to be read by the baby and which (somehow magically) forms the basis for his or her developing self-image. When the baby feels that he or she exists in mother's mind, then together they can explore and discover the world.

Susan Reid surmises that Georgie probably retained fleeting experiences of good-enough mothering, perhaps even remembering prenatal experiences of unity with his mother and the feeling of security that goes with it – something that was the seed for later experiences with her in the therapy. She suggests that Georgie's autistic defenses could be seen as a means of protecting the good within himself against the onslaught of and bombardment by his mother's unbearable persecutory projections. These defenses became almost impregnable so that by the time he reached his foster family, gestures of kindness and goodness from outside could not reach him and he was in danger of dying.

In their book *The Apprehension of Beauty*,[18] Donald Meltzer and Meg Harris call this split between the apprehension of beauty and the defenses against it, the "Aesthetic Conflict." They suggest that babies' first encounters with the world almost always contain blissful and beautiful moments of ecstatic wonder alternating with negative, aversive experiences that are highly threatening. The mother is an object of "overwhelming interest" to her baby. Her outward beauty, "concentrated . . . in her breast and face," opens the baby to the world. Even "proto-aesthetic experiences," they suggest are likely in-utero as the baby is "rocked in the cradle of the deep of his mother's graceful walk; lulled by the music of her voice."[19]

But, according to these authors, the mother is also an object of overwhelming terror. Unmediated moments of anxiety may attack the fetus, instigated by the mother's stress, rage, despair, addiction to substances, and so on. And in the case of an abusive, disturbed, or absent mother like Georgie's (or for that matter, Jennifer's too), Meltzer and Harris suggest that powerful defenses against the experience of beauty inevitably develop. They employ Bion's vision of the absent object becoming a present persecutor[20] and suggest that, augmented by the child's unconscious rage, such defenses become violent and overwhelming. These patients, they suggest, "split the joyous and terrifying components of the apprehension of beauty into two parts, one persecuting the other."[21] The child's vulnerable and fragile psyche then becomes the locus for an epic struggle "between aesthetic sensibilities and the forces of philistinism, Puritanism, cynicism and perversity – what Bion calls minus K."[22]

To illustrate the dramatic struggle between aesthetic experience and the defenses against it, Meltzer and Harris cite the case of an autistic boy whose concrete obsessions seemed intractable – except for the fact that he found his therapist beautiful and began an ingenious attempt at seduction, begging her to take off her clothes. Another child, "Francesco" entered the room of his female therapist, stopped in astonishment before her and murmured, "Are you a woman – or a flower?" [In this, say the authors], "one could catch a glimpse of the reaction of the newborn to the first sight of its mother and of her breast [or face]."[23]

Meltzer and Harris are trying to express – in the cumbersome language of psychoanalytic science – what John O'Donohue says more poetically in the following comment: "Each one of us," he suggests, "has made a huge discovery that we have never gotten over. That is the discovery of the world [and its astonishing beauty]."[24] Whether in the language of psychoanalysis or poetry, it is agreed that this discovery for a vulnerable child is so powerful that it threatens to overwhelm the fragile ego. As Plato said in the Phaedrus,[25] we "shudder" and are struck dumb with awe and terror. It's as though we have looked directly into the face of the living God and we may not survive this – unless the experience is mediated.

We probably do not remember unmediated experiences of the beauty of the world. They probably were the developmental equivalent of sustained ego-orgasm – simply too much to hold. The only "remnant" of these early traumas may be our defenses – the way we inadvertently close down to our perceptions – the way we numb ourselves to our experience. As Meltzer and Harris succinctly summarize: "what our fragile child-ego's [sic] cannot sustain and are riven by, a lifetime of mediation by art, and culture and language strives to restore so that the beauty surrounding us may be looked upon directly, without doing damage to the soul."[26]

It seems that if our encounters with the beauties of reality are mediated by persons, then we may be able to grow in our capacities to apprehend beauty in general.

It helps if these persons understand something about the soul – about the fact that the beauties of people and the beauties of nature conceal an *inner* spiritual reality that we must hold in mind while we work as psychotherapists.

Susan Reid clearly did this with Georgie – holding him in mind as a lovable, beautiful child. The tender exchanges between them in that crucial session occurred in the play with water, where Georgie's therapist followed his every move patiently and identically and then smiled spontaneously and tenderly at him in the middle of their shared play. This was the moment when Georgie felt seamlessly at one with his therapist. This was the moment of unity and separateness together that literally lit Georgie up from inside . . . lit up his little soul. However briefly, the boundary between self and environment dissolved. Georgie could let go – submerging himself in this experience, and Mrs. Reid could, too. Suddenly she was reminded of an early childhood experience of her own – a shimmering early morning in a wood full of bluebells. What seems to happen in these moments is more than knowing – more than cognition – more like re-cognition. To paraphrase T. S. Eliot, Georgie and his therapist were arriving back at the beginning of their journey, now aware of it for the first time.[27]

It seems that there is no adequate way of describing such moments without admitting that two worlds – equally real, one spiritual, one material – come together then. Soren Kierkegaard[28] said that the human self is a tapestry woven of two strands – one material and temporal, one ineffable and eternal. We live, he suggested, with the blessing and the curse of this dual destiny. Jennifer and Georgie provide evidence of this dual unity – thin places between the worlds, where we see through into mystery. No other theory is adequate to our experience – at least not to me. As depth psychologists, we must not be afraid to claim this fact. And experiences of beauty bring this truth home to us.

## Trauma and healing through a dream

The third clinical vignette I wish to relate illustrates the beauty that sometimes comes to presence in our work as depth psychotherapists. This case illustrates something unique about Jungian work and its special appreciation for the beauty of the psyche itself.

The case is reported by my colleague Monika Wikman of New Mexico in her book *Pregnant Darkness.*[29] Her patient was a Hopi woman, raised in her tribe, who suddenly lost her mother and daughter in a car accident. This catastrophic trauma was so severe and the patient so dissociated, that she was unable to speak. In the early stages of her therapy, she had no access to feelings and had no dreams. Often the sessions were spent in complete silence. Her therapist spoke reassuringly to her and found herself telling her stories of other women who had found the strength to come through such tragedies. Finally, Dr. Wikman began to read to her – myths or stories with strong feminine characters. She was thinking about the alchemists who say that one must "dissolve the problem in its own water" and who describe an alchemical operation called *benedictio fontis,* or the blessing of the fountain. "If we do our part, the divine elements of the imagination may come." Dr. Wikman's best sense of how to do this was "simply to attempt to create a loving, warm environment that was open to the psyche, and wait."[30]

Soon the patient began to speak again and slowly to connect with her therapist. Her feelings began to thaw and come to life. Then, in one session she reported the following dream:

> I go to the spring at the river, to the pool I have always known since I was a girl. It is the spring of my mother's people. In the pool, you are with me and another older woman, mother's old friend from the pueblo. You two hold your hands underneath my body, and I float. Closing my eyes . . . I feel peace. Then my body, as I know it, is on one wing of a giant butterfly on top of the water. This butterfly gently flaps its wings together, apart, together, apart, together, apart . . . I seem to be chanting this while the wings so gently open and close. My mother's friend tells you not to take your hands away but to leave them under the butterfly that sits in the water between you and her. You flinched a little as my body became one with the wing of the butterfly, and you and she were upholding the butterfly in the water, instead of just me. I think she was trying to be sure you didn't let go.
>
> Now my body on the left wing, where you stand, is experiencing something new as the wings open and close. The right wing has someone forming in it. Just like my body is in the left wing, this new being is forming in the right wing. As it takes shape, it is evident it is a new kachina I have never seen. The wings open and close some more. I keep chanting with the rhythm, "Together, apart, together, apart." Each time the wings close, my body is pressed up to and touching this kachina. Then, finally, it is all different.
>
> I am standing outside the pool and am completely in my body. The butterfly is now small and comes toward me. It lands just above my belly. I have a hole there that is very deep. It sits there and drinks in some water and then beats its wings. I feel sad and empty. But I am back in my body and am comforted by this incredible butterfly sitting on the entrance to this hole in me. I am feeling clear-minded and large of presence gazing at the pool from which I have emerged and gazing then on down the river as it shimmers into the valley. I feel sober and peaceful, made new. I have been reborn. I wonder that maybe my mother and daughter experienced the same thing I just did, somehow, since we all come from this pool.[31]

It is difficult to imagine a more beautiful illustration of the psyche's symbolic wisdom and healing potential than this moving account. The patient's dream is so clearly a *response* to the holding environment supplied by Dr. Wikman's presence, yet its story immeasurably deepens the overall experience, weaving a tapestry of the *interpersonal* relationship together, warp and woof, with the *intrapsychic* depths that go all the way down into her tribal ancestry and the collective mytho-poetic roots of consciousness itself.

******

In the following remarks, I hope to highlight and enrich some facets of this "tapes-try" without compromising the music of this therapeutic moment with words. The dream begins with an immersion in the pool that belongs to her mother's people, that is, to her feminine lineage – precisely the source/ground of her feminine self where she was so terribly injured following the death of her mother and daughter. Immersion in the "living waters" is a classic image of renewal of life, as reflected in baptism rituals in the Judeo-Christian tradition and many others. Baptism always involves renewal of the Spirit by the Spirit. The patient enters this pool with her therapist and an old friend of her mother's who serves as a kind of psycho-pomp, the mistress of initiation, here guiding the renewal process.

The second healing image is, of course, the beautiful butterfly, which is another remarkable example of nature's totally unnecessary beauty . . . beauty that comes about through a miraculous process of transformation – *metamorphosis* is our word for it – in which the larval worm or caterpillar undergoes a change of form – "dying" to its old self, entering a cocoon or chrysalis of its own making, and emerging in the spring as a radiant winged being capable of flight. And not just any winged being. Nature could have made butterflies with bat wings, or mosquito wings, or cicada wings. That would have been miracle enough. Instead, Nature gave butterflies magnificent wings with delicately arranged multicolored scales, full of intricate symmetrical designs and patterns that defy the imagination – all reflecting brilliant iridescent colors – like flying flowers!

When I was a boy, I was so fascinated by the lifecycle of the Monarch butterfly that I would stake out a milkweed patch in a nearby field and watch the Monarchs lay their eggs on those plants, watch as the eggs hatched into striped caterpillars, watch as those caterpillars grew and grew, watched as they spun their beautiful green chrysalises and then harvested the chrysalises and kept them over the winter until the spring when the exquisitely beautiful orange-, white-, and black-winged beings would slowly emerge, dry their wings in the sun, and take to the sky. This to me was a miracle of beauty unfolding, and still is – not adequately explained in purely evolutionary terms as a result of random mutation and natural selection. Here, beauty is unnecessary to survival and provides no adaptive significance that we know of. Far better to say that the Monarch butterfly soaring in the summer wind is simply an emergent, self-unfolding expression of a patterned truth about the universe that we don't understand and will never understand. The universe celebrating itself and its own beauty.

The remarkable beauty of the butterfly is undoubtedly why in the Greek lan-guage the word *psyche* stands not only for the human soul, but also for butterfly, a symbol of the soul. Psyche, the beautiful human goddess in the Greek myth, is pictured with butterfly wings, and she is so *beautiful* that even Aphrodite's temple altars are neglected in her favor. Psyche's partner is, of course, Eros in the myth – another winged being – and their partnership stands for the inextricable union in human experience of the reality of the psyche and its transformative potential, made possible by a union of human and divine, of feminine and masculine, of self and other, of beauty and love.

In our specimen dream, the patient's body is now carried on one wing of the miraculous butterfly and is slowly being healed as the butterfly opens and closes its wings – together, apart, together, apart – each time pressing the patient's body against a kachina, slowly forming in the other wing. In the Hopi culture, kachinas are material/spiritual beings who were understood to have been present from the beginning of time and who taught the Hopis how to live on earth after their original emergence from the bowels of the earth. Representing the spiritual essence of everything in the world, the word *Kachina, Katsina,* or *Quatsina* means "life bringer" in the Hopi language. As the butterfly's wings open and close, carrying her body to its kachina, she is "re-enspirited" with her own human/divine life-force – made especially in her image. Life begins to flow once again. The patient's lost soul slowly returns and takes up residence in her body. She can now begin to feel her grief (sad and empty) and a normal human mourning process is initiated – companioned by her trusted therapist.

In a final beautiful image, the butterfly, now small, returns and lands on her belly, sitting at the deep hole there drinking from her wound, beating its wings again. This image suggests that *the psyche is nourished by our conscious and contained suffering* – it is drawn to it. The patient is no longer overwhelmed by her trauma and dissociated – she can now house the injury that previously constituted an unfeeling abyss into which she had fallen and disappeared. Now *her* life contains the wound. Now she feels "sober, sad, and empty," but also "peaceful and renewed." She has been held by both her therapist and the psyche through a tolerable grief process, and her trauma has been healed. The process is nothing if not beautiful!

## Concluding thoughts

In concluding these remarks I don't want to spoil these stories with stilted words or lose the melody in between the written words that frame these accounts. For those who have heard this "music," I want to say that this is why we do this work. We are trying to make space for that music – humming about feelings like Georgie's therapist or reading stories like Monika Wikman to her Hopi patient – trying to reduce trauma's legacy of fear and dissociation in order to create a holding space so that the psyche has a chance to restart its symbolic process and beauty can be found once again. Rumi said, "Let the beauty that you love be what you do."[32] That, I believe, is what we strive for.

Practically speaking, as Susan Reid reminds us, we hold in our minds an awareness that somewhere inside the catastrophically wounded and traumatically defended patient who sits across from us, surrounded by a thornbush of defenses, is a beautiful "child" – a child capable of living in this world with a passion for beauty. A child, who like Jennifer, even with darkness closing in, can find the light and say, with all her heart and soul, "I want to color!" – and who then, years later, can tell that story again and reconnect with her soul. We are "psychotherapists," which means that we serve and care for the soul. In the words of Louis Howe (as reported in Hazel Rowley's book *Franklin and Eleanor*), "We are at heart, minstrels singing outside the window of beauty."[33]

Each individual life carries this apprehension of beauty at the core – a divine spark thrown into the material tinder of life. Often the spark smolders and never catches fire. Perhaps it has never had a chance. Often no one has blown on that spark or helped with the kindling process, or sat with a child long enough for a true birth of ensouled selfhood. Then defenses develop against this beauty and the psychic depths that it mediates . . . defenses against feeling its "possession," its "measure of awe," and the "shuddering" that Plato said is an inevitable part of the raw experience of beauty. In such cases, one has to create a safe space for the re-experience of beauty, and this may mean doing battle with the forces of resistance and defense that try to insulate the patient from his or her own intolerable vulnerability. This can feel like an ugly process but the struggle toward transformation sometimes pays off, as the these three cases illustrate.

When I sit with a patient, I am looking for the glowing coal of that vital spark inside – the potential for a genuine apprehension of beauty – through all the smoke and distraction that masks it – the noise of defenses. I am listening for that music and trying to find it in myself. If the patient is telling me a story and there's no music in it, I try to imagine where the music might be or maybe I am silent to make a space for the spark of truth or beauty that is hidden. If I say something and get a defense back, I point this out and struggle with the defenses and the patient's fear in order to liberate myself and the patient from a useless, beauty-destroying process. Sometimes it's hard to tell "who" in the patient is speaking – the vital core or its defenses. Sometimes the music has no vehicle except the squeak and squawk of rusty armor – heavy metal instruments. But then again, sometimes the psyche presents the beautiful hidden truth in a dream and the struggle with defenses stops – like in Monika Wikman's case, the butterfly is there and the healing waters and the kachina and some direction from the psyche about how to hold the patient.

That's the miracle. When we touch it, it's beautiful. On our best days – when we're doing our best work – I believe we are at heart "minstrels singing outside the window of beauty."

## Notes

1   Plato, "Phaedrus," in E. Hamilton and H. Cairns (eds) *The Collected Dialogues of Plato*, Bollingen Series LXXI, Princeton, Princeton University Press, 1961, para. 249d.
2   Paul Klee quoted in John O'Donohue, *Beauty: The Invisible Embrace*, New York, Harper Collins, 2003, p. 85.

3  Ibid., p. 82.
4  *The Holy Bible,* Exodus 33:20 (King James Version).
5  P. B. Shelley, *Adonais,* first published 1821, quoted in Ann Wroe, *Being Shelley: The Poet's Search for Himself,* New York, Pantheon Books, 2007, p. 222.
6  C. G. Jung, *Memories, Dreams, Reflections,* ed. A. Jaffe, trans. R. and C. Winston, New York, Vintage Books, Random House, 1963, p. 6.
7  Ibid., p. 199.
8  Harold. F. Searles, *The Nonhuman Environment in Healthy Development and in Schizophrenia,* New York, International Universities Press, 1960.
9  Ibid., p. 6.
10  Ibid., p. 11.
11  C. G. Jung, *Letters, Vols. I and II,* ed. G. Adler, Princeton, Princeton University Press, 1975, p. 540.
12  Susan Reid, "The importance of beauty in the psychoanalytic experience," *Journal of Child Psychotherapy,* 1990, vol. 16, no. 1, 29–52. I am indebted to Jungian analyst Carl Boyer, MD, for bringing this paper to my attention and for his larger work on the *Archetype of Beauty* in his diploma thesis for the Inter-Regional Society of Jungian Analysts.
13  Ibid., p. 34.
14  Ibid., p. 35.
15  Ibid., pp. 35–6.
16  Ibid., p. 37.
17  Ibid., pp. 39–41.
18  Donald Meltzer and Meg Harris, *The Apprehension of Beauty,* Strathtay, Perthshire, Clunie Press, 1988.
19  Ibid., p. 17.
20  Ibid., p. xvi.
21  Ibid., p. 5.
22  Ibid., p. xiii.
23  Ibid., p. xvi.
24  John O'Donohue, *Eternal Echoes,* New York, Harper Perennial, 2000, p. 21.
25  Plato, "Phaedrus," para. 249d.
26  Meltzer and Harris, *The Apprehension of Beauty,* p. 6.
27  T. S. Eliot, "Little Gidding, V," *Four Quartets,* London, Faber and Faber Ltd., 2001, p. 43.
28  Soren Kierkegaard, *Either/Or,* Vol. II, trans. Walter Lowrie, Princeton, Princeton University Press, 1972.
29  Monika Wikman, *Pregnant Darkness: Alchemy and the Rebirth of Consciousness,* Berwick, Maine, Nicolas-Hays, Inc., 2004, pp. 53–5.
30  Ibid., p. 53.
31  Ibid, pp. 53–4.
32  Rumi quoted in John O'Donohue, *Beauty: The Invisible Embrace,* p. 3.
33  Hazel Rowley, *Franklin and Eleanor: An Extraordinary Marriage,* New York, Picador Press, 2011, p. 206.

# 3

# INTRODUCTION TO *THE KORE STORY/PERSEPHONE'S DOG*

*Craig San Roque*

> . . . we are dreaming creatures . . .
>
> (Salman Rushdie, BBC radio, 17 September 2012)

## On the poetics of being

Imagine original beings walking the earth, archetypal forms in the making, emerging out of the land. Emerging simultaneously from the human psyche. You might ask – am I discovering these beings walking toward me across the land, or am I creating them?

It is a human thing to dream creatures. Yet perhaps not every original being is invented by human beings. Perhaps the force of nature has a life of its own and comes to meet us in forms that nature chooses, firing our imagination as it does so. A special kind of sung poetry has developed among many peoples of the world that mingles the reality that we see with the reality that we create. There may not be one clear term in the English language that describes this intermingling of that which we imagine and that which is independently there. I prefer the term *ontopoiesis* – or, more simply, *ontopoetic* – suggesting a mingling of the Greek concept *ontos* ("that which is" – "I am" or "being") with *poiesis* ( indicating "coming into being" – "creation" or "bringing forth").

Together these words *ontos* and *poiesis* synchronize into a sense of the poetic, creative relationships between beings. This intermingling is an intricate etymological and psychological matter and my sentence here merely hints at the subtlety of *ontopoetics*. Let us say that the term draws our attention to the poetic infrastructure of creation, the beauty and symmetry that may be found in the order of an insect, in the structure of seeds, in the composition of bird song, in the camouflage speckle on the skin of trout or deer . . . And then there is the response that a human being makes to these symmetries, for the human is a part of this design.

I seek for words in English that hold the notion of human communicative participation in the breath of nature, in the walking of archetypal forms, moments when human creatures and nature's forces collaborate, comingle. The philosopher Freya Mathews coined this term – *the ontopoetic,* lovingly acknowledging that the world itself is open – "intimately psycho-active and disposed toward communicative engagement with us."[1]

This *Kore Story* is, for me, subjectively, an instance of ontopoetic collaboration. It was composed at a marvelous ancient site, with no preconceived expectation. I had prepared the ground, as a painter prepares a canvas, but the words began to flow from voices in my inner ear, describing to me the two women traveling in that landscape at Delphi; and I obeyed, writing down the lines as though from dictation.

## A note on style and context

The style of this text follows the mode I developed for the *Dionysos/Sugarman* performances in Central Australia, in 1996–9, two extracts from which appear in this volume as the invocatory *Creation Story* and the closing *Traveling Ariadne.* The mode is influenced by the rhythmic, colloquial humor of local storytellers. The narrative structures of *Kore Story* echo, but do not copy, the tone, simplicity of movement, and repetition that you might hear in Australian indigenous ceremonial song cycles. These involve chanted verses, accompanied by rhythmic beat and dance, revealing specific acts and travels of mythic, original creation beings. Such activities take place in ancient or ancestral time and continue in the present. Cultural lore and memory is held in place through such story/song lines, known in some Central Australian desert languages as *Jukurrpa* or *Altjerre.* These are the creation sagas of a hunter-gatherer people who live off the land.[2]

Similar compositions of cultural lore and memory are held in the song cycles and mythic narratives of old Europe. The Demeter/Persephone myth is one such cycle. A traditional version comes down to us through the Homeric Hymns. More primitive or folkloric forms of this story would have been circulating among the peoples whose hands were accustomed to digging the earth, bringing plants and vines to fruition. It is likely that the Demeter/Persephone story is located historically and mythically at a time of crucial transition in European life. It is a poetic account of the experience of peoples moving from the hunter-gatherer way of life toward a settled agricultural way of life.

I acknowledge the influence of Australian indigenous style and ontology upon my (echo) version of the Persephone story. The connection between Ancient Greece and modern Australia is made for practical reasons. It is about hunger. This re-visioned story forms part of a contemporary food-security and land-use project in which I am involved in arid Central Australian Aboriginal regions.[3] The project is concerned with how people in remote areas of Australia can produce decent and nutritious food from their land, now that traditional hunting is unreliable. Food supply has become an acute problem in Aboriginal life. Remote area food stores are very expensive, fresh food is hard to get, processed sugar-rich foodstuffs and alcohol generate diabetes and obesity. The rigor of walking for hunting and gathering has been replaced by the convenience of motor vehicles and shops.

My purpose here is not to explain in detail the circumstances and complicated nature of developing and managing agricultural (and pastoral) developments on indigenous land in Central Australia – but these matters lie behind my interest in revisiting the European-Caucasian transition from a hunter-gather life to an agricultural life. Suffice it to say that a hunter-gatherer society develops specific, pragmatic ways of organizing land, waters, and social systems for food gathering and distribution. By contrast, farming/pastoral/industrial societies organize land, resources, and social relationships for food production and distribution in a different way. Over many generations people get into the habit of thinking as hunters or as farmers. The occupation breeds a mentality. If circumstances begin to change . . . if people lose control over their own food production and/or lose control over their own land and waters and trade . . . if the way of thinking upon which they depend becomes redundant . . . what happens then?

In Aboriginal Australia, there is acute and insidious conflict arising around this theme – hunter-gatherer practices are forced to give way to an industrialized food-supply system over which the hunters and gatherers have little or no control. The shop gives you food in exchange for money. The shop is not moved by "increase ceremonies," and it matters not that the old man who bellies up to the shop counter is a man with vast cultural knowledge, who, in a hunter-gatherer economy would be supplied with food by men he had initiated into esoteric knowledge. Now there is no opportunity for trade, for the white people own the goods and the means of production. The equation of "food for money" and "money for work" is the equation that rules.

In Aboriginal Central Australia, the rules of food gathering are changing – including the rules of food distribution among specific kin – a system that prevails in the carefully managed indigenous hunter-gatherer economy. Furthermore, a cohesive poetic of being interweaves hunter-gatherer management of land, water, fire, animals, and the processes of natural cycles. Swift and blunt economic change, however, is changing the hunter-gatherer economy and the embedded ontopoetic mentality, as represented in the songs and ceremonies of *Jukurrpa/Altjerre*.

Psychologically, the hunters now rattle around in a state of cultural anxiety, marked by a sullen kind of existential anguish, intoxication, interpersonal violence, and passive aggression. This is not surprising.

Well then, how does an Australian hunter-gatherer family group get to think and work like a European farming family and run an agricultural company? Making a successful transition in civilization from one form of food production to another is not simple. How does one move from hunting to animal husbandry, from gathering to planting and cultivation? How long might it have taken the Caucasian or Semitic peoples to make that change? In what circumstances? By what steps did that adaptation proceed? Such questions are a part of the context of this *Kore Story*.

## Cultural mentalities

Consider how the stories of the Peoples of the Book are entwined with the story of pastoralists and farmers. Many Judeo-Christian spiritual metaphors are linked to land-use. The histories of the Children of Abraham, the parables of Jesus, the metaphors of sacrifice, the lamb, the shepherd, the vine, the bread and the blood, are metaphors specific to a mentality formed by the everyday processes of cultivation, animal husbandry, land management, flock management, the settlement, and the kinship systems of such cultures. Indigenous Australian culture evolved from an entirely different system of environmental management. Thus do their mentalities differ.

A cultural mentality slowly becomes encoded into myth. This is why I am exploring a cultural story (a myth) from the time when the Caucasians changed food production toward agriculture. Australian indigenous people also structure law and culture around myths. A people's mentality is revealed in the myths upon which they draw.

The old *Demeter Persephone/Triptolemus Story* marks a significant point of transition in European civilization. Understanding that historical transition may empathically help us appreciate the difficulty and the potential of what is being experienced today among Australian Aboriginal people, especially in settings where agricultural projects are being ambivalently developed around specific indigenous communities north of Alice Springs (Ti Tree and Ali Curung).

This is a complicated lead-up to saying that my purpose in retelling this old Greek story is to set out characters, images, events, and a mood that can be drawn on as we think together on themes of hunting, gathering, and farming practices. The *Kore Story* is part of a project in sharing or bridging cultural mentalities within a Central Australian region that is teeming with song lines (*Altjerre/ Jukurrpa*) related to native food and animal beings, including the important *Alekarenge Story*, which features the activities of mythic traveling dogs. The thought of exchanging cultural stories in a culturally rich region like Central Australia is not unusual. Indeed, such an exchange is common sense. Understanding the myths that support the mentalities of both the hunters and the farmers may help these two peoples work together more efficiently to solve the hunger problem. At present, I observe that two ways of thinking (that of hunters and that of farmers) are in oppositional resistance.

## Caution and connection

I am not naïve enough to believe that a "fairy story" from the past will make people change their behaviors in the present and turn them into farmers. This Kore project is not a propaganda exercise. I tell this story only so that people from diverse cultures can hear it, match it with indigenous experiences, and perhaps be stimulated to talk with each other, acknowledging the anxieties around food gathering, production, and distribution. Local indigenous people have hundreds of stories about plants and animals pertaining to the nurture, gathering, distribution, and preparation of local foods, just as the Europeans and Asians also have cultural mythologies pertaining to the cultivation and uses of cereals, fruits, medicinal plants, flowers, fish, animal meats, fermentation and brewing, and all that sustains life.

There is a deep problem that needs to be signaled, even if not analyzed here. The indigenous Australian is deeply versed in hunter-gatherer mentalities and conservative habits of thinking that have sustained life for millennia. Most admit that some kind of collapse of the culture is now taking place. Concerned economic and social development people, deeply versed in procedural mentalities that have served the European empires for centuries, also observe the social collapse. Concerned government agencies, desperate for a solution, habitually revert to pushing forward the "evidence-based" economic solution (aka "the white man's solution"). Well-intended economic development agents revert to habits of thinking that have sustained European life. They cannot imagine any other solution. The hunter-gatherers, in turn, defend their habits of thinking and may not be able to imagine any other solution either. Two forms of habitual thinking are locked in a passive-aggressive dogfight.

The managers of the agricultural project in Central Australia with which I am involved are looking for links in thinking between these two completely diverse groups of peoples and their respective mentalities. Good business, they say, depends on good thinking – and on consensus in the minds of those involved in whatever the deal is. Good business involves linking the thoughts of indigenous hunter-gatherers with the thoughts of farmers. Good business also involves "left brain" rational, numerate ways of processing experience and managing money; linked with "right brain" imagistic, emotionally toned, artistic ways of processing experience and managing people. Communication between peoples of two distinct cultural histories means using all parts of one's brain and all capacities of the active human body – the practical, the intellectual, the emotional, and the poetic.

You do not need to understand the complexity of this Australian situation, nor be convinced by my formulation. It is enough to know that this re-vision of the Demeter myth was evoked by a problem of hunger in desert communities. The text was set down during a visit to a significant European site (Delphi),[4] and I tell it here out of respect for my European cultural history.

## Placing Kore

I have taken Persephone's story as a version of a Mediterranean cultivation narrative. I see Persephone's return and the subsequent Triptolemus ventures as linked with similar Dionysos legends that recount the spreading of the vine culture.

From these myths, we get a sense of those peoples' preoccupation with loss, disappearance, violent death, dismemberment, lament, yearning, and resurrections. Such preoccupation, linked with organic fertility cycles, sexuality, birth, and nurturance lead us directly into themes of the old Mystery cycles, in which Egyptian

51

Osiris/Isis, Sumerian Inanna/Dumuzi, Grecian Dionysos and the Eleusinian Mysteries all have a place.

The Eleusinian Mysteries include ritualized, seasonal death and regeneration ceremonies and illuminations that were continuously celebrated for over 2,000 years until the Christian era. These events were located at Eleusis, near Athens, an acknowledged site of Demeter's search for her daughter Kore and then Kore's return. This central ceremony of the ancient Mediterranean is no longer celebrated at Eleusis. The place itself is surrounded by industrial suburbs. It is a memorial to loss.

It seems that the European Christian orthodoxy gradually came to prefer a mythologem of eternal return, not of a daughter like Persephone who dwells in the soil, but of a recycling spiritual son portrayed as an emanation of a divine father dwelling (elusively) in heaven and on earth. So be it. I feel, however, that *The Kore Story* holds the older line of the land-dwelling mothers who cross country on foot. Land-dwelling mothers who cross country on foot are alive and well in contemporary indigenous Australia. Those mothers might appreciate this story of two traveling Caucasian women and their dog, seeking out plants and good things to eat.

Demeter's grief story probably marks a significant shift in the Caucasian people's security about the management of food supply. Something happened that brought about that shift. What was it? Perhaps a flood, an ice age, an invasion? Darkness and famine pervade the land – and then the daughter returns and all seems well again. Demeter commissions a young man, Triptolemus, to begin spreading the art of managed agriculture. He meets resistances. This is to be expected. The transitions from unreliable hunting and gathering to sometimes reliable agriculture would have been gradual, sporadic, ambivalent, and depressingly hard.

There are many variations of the Demeter/Persephone myth – fragments recorded on vase paintings, in sculpture, and in writings from early Greek sources. There are also many interpretations. I acknowledge in the notes the several authors whose works helped me absorb this elusive material.[5]

## Names and definitions

The names of mythic characters tell much about their nature, and if one truly understood ancient Greek, one might perceive subtle, complex meanings. I give here some simple etymology as a guide.

### *Kore*

The term *Kore,* in original Greek, denotes a young girl/woman/maiden before marriage. *Kore* is conventionally used to refer to young Persephone in the Demeter myth. Jules Cashford notes:

> I've always taken heart from the fact that *kore* is the feminine form of *"sprout"* – *koros* – And that the *"De"* of Demeter may also come from the *"dyai,"* barley grains of Crete, where the Homeric Hymn has her originating. Agricultural

meanings are already written into the etymology, giving us familiar images of a human plant waving in the wind, dropping its seeds – barley, wheat or corn – and coming back up as sprouts in one eternally returning cycle of life.[6]

### Demeter

The term *De-Meter* signifies divinity + mother (*Meter*) with the prefix *De* or *Dyai,* suggesting a divinity and making an association to life-sustaining cereal plants (barley). Cashford also informs me that "it is important to note that primarily the two forms of the Earth or Corn-goddess are not Mother and Daughter but Mother and Maiden, the older and younger form of the same person."[7] In this sense, Demeter/Kore is a unity and a couple, the older and younger aspects of the same feminized force of a natural living process. In storytelling, you need the play of personifications of archetypal processes. You need different characters to play out the drama, even though in ceremony and song the characters represent natural processes that are not "persons" as such. Because of the needs of drama, the characterization works better as mother and daughter – two characters, not one.

### Persephone and her consorts

The etymology of *Persephone* is intriguing and somewhat obscure. Felix Guirand[8] suggests:

> it is believed the last half of the word Persephone comes from a word meaning "to show" and evokes the idea of light. Whether the first half derives from a word meaning "to destroy" – in which case Persephone would be "she who destroys the light" – or from an adverbial root signifying "dazzling brilliance," as in the name of Perseus, it is difficult to decide.

Names of mythological characters often have descriptors of their nature (epithets) attached. One version of a descriptor for Persephone suggests "wedded to destruction." I draw on this description in the marital scene with Aidos (conventionally named Hades in English). Guirand suggests that Aidos' name, in Greek, is derived from the prefix "a" + "to see" – indicating "not seeing" or "not seen," that is, "invisible." Aidos' other name *Pluto* indicates "riches" hence, "he was then considered the god of agricultural wealth. From the centre of the earth he exerted his influence on cultivation and the crops."[9]

You will note that I have taken up and enhanced this fertile and productive notion of Aidos/Hades in my version of the story, rather than going for Aidos/Hades as the dark incestuous abductor from the underworld – a terror version favored, no doubt, by Demeter in her distress. The paradoxical double edge of the Greek naming system helps us grasp how Persephone, in her annual cycle, can be wedded to destruction and wedded to productivity, wedded to darkness and wedded to light and illumination.

"Triptolemus" usually figures as the son of the family at Eleusis who helps Demeter find her daughter. His name may signify "to plough or dig three times." This makes sense when we think of Triptolemus as an agriculture mentor.

In this particular way of decoding the names of Demeter, Aidos, Persephone, Eleusinian Triptolemus, and associated characters, the figures present as essential elements in a comprehensive story about plant behaviors, ecosystems, and cultivation. It is all close to the ground. In the same manner, much of the Australian desert myth is close to the ground.

Before the art of writing was consolidated, our ancestors transmitted their observations in folkloric forms, probably in the same way that indigenous Australians transmit knowledge in song, dances, painting, and ceremony, suffused perhaps with magical and pantheistic ways of sensing the interweaving of natural process. Poetic sensibilities and scientific observation can tenderly match each other's potencies. This tends to be referred to locally as "two way thinking." I am all for "two way thinking."

## On the geography of Kore

... the fields of song are laid out ...
(Homeric Hymn to Apollo, Line 21)[10]

The reader may need to consult a map and note routes and places to which I refer in the story. Demeter is said to have come ancestrally from Crete to the mainland and thus to Eleusis. Carl Kerenyi[11] explores this notion in his work on Dionysos' Cretan origins. George Mylonos,[12] in the introduction to his book on the Eleusinian Mysteries, outlines and also questions the diverse notions of four possible origins of the Demeter cult – Egypt, Thessaly, Thrace, and Crete. From an archeomythological point of view, sorting out the reality of origins and arrival points and times is important. From a tribal point of view, however, what counts is that the divinity arrived in this or that tribe's country from such and such a place in a particular manner. This story becomes the folklore and legend of place and declares local ownership and participation in that divinity's story. The sense of participation is what counts. I think this is the ontopoetic thing, where people communicate with numinous creatures who are felt to inhabit the landforms. Mystical participation with and identification with traveling gods in the ancient Greek stories is similar to the sense of psychic participation with traveling beings who dwell in Australian *Jukurrpa/Altjerre* stories.

It is natural to imagine and describe Demeter and Kore's creation activities taking place at specific sites, close to the ground, at rocks, caves, and chasms, including the place where the Omphalos stone landed. The fateful mythic place where three ways cross near Thebes is a real place, not imaginary. The beach and caves of Eleusis are natural places and, at the same time, mysterious; timeless events take place there.

My story acknowledges the mother and daughter arriving from Crete, landing at Krisa below Delphi, and then ascending the cliff route to the Gaia rock site, now known as *Athena Pronaia*. Pythia's cave and the natural features are as they are today, before temples and paths, ovals and theatre were constructed.

There is another track implied in my story – a walking track coming from the north, and Mt. Olympos, seat of the Olympian divinities, and thus another seat of Demeter. I think Hekate lives up there, too, in her cave where Demeter calls on her, dragging the reluctant Kore behind her. The present road from the north comes down through Lamia, Amfissa, toward the bay of Corinth, into Boeotia, and thus to Delphi. One assumes such routes follow early walking tracks, as would the routes heading east and south via Mt. Cithaeron/Kytheron. Thebes figures in the colonization legend of Phoenician Cadmus and is, of course, the site of Jocasta and Oedipus' ill-fated city. It seems right that Demeter stopped there, for Thebes is a city where many children were lost. The traveling women stop at Eleusis, near the coast, just west of present-day Athens. Eleusis, or *Elevsis* or *Elefsis* as it is named on the road signs, currently struggles to survive as an ancient sacred site, now threatened by industrial asphyxiation in the same manner as many similar sacred sites in Australia are now demolished, overbuilt, or ignored.

From Eleusis, in my story, Demeter and Kore walk through the peninsula, east and south of where Athens is today, to the promontory dedicated to Poseidon, who, in some myths, is a consort/lover to Demeter. There, you might find yourself gazing over the sea toward the Cyclades, volcanic Thira and Crete to the south. It is along this walk to the sea that I have imagined an event that establishes an origin of the olive.

Demeter/Persephone, as cultural personifications, would have traveled other routes, just as Australian mythic women traveled a maze of routes across the continent of Australia. Whichever country the icons travel through, the people of those countries claim them and their activities. It would not be surprising then, to find sites of Persephone's descent and return located at many places and in many time zones.

My story sites are limited to Delphi, Hekate's cave near or on Olympos, the Eleusis site, Mt. Kytheron, and the country along the coast toward the Attic peninsula. The Delphi site itself is on the cliffs overlooking the Pleistos river. This stream forms the Parnassos gorge. Two sites at Delphi must be mentioned. The original Delphi seems to include or be a site of primal maternal *Gaia* (now *Athena Pronaia*). This is where, in my story, Kore and Demeter visit the "Mother Sitting," which may have been represented in ancient times as a large, animated rock – as are Australian mythic sites. There are now several formidable old olive trees on the Gaia/Athena site and the river flats and slopes below are rich with cultivated olives.

Higher up are places associated with the original, prehistoric, serpentine Pythia. There may have been several locations, over time, where snake nests, gaseous emissions, sibylline voices, and awesome enchantments were experienced – with or without the aid of hallucinogenic fungi.

Kore's vision of the cosmic seed refers to the legend of the stone that falls from the sky/Zeus and rests at Delphi as *Omphalos,* that is the central navel/womb/seed of the world. I feel this as a composite image of original sperm/*panspermia,* ovum, womb, and navel of the Original Mother – evoking Delphi as mythic locus of a Creation Point – a point from which creation emanates.

## Text, time, and precedent

In many traditional story forms, including in Australia and Oceania, narrative lines follow a discipline of rhythmically told accounts of actions by mythic beings. The actions tell the story. That is to say – "He did this . . . "; "She did that . . . ". We get accounts of what he or she said or sang and sometimes thought, but this is mostly without intellectualizing, without abstract philosophizing or introspective reflections. The action tells the story. *Kore Story* is an action story.

In the Papua New Guinea highlands,[13] similar story forms are in use where travels, sites, seasons, hunting, farming, conflicts, and adventures map into the country stories that imbue memory and ratify cultural practices and law. And in Papuan stories, mythic time is not chronologically bound to the past. As in *Jukurrpa/Altjerre,* characters walk in ancestral mythic time and walk in the present. Persephone and her mother walk in ancestral time and walk the active present.

*Kore Story/Persephone's Dog* was not composed in order to instruct or influence indigenous people to become farmers. It is to remind those of us of European descent, who live on the surface of Australia, that we, too, have an old culture, and a history of struggle with the elements, a struggle with survival, collapse, and recovery – and we have a lineage of sung poetry that keeps the mind going.

This is a story about a mother and a daughter and a dog, and I hope you like it. I hope it keeps your mind walking a little bit further.

## Acknowledgments

Alice Springs Centrefarm team, the indigenous directors, and members of the Alekarenge Horticultural Company. The participants in the *Ancient Greece, Modern Psyche* Conference at the Nomikos Center in September 2012. Thomas Singer, Jules Cashford, *The Chorus of Women,* Glenda Cloughley, Freya Mathews, Marlene Nampijimpa Spencer, Lila San Roque, Jude Prichard, our family dogs, and the view from the *Hotel Hermes,* Delphi.

# THE KORE STORY/
# PERSEPHONE'S DOG

## *Craig San Roque*

When Aidos lies down, earth rumbles, when Hades lies down, islands erupt.
Things go on beneath the ground. There is need to fear these things.
Things go on beneath the ground. There is no need to fear these things,
Things live, things die. This is the way of it.
(*Invocation to Hades*, Thira, 10 September 2012)

I begin to sing of her and her daughter, the surpassingly beautiful Persephone.
(*Invocation, Homeric Hymn XIII*)

### Story sequence

Coda

# 1 At Delphi Parnassos

*Demeter and her daughter Kore arrive at the site of Delphi; they mark the gorge of the Pleistos river, Gaia's seat on the edge of the gorge, later known as* Athena Pronaia. *They visit Pythia's cave. Kore's birth and the secret of the Omphalos seed/stone that falls from the sky is shown to Kore.*

Demeter was travelling. She came from the north. She came down through the mountain, Demeter, travelling with her daughter. Two women travelling; together, down through the mountain. They stopped on the hill. They looked to the south. They looked to the cliffs; they looked down. There is the gorge, she said, two sides of the cut. Remember this. Two sides of the cleft in the grey rock; they saw them. They named them, two sides of the mountain, two sides of the cut. *The Shining (Phaedriades)*, Demeter said. *The Shining*, said Kore, I remember this.

Looking at these things, the eyes of Kore began to form. This is how the eyes of Kore began; the scent, the taste of things, the touch. This is how these things began. Her mother showed her things and eyes formed in the body of Kore. Hearing formed in the body of Kore.

Listen, said her mother, you will hear the world beginning. Listen, Demeter said, your grandmother is here, Ge is here. This is the beginning; this is where all things begin. I love this place. Remember this.

Demeter climbed the hill. She sat down; she sat down over Delphi. She looked over the valley. Together they looked down. They could see below on the edge of the cliff, below *The Shining Ones,* they could see the Mother Rock. They could see the stones, rock on rock, circle upon circle. There on the cliff, Ge is there. She is there. Remember this.

What is this, said Kore, I see old rocks; I see nothing. How can this be? She said. Old rocks; how can your mother be born from rock? Demeter turned to her daughter, she smiled at her. This is your grandmother sitting. This is the first mother – she does not move. The rivers move. The mountains move, but *She* does not move. She is sitting where everything begins. She is sitting where everything comes out. Everything comes out from her – smoke, mosquito, lizard, fish, snake, bird, kangaroo, dog . . . they all move, but she does not move.

Look, she said to the daughter. Look, she said to Kore. That is where you begin. Here is your grandmother sitting, the first mother. In the beginning. This is the place. Kore looked. She crossed her arms; she placed her two hands over her breast; like this. She said nothing. She was quiet. I will wait, said Kore.

They turn together, they lift their eyes, they look up to the python cave.

There on the cliff, said Demeter, there on the cliff, let us go up. They climbed to the python cave, they climbed the grey rock. Kore looked in the python cave. This is Pythia? she said. She said to her mother, is this the place? I see nothing, there is nothing here. This is the place, said her mother, you shall see. There . . . Pythia there . . . the snake; she can see you. Look, the smoke. The voice is there, there. Remember this.

Smoke comes up from a hole in the rock. The python turns like smoke in the wind. The python turns an eye to Kore. The snake turns her eye to Kore. The world begins. Look – said the python, look, said Pythia. This is the place, Kore, open your eyes to the smoke. Kore, open your breath to the smoke. The python opens her mouth, Kore sees inside, inside the open jaws of Pythia the python, Kore sees the world beginning . . . In the beginning.

She cried out – Mother, you grow bigger, you grow greater than the mountain. You rise up. You cover the sky. Her mother Demeter covered the sky. She rose up, she covered the whole world. The whole world inside her body; in the beginning. The whole sky inside her body. Two eagles flew around her, inside her. One flew to the east, one flew to the west. The two eagles flew right around the body of Demeter. They flew right around inside the skin of the sky; inside the body of the first mother. It took them days and days.

The eagles flew in circles. They cried. All the birds heard their cry – the cry and clatter of wings. All the birds of the world rose up. Clouds formed, and smoke. The lightning cracked . . . This Kore heard. This Kore saw.

The two eagles meet; in the sky over Delphi they meet. They circle the body of Demeter, the mother. They meet in the sky over Delphi – the cry, the clatter of wings.

*Demeter spoke –*

59

"I am the womb of the world, I am the seed of the world.
Today I give birth to women. Today I give birth to Kore."

This Kore heard. This Kore saw. She saw her own birth, she saw her mother, she saw the four wings of two eagles, beating, beating; the wings beating. The beating settled. In her own heart it settled. This Kore heard. This Kore saw. A seed fell from the sky, a seed fell. It nestled in Delphi. It nestled in Kore. In her own heart it settled, it spoke; "I am the seed of the world. You are the seed of the world. Nurture us."
This Kore heard. This Kore saw.

The smoke lifts, the python rolls. She closes her mouth. She closes her eye. She gives Kore a drink. Here, she said, you need a drink. Yes, said Kore, I need a drink.

## 2 Digging stick

*Demeter marks out places. She makes the geography of the Pleisto river that runs in the gorge beneath the cliffs of Delphi.*

Two women are travelling, they keep moving. Demeter looks out along the mountain line. They come down the mountain. Kore comes down from Pythia's cave, she turns for one more look; she thanks her. Demeter takes up a stick; she takes up her digging stick. She names it. *I remember this place.* Naming the digging stick, she says. *I remember this place.*

She marks out a line deep between the mountains. The shining mountains, she calls them. She makes the line deep. It cuts through her body. She cuts a long cut between her breasts. Water runs always along this cut. Down this line a river will run, she says. It will run to the sea, it runs all the way down. She names it – *Pleisto* – the best. This is the best of rivers she says. This river, I love.

What Demeter makes becomes.
What you see today, Demeter makes for all time.

The lines Demeter draws are the lines we should not change. The places Demeter has placed are placed here for a reason. Those places hold the world in balance. The cave, the granite, the tree, the river and the flow of clear water. She says, "I love this place," and so, *we* love this place. She says – this is the time in which I walk, I love this time the most. *This is the beginning.* Remember this, she said to Kore. I will come here always; this is the mother place. People will come. They will walk up from the sea. People will come, they will walk down through the mountains. Coming here, they will remember the beginning of the world. I love this place.

What are these "people?" said Kore. What are these "people" of which you speak?

Never mind, says Demeter, they are yet to come.

Two women are travelling. They go along the valley. They scour out the valley. Look, says Demeter, seeds. These seeds, taste them. Kore gathers the seeds. She grinds them in her teeth. She smiles; I like them. Take them, says the mother; these are the seeds to remember. With these seeds you will make bread for the people to eat. With these seeds you will make bread, so the people are fed.

Kore says; what are "people?" Never mind, says Demeter, they are yet to come.

## 3 Demeter sings the country

Demeter held the seeds in her hand. Give them a name Kore. And Kore gave them a name. As she walked Demeter hummed. Bees flew from her eyes. As she walked Kore sang; she carved the ground; she rustled the seeds. She walked. She turned her head this way and that. She smiled. As she walked she sang their names. Plants grew behind her. Kore carried her digging stick. She named it; *I remember this.*

Demeter lifted her eyes, she gazed over the country; she looked over all the plains. Demeter said; people will come. In the caves they sleep, in the caves they live, they walk around. They'll be hungry; they'll find these seeds, Kore. You show them the grinding stone. You teach them, poor things. "Grind the seeds for your bread," you say. They are not like birds, she said.

## 4 Demeter teaches Kore

They walked on; they went this way and that. Look, said Demeter, and she showed Kore all the seeds in the country. She showed her the seeds to collect; seeds good to grind, seeds good to mix with water and honey, good to roll in little cakes; the seeds good to bake. They will need hot coals, Kore; teach them to make hot coals. They are not birds, she said.

The plants of the country, she named them all, she named them in words that later the people would speak, old words that form the language of Kore's lands, words falling from the tongue of Meter. Words laid down in the mind of Kore. They covered the country; together, they covered the country. Kore smiled. We are like birds, she said.

Demeter showed her daughter where everything grows. Teach the people to walk, she said. Teach them to gather and crush; teach them to winnow and grind. Show them the grinding stones, teach them to mix and bake. Show them the basket to carry the seeds.

Teach them the way to live, she said. They are not birds.

## 5 Mt. Kytheron

The mother travelled on. They were travelling fast. Down to Mt. Kytheron.[14] On the way down they came to a place. Look, she said, tracks; vulture, lion, and dog; three tracks meeting. They passed through a narrow gorge. Demeter sat on a rock. She cried. She said, terrible things will happen here. People will die, she cried. Show them a better way to live, she cried.

## 6 Pan's dog

They walked on down the mountain. They walked on through the valley, they were travelling through trees; Kore stopped. She saw a tall creature in the sunlight; she saw a small creature. She could not be sure, his shape changing. The creature had goats crying all about him; the goats licking his face, they were licking his beard. Who is that? said Kore. That is Pan, said Demeter, he is everything; he goes everywhere. You should marry him. You'll be happy.

Kore looked at the creature, sometimes tall, sometimes small; his face was smiling. She loved his face. I am not ready to marry, said Kore, but I love his face. Pan smiled at her. The goats followed her. A dog followed her, a beautiful dog, long and lean, soft red fur, bright eyes, clever eyes. Pan's dog followed her. The dog stopped. He turned back his head; he looked back to Pan. Go with Kore, said Pan. Go with Kore, he whistled.

## 7 Dog travelling

*They come down to a place now known as Eleusis, overlooking the bay of Saronis.*

The dog travelled with them, the dog travelled with Demeter, the dog, travelling with Kore. They're good travellers. They travel down to the sea. This is a good place, said Meter. Name it, she said to Kore, and Kore named it. She named it *Eleusis*. I do not know what it means, she said, but I love the sound it makes on my tongue. Good, said her mother. Remember that sound; remember this place.

The two travelling women sat down at Eleusis. We will come here again, one day, said Demeter. I remember this place.

She stuck her digging stick in the ground; upright it stood. It gathered darkness; it grew leaves. It became a tree, dark and shapely, outlined on the hill. It gathered in the scent of pine, dark and shapely, outlined on the hill. I will call it *Kyprissa,* Demeter said, when people see this beautiful shape, they will think of you, *Kyprissa Koreai.*

She stood, she sighed. Why am I sighing, she said. You are tired, said Kore. Perhaps, said her mother; she turned her head, gazing back at the dark shape of the cypress tree, outlined against the hill.

She came down to Eleusis. At Eleusis she sat down. She sat there singing. She sang a sad song; she sang a lament. It was the first time she sang a lament. Why am I singing a sad song, said Demeter. I don't know, said her daughter. Keep singing. I will remember.

They walked on. They walked southeast, along the coast toward Poseidon. They were thinking about water, they were thinking about sea. I will show you the foam on the sea, said Demeter. They walk on.

The mother showed the daughter the wild berries growing in this place. Things are different here, she said; these things grew as I walked down to the sea. She showed her all the native fruit that grew along the shore. They walked along the hills. Look, she said, this one, the green one; this different berry. I like this tree, said Demeter. I like the silver leaves, said Kore. I like the old black berries, said the dog. He snuffled along the ground, he snuffled like a pig.

I tell you now, this tree they saw, it was an olive tree – the only one; the first one.

Before that day, the two women hadn't tasted those berries. They look like little plums, little peaches, she said. Demeter was worried about them. They came out of me, she said, but I forget what kind of day it was. I'll taste it, said Kore, watching her dog snuffing at green and blackening fruit scattering the ground. He picked up a black one in his teeth, he bit into it; he swallowed. He kept walking, his tail wagging. Looking for more, and maybe, looking for lizard.

I'll taste it, said Demeter. She reached up. She took a ripe one; her teeth bit the black flesh, she spat it out. The people won't like this, she said, it's only good for dogs . . .

The olives fell to the ground. Wherever Demeter walked, the olives fell to the ground. She walked over them but she would not eat them. Some things are too bitter, she said, spitting them out. Where she spat them, more olives grew. Soon all the hills above the sea were covered with olive trees, but she did not eat them. Kore followed behind. The dog followed Kore. They walked among the trees. Kore collected olives; she wove a basket with grasses. She carried them in her basket.

This is my Khora, she said, this is my basket. I will carry this Khora wherever I go.
I will keep things in this and carry them. I will think about them.

She broke off a branch of the olive tree, She made a cutting; she carried it to a secret place. She stuck it in the ground, in a cleft of the rock, water flowed there, clean water; I will remember this, said Kore. This tree will grow here, she said, this will be a good one; I will call it "the beloved". This is the one to feed the people to come.

She took the ripe and bitter olives down to the sea; she washed them.
She thought about olives soaked in salt water.

She held her two hands to her head; one on the left, one on the right.
She was learning to think like a human-to-come.
She saw the way to soak them; she saw the way to make them kind to taste.
She saw the way to wash away the bitter taste. She said to the dog, some things my mother says are right, but she is not right all the time. There are ways to change things . . . and she held her two hands to her head. I will learn to think, she said. I will teach the people to think. My mother travels; she does what she does. My mother makes, but she does not think. I will teach the people to think.

## 8 Kore and the pomegranate

She went travelling alone with the dog. They went tasting things.
They watched the birds. They stopped at a tree with red fruit. The shell of this one is hard, said Kore. But the birds still get in, said the dog, open it and have a look. I'll take it to my mother, said Kore; let's see what she says about this one.

She put some in her basket. She put the basket on her head. She carried it to her mother. Demeter said – this is *Pomegranate,* this beautiful fruit. Open it – see the red seeds shine in the sun. Touch the juice, it runs down your hand. I love it. When you open the skin, look inside and remember me. I am the womb of the world, she said. Take; eat this in remembrance of me.

## 9 Kore and the dog observe the world

In this way Kore travelled with the dog. The dog sniffed things, the dog licked things. What the dog licked and the tail wagged, Kore happily tasted. What the dog sniffed and turned from, Kore marked and turned away. This way they learned many things about the things that grew in the tracks of their mother. They learned the mother's moods as she crossed the country, this way and that. They followed old tracks of Demeter, where Demeter walked before – grasses grew. Where Demeter walked before – native fruits grew. Plants strung out in lines, singing, right across the country.

One day Kore said to her mother, when I follow your tracks I find white flowers.
In a different place I find yellow flowers. When I follow your tracks, sometimes I find red flowers, I find poppy, anemone, I find red pomegranate, sometimes I find quiet places near caves where figs grow, I find secret places hidden where vines and trees grow strong and tall. Why is this, she said, why do some plants grow in some places?

Demeter said, where the white grows, there I spit. And she kept on walking, turning her back on Kore. Don't talk rubbish girl, she said, things grow where they grow. I don't know. The dog sat back on its haunches, sometimes your mother talks rubbish-shit, the dog said to Kore. Does she think I don't see where she goes; does she think I don't see what she does. Where the yellow grows, there she stops for a piss. Where the red poppies grow, there she bled. Where the trees grow strong in quiet places; there she stopped to shit. Don't you see these things?

And the figs, said Kore. The figs, said the dog, that's where she stops and lies down.
She thinks about her . . . what's his name?[15] Sometimes your mother cries, she goes sorry.
Her lover boy was killed, she lost him; your father killed him. He's too jealous, your father. Where she stops to remember her man, the figs grow. She won't tell you this. You have to look.

Kore heard these things and she kept them in her heart. She thought about these things. She marked the places where plants grew best.

## 10 Eleusis again

On this journey the dog and young Kore walked all the way to Poseidon's country. They went for a swim; then they turned back and walked along the

coast till they came back to the cave above Eleusis. There was no one there. Where's she gone? said Kore.
The dog looked at the tracks. Maybe she's gone to visit that old echidna.[16]
The dog sniffed the wind. Or maybe she visits that sister; what's-her-name?
OK, said Kore, she'll be gone some time, let's go down to Eleusis; let's go down to the beach.

The mother'd gone gossiping, Demeter was sitting down with her old sister, Hestia. She was helping her make a kitchen, the first one ever. Demeter said, what is this? Hestia smiled, she said, it's the cooking fire; don't you see? Some people are coming for dinner. I've nothing to cook with. People are on the move; the people are coming. The people are here at last. They've nothing to cook with. It's like you said to Kore, they have to learn to make hot coals, they have to learn to crush the seeds and roll the bread. I'll help you, said Demeter; we'll work out a way to do it. We'll make the people happy, said her sister; gathering sticks for a fire.

Walking toward Eleusis in the morning, the dog stopped to sniff something. The leaves of the oak tree rustling in the wind. The dog sniffed around the roots of the tree. What's that? said Kore. Don't know, said the dog, smells good. It tastes ok, like old meat . . . and ate it. The dog staggered on its feet, the dog's eyes went white; the dog staggered and rolled over. The dog tried to vomit, but it was too late.

The dog lay still. Everything stopped.

Kore looked at the mushroom. This is poison, she said; you stupid dog, it makes you sick. She cursed the fungus; she gave it a name, *amanita phalloides* (*death cap*).

Kore cried out for her dog. Her dog did not move.
The wind moved, the sea moved, but the dog did not move.
What is this, said Kore, I have never seen this before.
She held her dog in her arms; she walked into the rocks.
She laid her dog down in the shade,
In a cleft in the rock, she laid her dog.
She crooned out for her dog,
She sang laments for her dog.

She saw the spirit of the dog move.
She saw the spirit of the dog rise,
She heard the spirit of her dog whimper.
The dog-spirit turned its head.
It turned to look at her. She saw the eyes.

Where are you going, she said.
I'm going to *Aidos*/Hades; he's whistling me.
I'll come too, said Kore.

She looked down the crack in the rock, she could see deep inside a cave, a cave going down in the dark. I can hear spirits crying down there. I can hear *Aidos* whistling, said the dog. I can hear dogs howling, said Kore, I can hear mothers howling for children.

I will come with you, she said. She went down, following the spirit of the dog. She carried the body of her dog in her arms. This is how Kore went down.

(Some say *Aidos*/Hades came and grabbed her. Some say he raped her. Some say the death cap was him; some say *amanita phalloides* (the poison penis) was him; "that poison toadstool ruined her for sure;" they say. All the women rip their hair, they cry out. "He came and took her away!" They say. They tell that story to keep their girls at home. Some people will say anything. But this that I tell you, this happened; Hades did nothing bad to Kore. He only had to whistle for her when the time was right and she came, carrying the body of her dog. Hades had a reason. Remember this.

## 11.i Kore underground

Kore went down. This is Aidos' Cave, she said. It's like Cave Hill.[17]
All the walls are black with smoke. There are drawings on the wall. What are those marks? said Kore. They are for you, said Aidos, these marks are there to teach you, he said. Look, he said; these are the plants, the ones you see up on country. These are the plants from outside; the plants from up above. Those are the ones you see when you follow your mother. Here are the plants from inside. Here are the marks. Here are the plants inside the skin of the world. These are the roots of things, the seedbed. You are very dark, she said, I can hardly see you; your hands move along the rocks and disappear. I am very dark, he said; you can hardly see me, you can feel me, he said; my hands move along the skin and disappear.

And he showed her drawings made in charcoal on the red walls of the cave. Charcoal and red and ochre white. Here, he said, here are the bison, gazelle, goat; all the animals with blood. Here are the fish, he said, and the serpents. Here is the serpent brain, he said, and the lizard. All these things are in your body now Kore, said Aidos, touching her forehead, his invisible fingers touching her solar plexus; I am placing these things inside you now – and all these things are inside the people to come. The people have come from this beginning; he said, touching all the marks of plant, insect, serpent, fish, bird, animal.

67

The people still are coming from this. All these things die. And begin again. I continue, Kore, I am the continuing of things. He showed her circles, he drew circles on the wall of the cave, he drew circles and lines turning and turning. You do not die, he said, you and I, we go on forever, we hold these things, we change these things; they turn and turn in our hand.

Here, he said; here are the seeds and roots. He drew the shapes. He drew lines and circles; he drew lines that flowed and lines that jaggered like the teeth of lightning. He drew the flow of waters underground. See how the plants grow underground, see how they suck and curl. Did your mother show you this? No said Kore. No said Hades, that is because everything grows where she walks, everything grows where she sings. Your mother is beautiful but she does not know how these things are done.

When she sings, things listen. Things nestle here and wait for her, and as she passes they wake. Good; they say she is coming again and they wake – but what if one day she forgets, what if one day your mother forgets? What if one day she gets angry and does not come? I know how these things are done. You must learn how these things are done. Look at this and learn. You are here to learn. When you have learned everything, you go home. Then go home.

Hades and Kore travelled underground. They travelled the world inside the world.
The spirit of the dog travelled with them. Kore learned how the water flows underground. Where the fires flow underground. You are the one to teach the people, he said. You are the one "wedded to destruction." In my hands you are destroyed. In my hands you are made again. My hands show you this. You are the one to show the people how life goes on.

I will show them dances, said Kore, I will show them how to remember all these things in a song, she said; and she began to practice a dance. And some words came to her with music, like a mirror in a mirror.

*"When Aidos lies down, earth rumbles, when Aidos lies down, islands erupt.*
*Things go on beneath the ground. There is need to fear these things.*
*Things go on beneath the ground. There is no need to fear these things.*
*Things live, things die. This is the way of it."*

## 11.ii Persephone's table

One night she rolled over in her bed; she said to the dog, I love Hades.
She thought about figs. One night Hades rolled over in his bed. He said, I love the daughter of sister Demeter, what am I to do?

In the morning, when it was dawn in the world above, he said; one day I will give you a new name. You will come to live with me. What is that name, said Kore.

He said not a word. He took up a great rock, he laid the great, flat and shining rock before her, he spread out a table. He covered the table in fruit; he placed grape, pomegranate and bread. He placed figs. He invited friends; he invited witnesses.

He addressed her.

"You will be called Persephone"; said Hades, and you will come to live with me.

Your dog died and you took care of him. The people will come, they will die; they will come here to Aidos; they will come in the same way as your dog came when Aidos whistled. When they come, they may be afraid, they will look into my eyes and they will say "we are being destroyed"; but you will say "I am married to destruction and I continue on," and you will place your hand upon their heads.

Humans get lonely. You will take care of the human spirits. The ones who fall from the trees, the ones who fall from the rocks, the ones who fall in the hunt, the ones who die in childbirth, the ones who fall as seeds fall from the hands of the wind. Will you do that? he said.

I will do that, said Kore.

He placed wine before her. Take this. Drink this and remember me.
What is this? she said. This comes from your brother, Dioniso from the slopes of Nysa. Volcanic country, very fine, he said. Take this in remembrance of me.

I will do that, she said.
And she took the cup . . .

For a long time she forgot her mother. For a long time she forgot her mother. That was how it happened. I tell you, that is how it happened. For a long time she forgot her mother.

## 12 There's always another story

People tell you different stories. What happened to Kore? It was nothing like that; they say. Well, those stories might be true. But this is how it happened; this is how I heard it. There's always another story.

The lizard from Eleusis tells a story – "I saw Kore coming down the rocks, that dog was after her. I hate that dog. Her uncle was watching every day for nine days; he was hiding, watching her – the lizard said. Kore came down the rocks. The sun was setting, the shadows long like us lizards, lizards lying quiet, all along the beach, birds drop in the water, fishing. Mother's spit on the hill, pretty white flowers catching flies. Stupid things, pretty smell . . . the black man came for her. He grabbed her hair. He snapped her up like me, lizard, snaps a fly. He took her away. The dog barked out. He threw a rock. Killed that dog. I hate that dog. No one saw, only me; lizard on the cliff saw this. He kept his mouth shut. Lizard. Me."

That's the story they like to tell. A dark thing took the girl away. He took her down a hole; a crack in the cliff; a hole in the ground . . . this is the place, they say. This is the place where Kore went down. The dark man, dog barking, girl screaming – nobody listens. That's how it goes.

"This is true," the lizard says. "That's what happened. You, you give me money now," says lizard, licking his lips.

That's not the story I heard, I say; I heard another story from the beginning. I'm not paying you for this. You hear what you want to hear, says lizard, (looking round for flies) only lizard tells the facts; me, I tell you facts. Now you give me ten dollars. That's how it goes.

## 13.i Hekate and Demeter

Two sisters are sitting down, two old sisters. The mother and the dark one, the old lady, Hekate; maybe she's an old echidna. You can see them there sitting on the hill, looking down on the claypans; they see us, coming and going. Two women up there; gossiping. They talk about husbands; they talk about sisters. They slap their hands at this and that. The mother doesn't know that Kore is gone. Demeter sits. Hekate knows things, but she doesn't speak much. What she knows she keeps in the dark.

People like to say that when Demeter heard her daughter had gone she walked around tearing her hair, ripping her skin. They say she covered her head with dirt and hit her head with a rock . . . well not at first. It wasn't like that, at first. Demeter and Hekate are talking. Like a slow echidna unrolling, Hekate brings the talk round. Sister, when was the last time you saw your daughter? The mother doesn't answer that straight out. She remembers the day, not so long ago, when she went to visit Hekate, her sister, up in the mountains. She took Kore with her.

## 13.ii Demeter remembers

She remembers what happened. She can see it as clear as day.
I'm not coming, says Kore. You *are* coming, says Demeter; you are coming

to visit your Auntie. What Auntie? (Kore's eyes rolling) I'm not coming, the girl said.

Your Auntie Hekate has to see you. I don't want to see her, she smells; she lives like a rat in a cave.

They went along the mountain line, north up toward Mt. Olympos. The sun was going down way out to the west. They went north along the mountain line to Hekate's cave; to see the old lady. The mother and daughter had to go. They had to put three women together in the one place. The young one, the mother, and the old lady – one, two, three – they have to be three like that, sitting together. That way things can start happening – that's the law, said Demeter. What law? said Kore, I don't want to know anything about that.

*Storyteller as an aside.* – That's what happened between those two. Me, today, standing here, I'm showing you what happened, you look there across the country you can see where that mother and daughter went travelling a long time ago. You see that – that's the Hekate track, the sister visiting track, the line of the mountains from here to the north, the sun going down on the west; see there, the shadows coming in. You can see where they walk; where the daughter gives her mother trouble. There, that rock, that's Kore stopping. There she's pulling back – I don't want to go, she says. Not me. You see that rock, her head turned away, looking back; there her mother caught up with her. There they had a fight. They took out their sticks and beat each other. See the cracks in the rock. There, Demeter dragged her daughter along, there where the rocks have fallen.

Kore didn't want to see that old lady Hekate. She heard too many bad stories about her. She looks like a porcupine, said Kore. She has children with two heads, said Kore. She's a dog with three heads, said Kore. She's a witchdoctor. Here, on this cliff, Kore argued again. She put out her lip. Here; she put down her head and followed; two women heading north to Hekate. The little hills below the range, you see that? Those are the tracks of the dog following, sniffing the north wind. They went on heading for Hekate.

### 13.iii Hekate's cave, a long time ago

They came to Hekate's place, a cave in the rocks, just like Kore said, not fit for a rat.

She was lying on her side. She was with another old lady. Old lady Echidne comes to visit her. That's how the story goes. Echidne, going through Hekate's hair, looking for nits. Two old ladies. Echidne and Hekate. Kore was frightened. She closed her eyes.

Hekate took one eye out of her head. She looked at it with her left eye still inside her head. She held the right eye in her hand. She spat on it. She started polishing it, she polished the eye in her hand and she looked at Kore with the other one.

What's she doing? said Kore; shaking like a dog. She likes to look at you, her mother said, keep still. I don't like her looking at me, said Kore, trying to turn away.

Demeter smiled a bit. She remembers you; see . . . she's smiling at you. Go to her now. Touch her face; Hekate's face. Touch her eye. Let her smell you. See she remembers you from before. She remembers you as a baby. She looks out for babies.

*Interlude.* When Kore was a baby, Hekate took Kore in her arms,
She fixed her eye upon her. She made a fire with fragrant leaves;
Bay and mountain sage, myrtle and secret words, frankincense and myrrh.
She made a fire and calmed the coals and laid the leaves upon the coals.
Smoke rose up, fragrant. She held the baby Kore in the smoke.
Here, said Hekate, she gave the baby back to the mother,
I held the baby in the smoke; your daughter will live forever.

## 13.iv Back on the hill

And then quietly Hekate said – (back in the present time, up on the hill, looking down on the claypans; gossiping with Demeter), Hekate said; when was the last time you saw your daughter? Oh, said the mother, she went visiting; she might go down to Eleusis with that dog of hers . . .

Oh, said Hekate. Sister do you remember the smoking leaves and the song I sang for you, a long time ago? I forget, said the mother. When was that? You know, said her sister, when you brought your baby to be smoked. We smoked her so she'd live forever . . . here, said Hekate, here's a bag of those leaves. Don't forget how we did that. She reminded Demeter how to make babies live forever. The smoke, she said. The smoke.[18]

*Interlude.*
When Kore was a baby Hekate took her in her arms,
She fixed her eye upon her. She fixed the shining eye upon her.
She took her other eye. The calming eye. She gave it to Kore.
She placed her calming eye in the baby's hand,
She placed it at her throat;
She placed the power at all the joints of limb and finger.
She smoothed her legs and thighs.
She placed her eye on the labyrinth, her liver and kidneys,
Her guts, her womb . . .

Kore has these things, she has all these things just like animals, birds and people have all these things, but these things are different in the body of Kore. How are they different? I don't know, perhaps the blood of Kore is different.

Hekate placed her eye on the labyrinth inside the baby Kore.
Grow like rivers, like caves, she whispered;
She whispered that song so no one can steal that song.
The old lady Hekate blessed the body of Kore.
She placed her eye within the Kore.
She placed her eye inside the brain of Kore,
Where all things join together.

"My eye will always be here, comforting you,
Holding you. My care will never leave you.
You are my sprout (*kore*), my basket (*khora*), my dance (*khoron*)[19]
When you dance in the circle all things hold together;
Remember this."

You remember the day I did that, said Hekate. Little sister, Demeter, you remember that day? Yes I remember that day. Hekate rolled herself in her blanket. She turned her back on Demeter. When was the last time you saw your daughter? I don't know, said Demeter, poking ashes in the fire. Looking in the fire, the mother put a question to Hekate.

Can you see her in your eye there? I see her now, said old Hekate. She's found another way to live. You see that fella, she went to see that fella. What fella? Said the mother. That fella . . . the old lady showed her sister the face of her (maybe) son-in-law. Demeter couldn't see him properly; she turned her face away; avoiding him.

I don't believe you, she said (the mother said that); my daughter's not ready for that.
Oh, said Hekate, maybe yes, maybe not. She showed her Kore going down a hole like a lizard. Coming up through a crack in the rocks, looking for light. She's looking very pale, said the mother. Don't worry. She'll come out alright, said Auntie Hekate . . .

Suddenly it hit home. Suddenly it hit mother Demeter. Something's wrong with Kore! The mother nearly fell down in shock. Why didn't you tell me? Where is that place? What happened? Why didn't you tell me before?

You never properly asked me, said her sister. She rolled over and she spat on the ground. I told you I had my eye on her. Do you think I talk rubbish?

73

Demeter got up. She was really wild. She picked up her stick. She was really worried, I gotta find that little slut, she said. Hekate rolled herself in her blanket; the little coals were glowing in the dark. She picked up the bag of secret leaves; don't forget this bag, she said. She called out after her sister; her sister running down the hill, crossing the claypans in the dark. Hekate called out; her voice ringing over the claypans and the dark coming in; "When you get really worried, go to Eleusis, go to Eleusis, ask that lizard."

But don't believe a word he says; she muttered to herself, smiling a bit, rolling over like echidna, going to sleep.

## 14 Passing by Eleusis

Demeter went down to Eleusis. She went looking for her daughter, she was cold, she was boiling; she was full of anger. Where she walked, the plants died behind her.

She was trying to see that face, the face of the one who took Kore away. She got angry and angry. She walked for a long way. She went to all her relatives; she went to Kore's father. You seen that slut? What slut? You know, that slut of a daughter. She's no slut. You know nothing – she said to that father. She kept walking.

She went to her brothers. You seen that girl, she said. What girl? You know nothing, she said; turning her back. She went everywhere she could think of. Have you seen Kore? No . . . Have you seen Kore? No . . . You all see nothing, the mother said. Useless, she said, useless – and she kept on walking.

Everything growing in the world is connected to Demeter. Her womb contracting in fear and anger, everything growing in the world contracts in fear and anger. Everything in the world begins to crack. It all begins to boil, it all begins to freeze.

What's happening, say all the people? Nothing, don't worry, say Demeter's brothers. She'll get over it. That's how it goes.

It took the mother a long time to get to Eleusis. She was too proud. She looked down on the beach at Eleusis and saw the people camping; they had a little fire. Why go talk to those people? she said to herself. What would they know, camping in rubbish, down there on the beach; they just arrived from nowhere. What would they know?

## 15 Demeter's search

Some say she searched for nine days. Some say, for nine cycles of the moon. Well that makes sense in one way. Nine months, that girl was lost underground.

The old men in the cafe say; Hades had her for nine years. He kept away from his mother-in-law . . . For nine years he didn't have to face his mother-in-law, they say, laughing. Nine years, the farmers say; or maybe ninety; that's true. She'd need all that time to learn the secret life of plants. Agriculture's not easy, say the farmers.

Some say Demeter walked 900 years looking for her daughter; 900 years . . . (What do you think of that?) Some say 9,000; a long time ago. All that long time the world was covered in ice. Kytheron, Parnassus, all the mountain ranges covered in ice. The seas shrank down. The people of the world were walking, walking; they walked east looking for sun. They walked south looking for sun. People walked all over the world. Some say, where the sea is now there was no sea. People walked where the sea is now. Everyone was walking. Demeter was walking. She walked north and south, she walked east and west, travelling, travelling looking for Kore.

And behind her the people walked, looking for food, hunting, looking for firewood, looking for fruit, anything; looking for any seeds to crush and roll into flour. Walking through countries where no birds sing. This I tell you. Where Demeter walked, her feet stirred things under the ice, but nothing grew. The sun stayed black, calling out for Kore. The rivers stay still, calling out for Kore. Birds drop in flight, calling out for Kore. Small creatures go underground. Snakes and lizards crawl away; nothing moves. Bees lie frozen in the hive, flies drop dead, cicadas cease. Everything is silent. Countries where no birds sing.

## 16 Kore's father makes a deal

Kore's father could not stay quiet forever; Kore's father had the water to manage. He had rain to organise. Everything is out of season, he said. The men in the café said the same thing. He can't stay quiet forever, they said. Kore's father can't stay drunk forever. Nine days he might lie down, but you can't lie around in bed forever. Not for 9,000 years.

Kore's father got up. He got up off his mountain. He took his lightning in his hands, he rolled across the plains; he went south. He travelled this way and that; down the country, looking for his brother. Where is that hole, he said; where's that hole my brother goes down. He was chewing his beard, looking right and left. Where's that arsehole brother of mine? Where is that prick?

Two eagles travelled with him. The wind was too cold. We can't fly, the eagles said. You go on alone . . .

Kore's father found his brother. Where he found him and what they said . . . that's not our business. If they did a deal; that's not our business. I don't mess in stuff that's not my business, anyway . . .

## 17 Demeter and Pythia

Demeter went back to Delphi. She sat down. She cried. She cried to Aunt Pythia; the snake in the rockhole, remember. Where is my daughter? she cried. Pythia rolled; she lifted her head, she uncovered her eyes.

I can't no longer see your Kore. She's got a new name now; I can't see her; that new name's in the way. What's that name? says the mother. Tell me auntie; come on tell me. Did she change her skin? Yea, said Pythia, she changed her skin. I can't see her now . . . What's that new name? Come on Auntie . . . Pythia rolls some more, smoke comes out from her mouth. Something beginning like me, like *P* for Pythia . . . I can't say it properly . . . What's that new name mean? Oh, said Pythia. I can see what that name means, I can't say it, but I can say what that name means. Tell me, said the mother. Pythia looked at Demeter a long time, she blew smoke in her face; I'm sorry, she said. It means she's 'Married to Destruction' – something like that . . . [20]

Thanks, said Demeter; you've been a great help.

## 18 Dogs at Thiva

Demeter kept walking, Where she walked, dogs followed her. She came down the valley from Pythia's place. Maybe I'll go down to Kytheron. She walked down to the place where three tracks cross. She walked down the narrow gorge, a pack of dogs came after her, snarling, biting her ankles. The bitches are hungry, she said. She passed through a narrow gorge. The pack leader came up the gorge. He stopped; he bared his teeth at her. She struck him with her digging stick. She picked up a rock; she hit him in the eye, blood ran out of his eye, the dog backed off. She struck the place with her stick. She cursed it.

## 19 The baby at Eleusis

She turns south; she goes to Eleusis. She looks down on the beach. She sees people huddling by a little fire. She walks up to the cave. They let her in.

Have you seen my daughter? Nobody answers. It is too cold. Everyone is cold.

They have nothing to eat. Demeter sits by the little fire. A baby is crying. The mother is worried for her baby. The little boy. My son is too cold, she says, we got nothing to eat, my milk dries up. He's hungry – Demeter looks at the baby a long time. She feels in her bag for those leaves from Hekate's place. Go fetch me more wood, she says to the older boy. It's ok, he says, all the trees are dead, we got plenty of wood. They burn the wood. They make hot coals, they make ashes.

Demeter takes the baby. The poor little sick one. She rubs the baby. She sprinkles leaves on the coals, she is crying. Bay and myrtle, secret words, frankincense and myrrh. The same leaves Hekate used for Kore, Demeter used for the sick baby at Eleusis. She tried to cure him; she tried to make him live forever.

## 20 Killer

Some people say she gave that baby a new name; she named that baby, "killer" (*Demophon*). This might be true. (People get names mixed up; these things happened a long time ago, people tell different stories.) Some people say she smoked that baby to make him strong again – just so he'd be a killer, so strong no one could beat him. Some say she was thinking about payback for whoever that fella was who took her daughter. She was thinking about murder.

Some say, back then, that that mother wanted to kill every generation of that fella's family because he took her sweet skin baby away. She couldn't see his face but she knew he was there. That mother was maybe thinking revenge. Only just yet, she didn't know who really it was who took her Kore away. She didn't know the true story, did she? (She would have murdered her own brother.)

She was smoking the baby, singing the words to make him live forever. Rubbing his skin. The baby's real mother was worried. She could feel something in the air, she didn't know which way all this was going. She cried out to Demeter; don't say those words – don't say that, don't make that happen, give me back my baby. Give me back my baby, she cried.

When Demeter heard those words she cried out, she broke down, she cried very softly, sitting in the ashes, sitting in the smoke; "Give me back my baby" she cried. Then something happened.

People say that that was the moment when Demeter's heart broke and all the ice began to melt. All the water in the world began to run. Maybe it was then that Demeter stopped splitting the world, she stopped killing the world. She gave the baby back. Something in the air changed around. The wind is changing, said the older brother.

He picked up his spears. He stood up.

## 21 Give me back my baby

All the mothers of the country stood up at that moment. They stood up. They walked to Eleusis. They walked to the crack in the rock. The baby's older brother showed them all the way. Look, he said; that's the place. Where the lizards come and go. Look, he said. He picked up a grinding stone left by the women from before the famine. He named it, "Kore's Call." She will remember this, he said. He picked up that stone and he pounded deep into the crack in the rock. He pounded three times. It made a sound like thunder. The wind began to roar. "Dig out that rubbish; clear the ground. Clear the way." (This is the older brother. Remember him. They call him the grinder, the pounder, *Triptolemos* in the old language.)

Look, he said, look carefully; look at the place, see the tracks of the dog. See the tracks of Kore. She's heavy; she carries the weight of her dog. Look, some-one was standing, watching. See his footprint. (This young man is clever; his eyes are sharp. He sees things.) Demeter sees the tracks. She can tell the story. She knows those prints; she knows this place. She knows who lives inside the rocks.

Demeter strikes the ground. The rocks crack open. Listen. As the rock opens, the ice cracks. Demeter begins to rock back and forward, she begins to croon. The ice melts. The earth rumbles. The stones roll away.

*When Aidos lies down, earth rumbles,*
*When Aidos lies down, islands erupt.*
*Things go on beneath the ground. There is need to fear these things.*
*Things go on beneath the ground. There is no need to fear these things.*
*Things live, things die. This is the way of it.*

Demeter looks in the eyes of the mothers of Eleusis. She touches the baby;
He will be alright, she says. Now he will suck, she says. I am singing for Kore and she is coming up; now the babies will eat. She struck the rock again, splitting the rock like a fruit, splitting it open like a pomegranate. She took the young man by the hand. They went into the cave. She kept on singing for Kore. Her words rippled with water through the ground. Her words soaked with water, through the ground; down, down; seeds stirred. Kore stirred in her bed in the dark, Kore stretched.

## 22 Persephone returns

She reached for the fruit Hades had placed near the bed. She reached for the pomegranate. She split the hard shell of the red fruit in the way her mother split the fruit so long ago. She was lying there dreaming about her mother. She opened the pomegranate – she felt the seeds, thinking about her mother. She is "the womb of the world," she said.

In the dark bed, Kore reached for the red seeds. Sweet, red seeds.
"Eat this in remembrance of me." She slipped the seeds in her mouth. She rolled the seeds on her tongue. She remembered her mother. She rose from the bed.

The dog was sleeping on the bed. She patted the bed. Stay here, she said.

I think I'll give you a new name; I think I'll call you Hermes, she said, smiling at him. Stay here. I'll be back. Hermes raised his head; he whined a bit, his eyes followed her steps all the way.

She climbs up. Through the crack in the rocks, Kore climbs up. She has a new name now, remember. Through the crack in the rocks, Persephone climbs up. She can feel the water soaking her feet, she can feel water drip on her face. She can hear the singing of women. She comes up. Kore comes up.
She comes up through the crack in the rock, she is like a fig tree in the morning. The birds gather, wings flicker; birds shimmer in the leaves of the fig tree.

Coming up by the rock hole in the morning, Persephone, water shining along the roots, water shining on the leaves of the tree, birds flickering. She comes up.

I can feel on my tongue, the taste of my mother, I am coming out, she cried. I am coming out . . .

### *Coda*

Two dogs sit by the water hole,
Their bellies are full,
The dogs are happy.
Our bellies are full, said the two dogs.
Our bellies are full.

End
(To be continued)

### *Kore Story/Persephone's Dog*

*This version composed Delphi, September 2012 – completed Alice Springs, October 2013.*
*Copyright, Craig San Roque, 20 Lindsay Avenue, Alice Springs, Australia.*
*Dedicated with thanks to Frankie Yamma, Central Australian Singer – his CD* Countryman. *And to the influence of New York mythic storyteller, Diane Wolkstein, who passed away while on a performance tour, 31 January 2013.*

## Notes

1  Freya Mathews, "Invitation to ontopoetics," *PAN: Philosophy, Action, Nature, Special Edition on Ontopoetics,* 2009, No. 6, available: <www.panjournal.net.webloc>. See also *PAN*, 2011, No. 8.

A charming note on Wikipedia on *poiesis* is worth referencing:

> Martin Heidegger refers to it as a "bringing-forth," using this term in its widest sense. He explained poiesis as the blooming of the blossom, the coming-out of a butterfly from a cocoon, the plummeting of a waterfall when the snow begins to melt. The last two analogies underline Heidegger's example of a threshold occasion: a moment of ecstasis when something moves away from its standing as one thing to become another.

(Wikipedia, accessed 31 December 2013)

2  Craig San Roque, *On Tjukurrpa, Painting Up and Building Thought*, in J. Mimica, (ed.) *Explorations in Psychoanalytic Ethnography*, New York, Berghahn Books, 2007. Reprinted in slightly revised form in *PAN, Ontopoetics*, 2009, No. 6. See endnote 1.

3  This conjoint horticultural project is managed by *Centrefarm*, Alice Springs, Northern Territory, and the indigenous, Alekarenge Horticultural Pty Ltd., in Ali Curung. See http://www.centrefarm.com.

4  This "Delphic Kore" text was composed at Delphi, beginning at 5 pm, Sunday, 2 September 2012, and into the day of 3 September. The text that you read here "fell out" unexpectedly under the influence of the sites at Delphi. The penciled text was written for the recitation at the *Ancient Greece, Modern Psyche* event hosted in Santorini by the Nomikos Conference Center on 7 September 2012. It is still a work in progress.

Sections of *Kore Story* were subsequently presented in October 2012, with large accompanying paintings at a gathering of some 60 indigenous and white Australian adults and children at the Aboriginal settlement where the agricultural project is tentatively developing. Since then, the text has been expanded and refined after a performance workshop in Canberra, 1 and 2 February 2013, that included members of "The Chorus of Women." See http://www.chorusofwomen.com. The Chorus of Women is a community group of musicians and singers based in Canberra, Australia, who are engaged in social commentary and constructive cultural advocacy inspired by the model of the Greek chorus in Aeschylus' works.

See, especially, *The Gifts of the Furies*, composed by Glenda Cloughley et al., performed 2010, at the Museum of Australian Democracy, Canberra, Australia, and elsewhere. Also Glenda Cloughley, personal communications, and doctoral material from the University of Western Sydney, along with several presentations (2000–12) in which she cited Maria Gimbutas, Dorothy Cameron, et al., exploring archaeomythology sources pertaining to old Europe, the flood, and feminine-settled culture in the Black Sea regions.

5  The main reference sources consulted include Anne Baring and Jules Cashford, *The Myth of the Goddess: Evolution of an Image*, London, Viking Arcana, Penguin, 1991; Jules Cashford (trans.), *Hymn to Demeter* II, *The Homeric Hymns*, Harmondsworth, UK, Penguin Classics, 2003, pp. 5–26. Jules Cashford, *The Moon, Myth and Image*, London, Cassell Illustrated, 2003; Robert Graves, *The Greek Myths*, Harmondsworth, UK, Penguin Books, 1960; Carl Kerenyi, *Dionysos*, trans. Ralph Manheim, Princeton, Bollingen Series, Princeton University Press, 1976; George Mylonas, *Eleusis and the Eleusinian Mysteries*, Princeton, Princeton University Press, 1961; and Edward Tripp, *Dictionary of Classical Mythology*, London, Collins Reference, 1970.

6  Jules Cashford, personal communications, October 2012.

7  Ibid.

8  Felix Guirand, "Greek mythology" in *New Larousse Encyclopedia of Mythology*, London, Hamlyn, 1959–86, section on "Persephone."

9  Ibid., section on "Persephone and Aidos."

10  Cashford, *Homeric Hymns, Hymn to Apollo*.

11  Kerenyi, *Dionysos*, pp. 52–89.

12  Mylonos, *Eleusis and the Eleusinian Mysteries*, pp. 14–15.

13  A. Rumsey and D. Niles (eds), *Sung Tales from the Papua New Guinea Highlands*, Canberra, Australian National University E Press, 2011.

14  Mt. Kytheron is where Oedipus was abandoned as an infant, but then rescued, fostered, and brought up believing he was the son of the royal couple of Corinth. As a young man Oedipus consults Pythia at Delphi and here he learns his fate – "you will kill your father and marry your mother." He descends from Delphi toward Mt. Cithaeron/ Kytheron and Thebes.

   Tripp in his *Dictionary of Classical Mythology* writes, "not far from Delphi, Oedipus comes . . . to the Cleft Way where the road to Daulis divides from that of Boeotia" p. 421. In Sophocles' *Oedipus Rex* the fateful confrontation occurs where three roads cross, in a gorge where the young man encounters the older man in a chariot who, in the altercation, is killed by Oedipus. The killer/Oedipus eventually turns up in Thebes, answers the Sphinx's riddle, is rewarded with the hand of the deceased king's wife, Jocasta, unknowingly, Oedipus' mother. And so continues the fate of the House of Cadmus. The Sphinx (a composite body of lion, wings of bird, and head of a woman), is a daughter of Echidne. It is in that gorge that Demeter sits and feels the terrible fate of the future.

15  Guirand, *New Larousse Encyclopedia of Mythology*, p. 152. Iasion (Yasion) is referred to as a mortal lover of Demeter. It seems that the sexual relationship between a female/ maternal power and a young mortal male recurrently underlies agricultural fertilization and regeneration mythologies. Some say jealous Zeus killed Iasion and others say the young man lived with Demeter and introduced her cult into Sicily. The Demeter/ Persephone agricultural mystery cult characters include Iasion and Triptolemus, Iakkos and Dionysos as consorts to the female avatars/ incarnations of the triple goddess.

16  In my version Hekate and Hestia and Echidne (the Gorgon's sister) are Demeter's elder companions. Hestia is the originator of the hearth fire/the first kitchen, and I have associated Hekate totemically with an Echidna. Apparently the Echidna is named after the Greek mythological being. The Australian *echidna,* affectionately known as the spiny anteater, is, like a platypus, an egg-laying mammal. This is very unusual. Though externally similar in appearance to the porcupine, it is unique, as is the Echidna male's reproductive system. Echidna is a solitary, persistent, slow-moving spiny creature that (doggedly) burrows and curls into a spiny ball when alarmed, perplexing dogs that try to worry it. There is a sacred site of two hills overlooking claypans near Mbantua/Alice Springs devoted to an Echidna mother and daughter. Such a hill, is, in my mind, a suitable location for when Demeter gets the hint from Hekate about Kore's disappearance. *Echidne*, in primal Titan Greek myth, is depicted as part woman, part speckled snake, sister of Medusa, the Gorgon, cousin of the Harpies. See Robert Graves, *Greek Myths*, sect. 33. There are associations mixed up with the Moon and Pigs. Sometimes Hekate is associated with Echidne. I find this association fertile. Hekate is a complex figure, the dark aspect of moon cycles, deathly and prophetic, and paired with Artemis the young moon, wild and beautiful, as Cashford illumines in her references to Hekate in *Moon, Myth and Image*. She writes, "this complexity speaks of an ancient grandeur, for Hekate

and Artemis are both survivals of the old European Great Goddess" and "in Hesiod's Theogony, Hekate is given as the original triple Goddess . . . responsible for increasing herds and nursing the young" (p. 125). It makes sense (to me) that Hekate has her eye on Kore, the wild young daughter of Demeter, and that darkly serpentine Hekate knows what happens to Kore when she goes underground. Hekate and Hades have a subterranean kinship association. I prefer this more primal underground female version over the story that the sun/Apollo had his eye on Kore.

17  Cave Hill in central Australia is a special and beautiful cave with overlaid ochred circular paintings. This site is associated with the indigenous Seven Sisters story. There are many and varied rockface paintings in Australian country, for instance, "The Bradshaw Paintings," Kimberley region; the Kakadu rock galleries; and throughout the Central desert regions. Refer to the Australian Rock Art Research Association website, www.ifrao.com/aura/, and the Bradshaw rock art site, www.bradshawfoundation.com.

18  This matter of the smoke is a double cultural reference. It refers to the myth that Demeter placed the baby from the Eleusis family in the fire to make him immortal, and it refers to a central Australian indigenous custom where newly born babies are held over a special quiet fire by grandmothers and/or other close relatives and bathed in the aromatic smoke of particular foliage to cleanse and strengthen the baby spiritually. This is called "smoking the baby." Sometimes, people say, in the old days the mother might also have been smoked after childbirth.

19  As I have understood it, these words are variations on terms in ancient Greek and modern Greek that form part of the cluster of associations around the word and sounds of *kore: khora, khoros,* or *horos* (dance), *horoi* (dances) including *chorus* – hence a word net that places the figure of Kore/Persephone (and koroi/young men) into a cluster of meanings, for instance, seed, sprout, young men and women, basket, container, circular dance, song ceremony, and ceremonial chorus/singers. With thanks to John Kassoutas, Sydney, Australia, and to Jules Cashford; also see http://en.wikipedia.org/wiki/Horon_(dance).

20  The complex etymology of *Persephone,* which includes notions of light and death, beauty and being in the dark, being destroyed and coming back to life as cyclic is acknowledged here, but I feel that the term "married to destruction" is a bit too respectable. I think Pythia probably said, "It means she's really fucked over but look on the bright side . . . "

# 4

# DEATH AND NECESSITY AT THE THRESHOLD OF NEW LIFE

*Richard Trousdell*

My subject is facing death's necessity and the accompanying feelings of dread and helplessness that task often brings. I approach this subject in both fiction and fact: first, in a rather odd Greek tragedy, the *Alcestis* of Euripides, in which the necessity of death is temporarily suspended on behalf of a virtuous but incomplete man who still has much to learn; and then in an actual case of a modern woman facing her death through the imagery of her dreams. I tell these stories against the background of the ancient Greek concepts of death and necessity, *thanatos* and *ananke* respectively, not to assert their priority as definitive, but rather to play upon the fantasies of facing death still current with us. Among them is this paradox: we humans die and know we will, but religion, poetry, art, and science have never stopped looking for ways around that unwelcome fact. As poet and classicist Emily Vermeule puts it, the Greeks are part of a continuing human tradition of thinking that death may be inevitable but not necessarily fatal.[1]

Rather than begin with theories about facing death's necessity, I want to start with the human emotions out of which those theories arise, in particular, those familiar feelings of dread and helplessness. I remember feeling them as I sat with my sister Carol who was dying of cancer at what we both knew was likely to be our last meeting. The time was almost up, and we needed to say goodbye at a moment when it felt to me as if we were standing helpless together at the edge of an abyss. What more could I say in leaving to comfort her and – let's be frank – to comfort myself and feel less useless? I finally managed to ask if Carol knew that many people who have had near-death experiences have reported that at the end there is a feeling of light and lightness.[2] My sister, a former barmaid, paused for a moment and then said, "Yeah, the light at the end of the tunnel." That broke the tension and made us both laugh.

What a gift, that laughter, that tough mind of Carol's. Her quick-witted realism was like a gift of the gods that made life begin again. As we'll see, such humor about life's precarious situation is a psychological marker of what we call heroism. Carol is a hero for me. She made clear that one way to face death's necessity is to stay mindful, and in that we are not helpless. By acknowledging the darkness, she constellated its opposite, not some ideal light beyond, but the little light of the mind seeing what it sees and naming it true. Her move from evasion to directness is a vivid example of how facing death consciously can give human life a unique vitality and depth. Without knowing it, Carol was making real an ancient bit of wisdom. As Emily Vermeule tells us, wit's spark of reflective intelligence – what the Greeks called *nous* or mind – was the only reliable remedy for death.[3] Although darkness was the Greeks' central metaphor for both death and stupidity, the internal sunshine of wit could rescue a person from such darkness. My sister knew that.

While holding onto the idea of the mind's inner light, let's now meet death and necessity as they were personified in art and drama by the ancient Greeks. Who is Thanatos? Who is Ananke?[4] And what light do their images shed on our dread, as well as on our secret hopes for new life as we face inevitable death? A standard Greek image of death is pictured on the well-preserved *Euphronios Krater* (Figure 4.1), recently returned to Italy by the Metropolitan Museum of Art.

*Figure 4.1* The *Euphronios Krater* or wine-mixing bowl, c. 515 BCE, Museo Nazionale di Villa Giulia, Rome, showing Prince Sarpedon's body being carried toward burial by Thanatos (right) and his twin brother Hypnos (left) while Hermes stands in the center above the body. (Courtesy of © Soprintendenza per i Beni Archeologici dell'Etruria Meridionale.)

On this large red-figured vase, death is depicted as the god Thanatos, a darkly handsome young warrior with wings who is carrying the body of a dead hero, Prince Sarpedon, off the battlefield at Troy. This famous scene from Homer's *Iliad* is useful to our purposes because it shows the outcome of a struggle by Zeus, king of the gods, against death's necessity.

In Homer's account, Zeus wants to spare Prince Sarpedon from death because Sarpedon is his human son and favorite hero.[5] But Zeus is forced to give up that wish by Hera who reminds her philandering husband that even immortal gods must obey necessity's law that all humans must die, including divine favorites. Nevertheless, Zeus still manages to rescue his dead son's spirit from desecration by ordering Apollo to have Sarpedon's body carried by Thanatos toward honorable burial. This sacramental act will insure the safe passage of Prince Sarpedon's shade or ghost to the underworld.[6] In this way, Zeus acknowledges death's necessity for mortals while also rescuing a distinctive portion of human life from death. Called by the Greeks variously *eidolon* (ghost), *psyche* (breath), or *thymos* (spirit), this belief in a unique human essence that survives death lies at the core of most religious traditions. We should notice, then, that Zeus acts not so much out of petty defiance of Hera as out of his love for a hero who chose to face his death consciously. As we'll see in the *Alcestis*, Zeus's son Apollo will similarly try to cheat death of its absolute claim because of his love for a human hero. In the *Alcestis*, however, the favored hero has yet to learn what facing death means.

For the Greeks, the example of Prince Sarpedon represents one sort of death, a good one, a *kalos thanatos*, the sort won by heroic warriors that is honored by the gods and celebrated by poets and painters. Is it also, perhaps, the kind of good, brave death we'd all like to have? Not a passive death of dread and helplessness, but one in which we up and fight the good fight and, in some sense, "win." Not just for ourselves, but to join in life's common struggle against what Dylan Thomas calls "the dying of the light."[7] Contemporary obituaries still honor this heroic idea of a *kalos thanatos* when they describe how bravely the recently departed faced their final illness – as if to die any other way would be shameful.

Thanatos also seems familiar in a less heroic mode because he is paired on the *Euphronios Krater* with his twin brother, the god Hypnos, who represents sleep. As twins, Thanatos and Hypnos suggest that facing death is nothing to dread or fight; perhaps it is something to welcome as a release from life's weariness and pain – like a good night's rest. Not surprisingly, Thanatos and Hypnos are children of Mother Night (Nyx). They are born of her darkness, which, for the Greeks, was like the darkness that comes in the dwindling of light from the eyes of the dying. Darkness, like death, is simply part of nature's cycle from light to the dark and back again. When we die, then, perhaps we just go to sleep, as if carried away by the children of Mother Night into another world.

The soothing fantasies associated with Thanatos and Hypnos also overlap in the Greek iconography of death with that of Eros (physical love), another winged god who carries us away and causes us to lose consciousness, like the love that "knocks you dead," or – as in the French term for the post-coital state – that lulls you into "*un petit mort*" (a little death), a little falling asleep. We can feel other familiar fantasies in these overlapping motifs, in which dying is seen as a total surrender of self toward passionate merger with a longed-for other, a *Liebestod,* a love death that somehow brings completion. Conversely, coming back to life, mind, and intelligence might be like waking up again, coming to our senses, and being reborn with the dawn, the coming of light. Perhaps after death's sleep, there will be another dawning, another kind of awakening.

So much for a few ideas stirred up by Greek images of facing death as a *kalos thanatos.* By contrast, in the classical world's version of the dark tunnel, there is another image of facing death that is the opposite of a *kalos thanatos:* not a death that carries us toward a sense of completion, but rather a total death that reduces all life to nothingness. This is death as *ker.* In plural form, the *keres* were originally imagined as transformative soul-birds (*psychai*) or ghosts (*eidola*).[8] In that form, they were believed to be the still-living souls of the dead returning from their graves during the annual Anthesteria festival, a sacred if rather eerie event.[9] But in Homeric epic and thereafter, the *keres* were regularly demonized as evil creatures of death, represented as black-winged figures such as the Harpies, Furies, Sirens, or the Sphinx (Figure 4.2).[10] In these demonized forms, a dreaded *ker*-death

*Figure 4.2* Greek, Laconia, black-figured terracotta kylix or cup, c. 550–520 BCE, Museo Nazionale di Villa Giulia, Rome, showing the Boreads (left), sons of Boreas (the north wind), pursuing *keres* in the form of Harpies (right) and a Sphinx (below). (Courtesy of © Soprintendenza per i Beni Archeologici dell'Etruria Meridionale.)

(*ker thanatoio*) was anticipated as "more personal and vicious" than the tender carrying away by neutral figures like Thanatos and Hypnos.[11] The evil *keres* could devour the body like vultures or battlefield dogs, mutilate it and then pick the bones clean and scatter them, desecrating the human body as just another carcass. It is against this fate that Zeus rescues Prince Sarpedon.

A *ker*-death is an absolute death, a total erasing of the individual and its mind. Here's how the ghost of Patroklos in *The Iliad* describes her, suggesting in the process how easily *ker* overlaps with fate (*moira*) as humanity's necessary lot or portion. "The frightening *ker* who got me by lot when I was born has opened her jaws around me."[12] Swallowed by death, swallowed by darkness, over and done with: this negative image of death as *ker* vividly embodies feelings of dread and helplessness in their most nightmarish form.

Being swallowed by a *ker*-death suggests parallel psychological images. For example, if ego consciousness dares to face the darkness of the unconscious will an inner mind hold and carry it like Thanatos? Or will the unconscious tear the ego apart, swallowing it like a psychotic inner *ker*? The human mind is always grappling with that dark vision of a center that may not hold. But as Jungians, we struggle against the threat of disintegration to search for wholeness, gathering the lost pieces of living psyche hidden in darkness. Jung compared those pieces to *scintillae,* little sparks of light, little sparks of potential mind.[13]

Jung's belief in such inner light didn't come easily. He famously described his own initial confrontation with the unconscious as a terrifying journey into an underworld, a *Nekyia* – his ego's descent into a deathlike darkness similar to that of Odysseus into Hades.[14] In Jung's confrontation with the unconscious, he faced fears of suicide or psychic annihilation. But he continued the descent, holding onto his sanity by remembering what was essential to him – his wife and children, his street address – until he was able to face and survive the inner spirits that came into view. In this process, Jung faced the ego's dread of death, only to discover that the darkness of the unconscious contained *scintillae* of new life.

Jung's initial vision of drawing light from the darkness took intensely personal form in 1923 when he had a disturbing dream about his mother's impending death.[15] In the dream, Jung felt intense grief, but he also had jarring fantasies of music and laughter. In struggling to understand this emotional paradox, Jung came to see how death can, indeed, be seen simultaneously in two opposing ways, not unlike the contrasting visions of death as *kalos thanatos* or *ker* that the Greeks imagined:

> One side of me had a feeling of warmth and joy, and the other of terror and grief; I was thrown back and forth between these contrasting emotions. The paradox can be explained if we suppose that at one moment death was being represented from the point of view of the ego, and at the next from that of psyche. In the first case it appeared as a catastrophe; this is how it so often strikes us, as if wicked and pitiless powers had put an end to human life. And so it is – death is indeed a fearful piece of brutality . . . not only as a physical event, but far more so psychically . . . From another point of view, however,

death appears as a joyful event. In the light of eternity, it is a wedding, a *mysterium coniunctionis*. The soul attains, as it were, its missing half, it achieves wholeness.

I will return to Jung's analysis to suggest how facing death's necessity can deepen life experience to form an essential part of psychological individuation. But, for now, Jung leaves us with some understanding of how the ego, balanced by the transpersonal psyche, can hold the tension between life and death to glimpse a third possibility: that the ego itself must in some sense "die" in order to discover a larger wholeness that neither kills nor swallows, but rather contains and completes. From this theoretical perspective, death may indeed be inevitable, but not necessarily fatal. Still, at the hour of facing death, will theory alone be enough to hold and sustain us?

Ananke, the Greek personification of necessity, is harder to see than either Thanatos or *ker* because there are so few contemporary images of "her." So although Ananke was thought to exist from the start as primordial order – even before the Olympian gods – that she cannot be seen or conceived of by the human mind is clearly Ananke's most defining characteristic. No images, no words can easily represent her because, in some sense, she's unthinkable: Ananke is the void, the dark logic out of which the universe spun. For humans, she is irrefutable, indefinable otherness.

Here's how the Chorus in Euripides' *Alcestis* tries to say what Ananke is:[16]

I myself . . . have found
nothing so strong as [Ananke],
nor any means to combat her . . .
She alone is goddess
without altar or image to pray before.
She heeds no sacrifice.
Majesty, . . . all even Zeus ordains
only with you is accomplished.
By strength you fold and crumple . . . steel . . .
There is no pity in the sheer barrier of your will.

Unlike all other gods, then, Ananke is totally unresponsive to human appeals or empathetic emotion and, therefore, remains almost inaccessible to thought or imagination. But whereas Ananke might be impossible for the human mind to fully grasp, for the Greeks she did not imply nihilism or chaos, but just the opposite: Ananke's meaningfulness may be incomprehensible, but her implacable logic was there in and under everything, like it or not. Over time, various interpreters have defined Ananke as constraint, the limitless limit, the inescapable, that without which nothing else can be.[17] Inevitably, there is a close emotional connection between Ananke and death: they both represent fixed limit; they both are essentially unthinkable; and they both arouse feelings of dread and helplessness.

In his essay on Ananke as necessity, James Hillman evokes a traditional image of it as a yoke.[18] The expression "the rough yoke of necessity" goes back at least as far as Homer, but Hillman traces Ananke's root meaning to earlier Semitic languages where it can mean not only that which ties two oxen together, but also the neckband of a slave and the actions of strangling, choking, or restraining.[19] As we'll see, Euripides takes up the yoke image in the *Alcestis* to describe marriage. Beyond an implied joke, in what sense are marriage and necessity linked?

Those are just a few of the questions the ancient symbols of Thanatos and Ananke conjure up. And, for me, they raise this larger question: Is death an absolute form of necessity? A fate, a compulsion, a total limit? Try to step beyond that limit, and you will be torn apart, crumpled, swallowed. Or does the concept of Ananke give us a frame of mind that lets us see life and death differently, from the other side as it were, and thus with an expanded and more objective consciousness?

I want to look at such questions in two ways: first, in the *Alcestis*, which, for me, is the story of how marriage, as a joining of opposites through love, has the power to redefine death and to challenge the limits of necessity. And, then, I want to look at two dreams of a modern woman, an analysand I worked with, who chose to approach death by following her dreams as a path toward wholeness. And because her daughters later fulfilled her wishes by making her dream manuscript public,[20] I can tell you her name: Elizabeth B. Smith (Figure 4.3). Mrs. Smith thought of her future readers as her fellow "dream-makers." That is, she saw dreaming as a shared creative act, a gift to us from God, of his creative ability to bring light and meaning out of darkness, chaos, and the nameless void.

Both the ancient play and the modern dreams suggest ways of approaching death as a spiritual achievement, a *kalos thanatos*, redefined as the threshold of new life. As we've seen, the Greeks traditionally symbolized that achievement as a warrior in battle. But the *Alcestis* sets out to challenge this traditional idea of heroism by celebrating a new kind of *kalos thanatos*, won not in battle by a warrior but in a marriage by a woman. By shifting the context from battlefield to bedroom, Euripides redefines death's necessity from a feminine rather than a masculine perspective in which the *logos* of outer action yields to the *eros* of emotional relationship. In that change, our awareness of death's necessity is expanded to include all the subtle little deaths of evasion, selfishness, and insensitivity that haunt the shadow side of marriage in which husband and wife are yoked together emotionally and spiritually as well as physically. Therefore, if one partner dies, in some sense so, too, does the other "die"; or if one partner dares to live more fully and with greater awareness, the other is challenged to do the same or come up short and be left in the dark. There are deaths and there are deaths. Some are necessary; some may not be. In using the yoke image to describe how married couples are bound together in body and spirit, Euripides implies that the joining of opposites in marriage is itself Ananke, the human form of necessity, that without which nothing else can be.

Here, briefly, is the story. Admetus, the young king of Pherae, whose name means the "untamed" or the "unyoked,"[21] is supposed to die; it's his fated time.

*Figure 4.3* The cover of Elizabeth Smith's dream manuscript. (© Estate of Elizabeth B. Smith, by permission.)

But, because the god Apollo loves Admetus, he blocks Thanatos by getting the Fates (Moirai) drunk and making them promise to spare Admetus if he can get someone else to die for him. The only problem is that no one is willing to face death for Admetus, not his father, nor his mother, his friends, no one. But finally one person does volunteer: his young wife Alcestis. Her decision to die when she doesn't have to begins to undo the image of death as absolute compulsion by revealing how conscious choice can start to chip away at death's fixed limits.

But we can't help wondering what motivates Alcestis to offer her life, especially when we hear how calmly, even beautifully she dies, for as her maid tells us: "she wept/ Not at all, made no outcry. The advancing doom of death/Made no change in the color and beauty of her face."[22] Is this image of facing death too good to be true? Do such things happen, and if so, how are we to understand them?

Psychoanalyst Heinz Kohut gives us a modern example from World War II, one that echoes Jung's earlier insight about facing death as a celebration of wholeness.[23] Kohut describes the remarkably calm deaths of students in the White Rose Movement, an anti-Hitler organization at the University of Munich. Because of their open demonstrations against Hitler, all were arrested, tried, and guillotined.[24] On the morning of her execution, one of those students, Sophie Scholl (Figure 4.4), aged 22, was described by eyewitnesses this way: she was "calm and peaceful, her skin glowing and fresh, her face radiant . . . her lips were of a deep glowing red. She was without a trace of fear."[25] For me, this strikingly parallel account suggests the human reality underlying the fictional character of Alcestis.

What is that reality psychologically speaking? Kohut notices some of its outer signs: how the students' heroic behavior was marked by their empathy and sense of humor, as if their impending deaths linked them in a unique way to others, even to

*Figure 4.4* Photograph of Sophie Scholl (1921–1943). (© 2014 Manuel Aicher, Dietikon, Switzerland.)

their guards. Their behavior also implied an ironic confidence that their seemingly futile protests were being affirmed by the very executions meant to silence them. More deeply, Kohut speculates that the students' stoically self-sacrificing behavior grew from what he calls a "narcissistic balance" in the personality in which the ego consciously facing its death is sustained by the ideals of a nuclear self that will endure.[26]

In support of his conjecture, Kohut cites a dream that Sophie Scholl reported to her cellmate on the morning of her execution. In the dream, Sophie said the sun was shining as she climbed a mountain, carrying an infant dressed in white toward its baptism. Suddenly, a crevasse opened before her so that she just had time to deposit the child safely on the other side before she herself fell into its depths. She told her cellmate that the child represented our idea ("*unsere Idee*") that would survive despite all obstacles ("*wird sich durchsetzen*").[27]

The dream's symbolism – the child in white carried toward baptism, the sunshine, the mountain, and the contrast between deadly crevasse and potential life on the "other side" – all point toward spiritual meanings beyond the students' immediate political situation. In this sense, although I admire Kohut's sensitive understanding of the students' heroic behavior, I think Jung's earlier and more spiritually oriented analysis of an ego-self *coniunctio* gives us a fuller picture of what Sophie Scholl and her compatriots achieved. Although Kohut's structural analysis of an ego-self balance makes sense psychologically, Jung's idea of a spiritual marriage between the ego and the psyche carries us further toward "the other side," where the life beyond death of which Sophie Scholl dreamed is located. As Donald Kalsched said of this dream, the child that Sophie Scholl carried was, indeed, her imperishable soul.[28]

Does such hope for spiritual wholeness account for Alcestis' remarkable action, a longed-for inner *coniunctio* with psyche within the physical bond of her marriage? We can't know for sure because "she" is a fictional character. But we can notice what Euripides stresses about her actions as she prepares to die: she bathes in fresh running waters, she puts on her finest robes, and she prays to Hestia, guardian of hearth and home, for her children and their future marriages; she prays that they will be yoked to good mates.[29] It is to uphold and insure that promise of marriage – in her own and for her children's – that she dies.

Alcestis, then, shows every sign of having what Jung calls a religious attitude, a faith in things unseen that lie beyond the limits of herself and her moment in time, symbolized by her children. In the same way, a child symbolized a living idea ("*unsere Idee*") beyond fascist tyranny, one for which Sophie Scholl was willing to sacrifice her life. A conscious belief in transcendent values beyond the personal ego is thus a hallmark of an inner attitude that can make facing death a genuine spiritual achievement, a *kalos thanatos*.

But the idea that Alcestis dies to affirm spiritual values in marriage would not have been an easy sell to Euripides' audience. They traditionally assumed women were more sexually compelled and less spiritually motivated than men. Women couldn't help it: it was their nature, their fate. That's the point of Aristophanes' satire in the *Lysistrata*; the idea that women could renounce sex was simply laughable. As the men in Plato's *Symposium* tell us,[30] Alcestis may, indeed, be honored as a model of love, but only of a lesser kind: romantic physical love (*eros*), not the higher kind of dispassionate love between men called *philia*, as in *philosophia*, the love of wisdom.[31]

So how did Euripides get his audience to take Alcestis' self-sacrifice as a spiritual story and not simply as bedroom melodrama? He does it by describing how Alcestis struggles against the physical compulsions of conjugal love symbolized by the "marriage bed," where, as she says, she first "undressed my maidenhood."[32] She returns here after her prayers, crying out to the bed as if it were a person or a god, before collapsing on it in tears – not once but twice.[33] Clearly, what Alcestis is struggling against isn't fear of death, but rather the erotic powers of married love she has experienced in this particular bed with Admetus. By describing first how their marriage bed shatters her composure, and then by stressing the calm nobility with which Alcestis takes leave of the bedroom to face her death in public, Euripides suggests that she is not dying out of sexual love "for her magnificent young man," as her cynical father-in-law thinks.[34] Rather, by moving from the emotions of an inner private space, to the objective actions of an outer public one, Alcestis demonstrates that she is dying for *philia*, the higher dispassionate love honored between men, but now claimed by a woman. Thus, the Chorus later celebrates Alcestis as a blessed *daimon*, an immortal hero whose spirit will live on to inspire us all.[35]

The evidence of the spirit, so easy to see on the battlefield, is harder to discern in everyday life. One must feel it, be enlivened by it in relationship with others. Alcestis' spirit will live or die through Admetus' faithful awareness of it. Will he or won't he be up to her challenge? I'm going to leave that question open briefly to bring Elizabeth Smith back onto the scene because, like Alcestis, she believed in spiritual values beyond herself that she would leave in her writing for her future dream-makers. And like Alcestis, too, Mrs. Smith set out to prove that a woman could claim moral and spiritual achievements beyond anything that the society of her time necessarily recognized or encouraged.

Mrs. Smith was raised in the 1930s and 1940s and came to maturity in the 1950s and early 1960s. By any standards, and especially given that timeframe, she achieved a remarkable life: winning a superb education through the doctoral level, a successful administrative career, and a solid marriage in which she helped raise two accomplished daughters. But she had to fight to achieve all that in order to break through familiar glass ceilings in academic and professional life. She also had to confront conventional fears and criticism, including her own, that a good mother's place was in the home, not in graduate school or in a career. But she had the energy, talent, and discipline to prove she could, though often with feelings of guilt, conflict, and doubt.

Mrs. Smith prefaces her *Dream-Maker* manuscript with her poem "Another Icarus," in which, like Alcestis, she lays claim to spiritual yearnings beyond the limits of gender:

Oh, endless universe, it's you I need.
I must have all your space through which to fall
And never know a place where I might light.
To fly from nests they say brings joy to life,
Not to return, and I so far agree
That I would fly into the heat of suns
To lose my wings, to fall but then to miss the sea,
Indeed to miss the earth and yet to find
The universe sufficient for my state of mind.

What might easily be pathologized in this poem as ego inflation or a death wish actually represents Mrs. Smith's wish to live more fully by finding an inner universe beyond ego that could satisfy the yearnings of her mind. As her dreams suggest, she was looking for the kind of psychological balance between ego and an inner self that Jung and Kohut describe.

Two dreams, in particular, reflect this search for balance – first, the initial dream she brought into analysis, and then, from eight years later, a dream she called her "sign-off dream." Both dreams replay symbols from the Icarus poem of aspiring and falling, first as a terrifying conflict, and then as another kind of falling that brings balance and resolution.

Here's the initial dream:[36]

I was a high-wire performer doing my act on a unicycle with only a bamboo pole for maintaining balance and no net to sustain me should I have begun to fall. As I approached the midpoint on the wire there was a sudden burst of applause which was inexplicable by any dramatic change I had employed. I searched the darkness ahead of me, a blinding kind caused by the brilliant lights aimed at me. Suddenly, out of this darkness appeared a clown, barefooted, carrying only a tiny paper parasol, which he playfully carried as if it were a serious balancer. The audience was applauding him as he somersaulted so very cleverly to everyone's delight – except mine – for as he approached me he showered me with looks of murderous hatred. It was evident that he was out to tousle me off balance and to send me flying into the dreadful darkness below.

As in a *ker*-death, Mrs. Smith felt swallowed by darkness.

Much of this dream is an accurate feeling-toned picture of Elizabeth Smith and her life, that high-wire performance she had done largely on her own and without the safety net of social approval. And, indeed, when she reached the midpoint of her life (the wire), she worked with a much-applauded Jungian analyst Dr. Hans Westman, who famously played a clown trickster role in professional circles to debunk self-serving pretensions.[37] So here comes such a clown figure in her dream, but this time one whose murderous look is about throw her off balance to fall, not into a universe sufficient for her mind, but into the darkness that feels like a death of shame at being so ruthlessly tricked, mocked, and brought down.

There are many things to say about this dream, especially about the questions it implies as to whether she could trust the Jungian work she had already done or, indeed, could trust the work on her dreams she was about to do with me. Was her Jungian work "a serious balancer"? Or was it just airy pretension that needed to be brought down? The challenge facing us, then, was how to survive the dream's murderous self-hatred and to find some less shaming way for her to become more grounded in her search for wholeness. Could she come down from the high wire of the ego's willed achievement to trust psyche's ability to catch and hold lost pieces of her spirit that had been sacrificed to it? The cost had been high, not to her superb mind, but to her soul as a woman.

Donald Kalsched's work on the inner persecutor/protector figure was of great help to us as we tried to rescue her inner spirit from induced shame, doubt, and *ker*-like self-hatred.[38] If we could do that, we might fulfill the passionate longing of her Icarus poem, not as a flight beyond the human realm, but as a gradual return to a spacious inner universe to release its imprisoned spirit. In that way, perhaps, we could find some small sparks of light that would not blind us with their sudden brilliance aimed at the ego, but rather would help us to enter the darkness of the unconscious gradually to discern, absorb, and understand.

And now I'll let her final dream speak for itself. To Mrs. Smith it signaled not just the end of our work – this was, indeed, the last dream we shared – but it also forecast accurately, as she sensed, her actual death, which followed the dream by less than a month. In the dream, she was back in her childhood home, up in its attic:[39]

> Yes, I was stepping outside my attic window onto the graceful branches of a sturdy pine tree . . . I was without worries because I knew I was to be buried in this tree and otherwise prepared for rebirth . . . . Mother [was waiting] down below on the terrace, [she] watched and readily stretched out her arms to catch me when I came within her reach . . . she observed the easy flow of my body into her possession. She insisted on arranging for the design of a brass plaque to be placed on the bark of the pine tree. . . . She wanted the world to know about the special gifts the pine presented [by] the safe procedure of moving [me] from branch to branch. The tree deserved all the credit we could muster for it – as well as all the publicity throughout the whole world to whom the story was to be told.

And here we are retelling it because she wrote it down for us to share. Mrs. Smith didn't need me to tell her that the tree she was descending was the tree of life as well as the analytic tree of inner knowledge, nor did she need me to explain the pine tree's connection to the goddess Cybele and the archetype of the Great Mother; she had seen those things for herself.[40]

What I did help her see was how the dream fulfilled her unconscious longing for an honored initiation into her spiritual wholeness as a woman, which her own mother and the society of her time had not been able to do. Now the Great Mother archetype was witnessing and celebrating that achievement. Mrs. Smith was coming down into the objective psyche's welcoming embrace of what were simultaneously her death and her rebirth into a trusted symbolic universe sufficient for her state of mind. Mrs. Smith's experience suggests that ancient culture and modern psyches often dream the same dreams about bringing new light from the darkness of death's necessity as a spiritual journey, an initiation into wholeness – much as Jung described it.

Does the *Alcestis* end with a similar sense of spiritual fulfillment? As you may have guessed, Admetus does finally get beyond self-pity and blaming others for Alcestis' loss, to face the shadow of his own guilt. He comes to recognize that he let Alcestis do what he should have done: face his death. She'll live on as a hero, while he died right on schedule, not physically, but spiritually. In losing Alcestis, he has lost not only his reputation as a man; he has lost his real life, his soul. She was his *anima*, his enlivening spirit. He sees that now. In his recognition, the spiritual ideal of marriage for which Alcestis died has come true; Admetus has finally been yoked to necessity.

A poet like Sophocles might have ended his tragedy with this image of a hero's painful recognition of Ananke, but not Euripides. He suggests that we only get brief glimpses of such deep insight, and then they go, and so the struggle for meaning must go on. Accordingly, Euripides quickly undoes this moment of recognition with a comic reversal of fortune: the sudden arrival of a guest, Heracles! He had shown up earlier asking for hospitality just as Admetus was about to bury his wife. Although Admetus was all in black with his head shorn and tears in his eyes, he played the virtuous host by pretending no one important had died. Heracles could stay, albeit safely split off in separate quarters. But now here he comes again, like the return of the repressed.

When Heracles found out how Admetus had deceived him about Alcestis' death, he knew just what to do. Off he went to fight Thanatos and to now bring back a mysterious and silent woman, veiled in black, who presumably is Alcestis. Within the limits of the play, neither the audience nor Admetus will ever know for sure who or what she is. The play's pointed ambiguity about this figure's identity allows Heracles to do some meaningful deceiving of his own. First, he explains to Admetus how he got this woman: she was second prize in a wrestling contest. Others got horses, but he got some "oxen and a woman was thrown in with them."[41] Although Euripides is clearly having fun with the idea that women count for less in the world Admetus rules than a good pair of oxen, those oxen necessarily bring with them an image of the yoke that binds them. With that not-so-subtle hint about what's coming for the as-yet-unyoked Admetus, Heracles finally persuades him to bring, not just another woman, but life itself back into his dark and empty house:

*Admetus:* My lord, you are forcing me to act against my wish.
*Heracles:* Be brave. Reach out your hand and take the stranger's.

And so he finally does, surrendering his ego to the inevitable. In giving his hand to this dark ox-prize lady, Admetus is also submitting once more to the yoke of marriage, the yoke of Ananke, the necessary joining of opposites, perhaps including now his life with his postponed death. In this richly overdetermined gesture, we also see that sometimes it may be necessary to forget death's necessity to make human commitments in time.

Perhaps that's why Heracles says "be brave." He knows that to fully face either death or life takes courage, let alone to face both at the same time. "It sounds like my life, the kind of work I do," he says.[42] Hero's work: wrestling with death, confronting its necessity, without losing touch with life. It's also what my sister Carol was doing when she faced the necessity of her death without losing the spark of wit that still gave her life its freedom and savor. It's what Sophie Scholl was doing, calmly, even confidently, as she rescued the child of living ideas, her soul, from the dark tyranny of her death. And it was what Mrs. Smith was doing as she faced her final sign-off with generosity and courage to reach out her hand toward future dream-makers so that they too might find psyche's tree of life and its treasure of deeply rooted knowledge.

And so now Admetus reaches out to welcome the unknown. But Heracles warns him that he may not speak to the dark stranger for three days. And after that, what? Will this homecoming find a welcoming embrace, forgiveness, and rebirth as Mrs. Smith's homecoming was celebrated in her dream? Who knows? The play ends here. But maybe, like Admetus and Alcestis, and all the other guiding spirits we've met in this account, we'll find that a short time is all we have, and by facing that necessity (and occasionally forgetting it), we will try to make the most of life while we can.

## Notes

1  E. Vermeule, *Aspects of Death in Early Greek Art and Poetry*, Berkeley, University of California Press, 1979/1981, p. 6.

2  Jung reported his own experience with this near-death phenomenon in *Memories, Dreams, Reflections*. C. G. Jung, *Memories, Dreams, Reflections*, rev. ed., recorded and edited by Aniela Jaffé, trans. Richard and Clara Winston, New York, Vintage Books, 1961/1965, p. 321. Hereafter referred to as *MDR*.

3  Vermeule, *Aspects of Death*, p. 25. Vermeule illustrates varying representations of winged *psychai* and *eidola* from early Greek pottery (see pp. 9, 19, and 26).

4  Throughout this paper, I have used italics and capitalization to mark a distinction between a concept and its personification as a god, thus, *thanatos*/Thanatos, *moira*/Moirai, and so on.

5  Homer, *The Iliad*, trans. Robert Fagles, New York and London, Penguin Books, 1980/1988, XVI, ll. 522–34, pp. 770–90.

6  As Jules Cashford points out, it is for this reason that Hermes, conductor of souls to Hades, is shown on the *Euphronios Krater* standing above Prince Sarpedon's body. Jules Cashford, *The Myth of the Messenger*, London, Kingfisher Art Productions, 2012, p. 37. A version of this paper was given at the International Association of Analytical Psychology, in Montreal, Quebec, Canada, in 2010.

7  From his villanelle, "Do Not Go Gentle into that Good Night." Dylan Thomas, *The Poems of Dylan Thomas, New Revised Edition*, ed. Daniel Jones, New York, New Directions, 1971/2003, p. 239.

8  Vermeule, *Aspects of Death*, p. 8.

9  J. E. Harrison, *Epilegomena to the Study of Greek Religion and Themis*, Hyde Park, New York, University Books, 1912/1962, pp. 289–97. Note that *Epilegomena* is from the one edition printed in 1921; *Themis* is the second revised edition, published in Cambridge by Cambridge University Press in 1927. The first edition was published in 1912.

10  I am indebted to Jules Cashford and Tom Singer for helping me see how important it is to balance the demonized vision of the *keres* with their original representation as immortal souls (personal communications, Santorini Conference, 5 September 2012). Jules Cashford also helped me see that because the word *ker* meant heart as well as death it implied an afterlife, as in the weighing of the heart against the feather of *Maat* in Egyptian religious imagery (email, 29 September 2012). Such positive views of *ker*, in contrast to its commonly demonized representation, correspond to Jung's account of facing death from either the perspective of psyche or from that of the ego; see Jung, *MDR*, p. 6. For a more historically detailed treatment of Greek death, see Christiane Sourvinou-Inwood, *"Reading" Greek Death*, Oxford, Clarendon Press, 1995.

11  Vermeule, *Aspects of Death*, p. 39. Unlike the weightless gods, the *keres* were thought to have material weight and substance.

12  Homer, *The Iliad*, XXIII, l. 78; cited by Vermeule, *Aspects of Death*, p. 40.

13  C. G. Jung, "On the nature of the psyche (1946/1954)," *The Structure and Dynamics of the Psyche*, CW 8, trans. R. F. C. Hull, Princeton, Princeton University Press, 1960/1981, ¶¶388–9. (Hereafter references to Jung's *Collected Works* appear as CW and volume number.)

14  Jung, *MDR*, pp. 179–80, 189–93.

15  Ibid., pp. 313–14.

16  Euripides, *Alcestis*, trans. R. Lattimore, in D. Grene and R. Lattimore (eds), *The Complete Greek Tragedies*, Chicago, University of Chicago Press, 1955/1967, ll. 962–81. See also Euripides, *Alcestis*, edited with Introduction and Commentary by L. P. E. Parker, Oxford, Oxford University Press, 2007.

17  For a review of philosophical attempts to define Ananke, see James Hillman, "On the necessity of abnormal psychology: Ananke and Athena," *Facing the Gods*, Dallas, Texas University Press, 1980/1988, pp. 11–16.

18  Ibid., pp. 5–6.

19  Hector uses this image (*The Iliad*, VI, l. 546) in telling Andromache how he foresees her fate "with the rough yoke of necessity at your neck."

20  E. B. Smith, *In the Company of Dream Makers*, privately printed, Charlottesville, VA, 2007.

21  W. Arrowsmith, "Introduction," *Euripides' Alcestis*, ed. and trans. W. Arrowsmith, New York, Oxford University Press, 1974, p. 13.

22  Euripides, *Alcestis*, ll. 172–4.

23  H. Kohut, *Self Psychology and the Humanities: Reflections on a New Psychoanalytic Approach*, ed. Charles B. Strozier, New York & London, W. W. Norton & Co., 1985, pp. 12–25.

24  In a discussion of a version of this paper (15 March 2013), John Peck reminded me that among those swept up and executed as part of the White Rose Movement was University of Munich Professor of Philosophy Kurt Huber.

25  Kohut, *Self Psychology*, p. 21.

26  Ibid.

27  Ibid.

28  D. Kalsched, in response to a version of this paper, Santorini Conference, 5 September 2012.

29  Euripides, *Alcestis*, ll. 162–9.

30  Plato, *Symposium and Phaedrus*, trans. B. Jowett, New York, Dover Publications, 1993, pp. 7–8. I am indebted to Smith College Professor of Classics Justina Gregory for pointing out this connection to me ( personal communication, 27 September 2012).

31  For this reason, Euripides stresses the dispassion of Alcestis' behavior toward Admetus. Her cool-headed objectivity is easily mistaken by moderns for lack of love, whereas for the Greeks, it was likely a sign of her virtue in acting out of *philia* rather than by the compulsion of *eros*.

32  Euripides, *Alcestis*, l. 177.

33  Ibid., ll. 175–87.

34  Ibid., ll. 695–701.

35  Ibid., ll. 995–1005.

36  E. Smith, *In the Company of Dream Makers*, pp. 72–3.

37  On the second page of her manuscript, Mrs. Smith describes an anecdote about Dr. Westman at an Euranos Conference in which he was so impatient with a speaker that he left the room briefly, only to reappear outside a terrace door wearing a beanie with a spinning disc on top. He then pressed his grinning face against the glass to make the audience laugh. Whether this anecdote is fact or myth, it clearly represents Mrs. Smith's image of her analyst as a trickster-critic who exposed shadow. Its placement at the very start of her manuscript suggests its defining influence. Notice, for example, how a repeating image of "terrace" develops from a site of mockery in the Dr. Westman story to a maternal space of acceptance and celebration in her sign-off dream.

38  D. Kalsched, *The Inner World of Trauma: Archetypal Defenses of the Human Spirit*, New York, Taylor & Francis Group, 1996.

39  E. Smith, *In the Company of Dream Makers*, pp. 57–8.

40  The *Penguin Dictionary of Symbols*, 2nd edition, eds Jean Chevalier and Alain Gheerbrant, trans. John Buchanan-Brown, London, Penguin Books, 1994/1996, first published in France, 1969, pp. 755–6, adds this particularly apt amplification of Mrs. Smith's pine tree image: "In Japan, the pine (*matsu*) is also the symbol of irresistible strength tempered by a lifetime of daily struggle. It is also the symbol of those who have held to their opinions unaffected by the criticisms of those around them."

41  Euripides, *Alcestis*, l. 1032.

42  Ibid., l. 449.

# 5

# HOW HERMES AND APOLLO CAME TO LOVE EACH OTHER IN THE HOMERIC *HYMN TO HERMES*

## Imagination and form in Ancient Greece and modern psyche

*Jules Cashford*

There are three different images of Hermes in Greek art: a tiny baby, a lithe and sometimes bearded young man, and an older thick-bearded statue (Figure 5.1).

We might be tempted to read these images in the order of their stages of life, were it not for the fact that the child, in the Homeric *Hymn to Hermes*, is "born" long after the older thick-bearded Hermes, who had been in existence since at least 1500 BCE, where he was named on a Mycenaean tablet from Knossos in Crete. (Mycenaeans – named after Agamemnon's town of Mycenae – had been coming

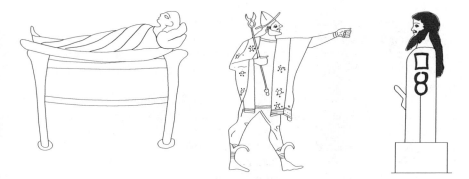

*Figure 5.1* Hermes as baby, youth, and elder. (Line drawings by the author.)

101

to Crete from about 1800 BCE onward). The *Hymn to Hermes* was written around 520 BCE, a thousand years later.[1] Reading the *Hymn* with these different images in mind may perhaps offer a new perspective on Hermes, one that suggests a complex relationship between the Greek myth and the modern psyche.

## I The older pre-Olympian Hermes

The Homeric *Hymn to Hermes,* simply read, tells a miraculous tale of a baby who was born in obscurity and in the course of two days becomes a god, and not just any god, but the god who guides souls on their journey after life.

> Born at dawn, he played the lyre in the afternoon,
> and he stole the cattle of Apollo the Archer
> in the evening, all on the fourth day of the month,
> the day he was born from the lady Maia . . . [2]

If we start from *within* the narrative of the *Hymn* we have to ask: how can that mischievous little baby, one day old, end up not just with a place on Olympos, but also as the god who made and played the lyre and the pipes; who invented fire; who traded his lyre with Apollo in return for Apollo's cattle, a magic wand, and certain powers of divination; and who was made the "only consecrated messenger to Hades" by Zeus (1.573)? Finding this question unanswerable, we are more likely to focus on Hermes' magical skill and versatility, his crafty tricks and wiles, and his shameless ability to get away with anything. These qualities have led to his being known as the "trickster" god, the one who cheats, thieves, deceives, and bargains, and who becomes the god of barter and trade. In this he is all too human, drawn closer to us than the other gods, and so able to move easily between gods and humans as "the messenger of the gods," who is also "the friendliest of gods to human beings," the one who brings luck. What we lose in this focus is the Hermes from ancient time when trickery was fused with magic, when the magical could take many forms and tricked humans who could not fathom the source of its mystery.

But if we begin chronologically with the older Hermes, then we are allowed a fascinating glimpse into an ancient *reimagining* of Hermes, in which the older established figure from Cretan Mycenaean, if not Minoan, times is brought into the new Olympian order of the patriarchal Greeks of the eighth century BCE, first recorded in Homer.

In *The Iliad,* Homer, writing in c. 700 BCE about the Mycenaeans of c. 1500–1300 BCE, called them *Achaeans,* who worshipped a god of thunder and lightning – Zeus – whose own name derives from the Indo-European word for light. Over the centuries, they entered the old Bronze Age culture and lands of the native Pelasgians, many of whom had themselves migrated from Crete a thousand years before. In 1953, Michael Ventris decoded the language of the Mycenaeans, which he called *Linear B,*[3] and the writing on the clay tablets showed that many

Greek goddesses and gods, assumed to be only Greek, came originally from Crete. Interestingly enough, in the Homeric *Hymn to Demeter*, dated to around 700 BCE, Demeter says she has come from Crete, and, in the Homeric *Hymn to Apollo*, Apollo will only have Cretans from Knossos as priests in his Temple at Delphi, kidnapping them from their ship to bring them there himself.

The Pelasgians, like the Minoans, lived an agrarian life, worshipping goddesses and gods with names now familiar to us from Crete, as though there had existed an unbroken continuum from the Minoans, many of whom would have migrated to Greece when the society broke down, probably because of the tsunami from the earthquake at Thera in 1450 BCE. They had their own version of the *eniautos daimon*, the Year God, whom the Mycenaeans called retrospectively Zeus. These goddesses and gods, and the values they embodied, merged with varying degrees of autonomy into the new Olympian order.[4]

Many of the divinities of the older mythology – whether Minoan, Mycenaean, Pelasgian, or Kabeirian – have two stories of their origin, and often two different parents. In the new version, Zeus typically becomes the father by marrying the various goddesses who long predated his arrival in their land – aspects of the one Great Goddess – and who are brought peacefully thereby into the new order. For instance, Zeus "marries" two Titans of the older stratum – strictly, in the new Olympian myth, his aunts – Mnemosune, goddess of memory, who then gives birth to the Muses, and Themis, goddess of divine law, who gives birth to the Moirai (who were also, as it were, "there already," as the three goddesses of the Moon – *Moira* meaning "part" or "portion").[5]

Consequently, in Greek myth, there are almost always two levels of sensibility, the older one typically obscured – as ancestry, etymology, epithet, and image – in the patterns beneath the newer heroic narrative overlaid upon them. And so it would seem with Hermes. At least a thousand years after the first mention of him, Hermes becomes the son of Zeus and Maia, bringing with him, inevitably, memories and qualities of an earlier, more magical, age.

In the new story, Zeus lies with Maia in a shadowy cave, far from the eyes of human beings, where she gives birth to "a child who was destined to bring wonderful things to light among the immortal gods" (l.16). Hermes' mother, Maia, was a mountain nymph of Kyllene, the eldest of the seven sisters of the Pleiades born to the Titan Atlas (son of the Titan Iapetus and Klymene, an Oceanid) and Pleione (also an Oceanid, one of the 3000 daughters of the original Titans – Oceanos and Thetys). Maia's name means "mother," "nursing mother," or "midwife"; goddess of birth and spring; and may also be related to *Maiores*, the Ancestors. Aeschylus identified her with *Gaia*, bringing her back to the beginning of things.

### Hermes as the herm

So who was the older Hermes? His name comes up in Linear B tablets five times – *E-ma-ai* – and once as *E-ma-ai Areias*, suggestive of Hermes the Ram, an old fertility god.[6] So also, to put this in context, do other goddesses and gods whom we

*Figure 5.2* Hermes as Herm, with caduceus, altar, and tree, showing the thick-bearded statue of Hermes from the oldest level of thought, reaching far back into pre-Olympian times. Red-figure lekythos. 450–400 BCE. British Museum. (From Jung, *Psychology and Alchemy*, CW 13, p. 132.)

already know from Greek mythology: Athena, as *A-ta-na Po-ti-ni-ja* (To the Lady of Athana); also, in recognizable form, Poseidon, Zeus *Diktaios* (from the Dikte mountains in Crete), Hera, Ares, *Erinyes* (the old version of Demeter), *Eleutha* (the old version of Artemis), and *Paean* (the old version of Apollo, retained as one of his later epithets).

The etymology of Hermes' name points us initially to the Herms and the stories behind them. *Herma* was originally a heap of stones, often found beside springs, offering a promise of water for the thirsty journeyer in the blazing sun, shown in Figure 5.2. Wayfarers would lay a stone – a *herm* – on the earth for other travelers, who thought themselves lucky to find it and would lay one of their own. Standing gratefully at a herm and, it may be, picturing the next herm, the next spring – leaping in the mind toward it – the journeyer takes heart and imagines his or her journey onward. Was it this disclosure of unexpected gifts, seemingly from beyond the human world, which allowed the heap of stones to shine forth as a god who brings gifts from the divine to the human realm – the herm becoming Hermes? The statue that took form out of the pile of stones was invariably ithyphallic, disclosing Hermes as a daimon of fertility, an *Agathos Daimon*, a Good Spirit, the rich spirit of abundance, bringing his gifts from the goddesses and gods deep within the earth.

### Hermes as Agathos Daimon, the Good Spirit

The *Agathos Daimon* was an ancient conception that, long before the Olympians, honored the protective daimon of the place to which the travelers came. Springs were especially sacred. The Good Spirit nurtured the flocks and herds and their magical increase and was often pictured as the ever-renewing snake, or, as in Figure 5.3, two snakes facing each other in embrace, with sheaves of wheat sprouting from both sides of their single "stem." This idea persisted into Roman times.[7]

Hermes was also called *Agathopoios*, "he who makes good," which was first of all "good for food": "When he shines forth the earth blossoms, and when he laughs the plants bear fruit, and at his bidding the herds bring forth young . . . He brings together food for gods and men."[8] This explains why the herm was also a boundary stone that stood at the entrance of a temple or a home, granting a fruitful life to those within. Words inscribed on a herm from 465 BCE call Hermes *Kalos*, good, and *Glaukos*, gleaming, to which was occasionally added a bird, whispering wisdom. This dual nature of Hermes – combining the deep-rooted fertility genius

*Figure 5.3* Coin of Claudius. (From Jane Harrison, *Themis*, p. 279.)

of the local place with the unfolding path of the journeyer – allows Plotinus, in the second century CE, to say: "According to the mystical wisdom of the ancient sages, the phallic symbols on terminal statues of Hermes suggest that all generation derives from the mind."[9]

As god of journeyers, the older Hermes was also god of boundaries and thresholds, the one who is necessarily *beyond* the boundaries he draws, who knows both sides of the line. So Hermes offers a perspective on boundaries: what is included or excluded, where a line is to be drawn, and how to mediate between different realms. Rilke's meditation on angels invokes this when he writes that the angels give him a spiritual space in which the usual boundaries of what is important, and what is not, are lifted. "Every angel is terrible . . . You must change your life."[10] Angel, coming from the Greek *angelos*, originally meant "messenger," which was what Hermes was to be called in the Olympian age. Any piece of luck became a *Hermaion*, literally, "a thing of Hermes" – a godsend, a windfall, a message from the gods, something good coming out of nowhere.

Since the ideas of journeys and boundaries are intrinsically related, these journeys, as Plotinus and John Keats both propose, were also journeys of the mind – traveling "in the realms of gold," as Keats begins his poem, "On First Looking in to Chapman's Homer":

> Much have I travelled in the realms of gold,
> And many goodly states and kingdoms seen;
> Round many western islands have I been
> Which bards in fealty to Apollo hold.[11]

William Wordsworth, in *The Prelude*, brings these ideas together:

> I love a public road: few sights there are
> That please me more; such object hath had power
> O'er my imagination since the dawn
> Of childhood, when its disappearing line,
> Seen daily afar off, on one bare steep
> Beyond the limits which my feet had trod
> Was like a guide into eternity,
> At least to things unknown and without bound.[12]

This poem leads us into all the boundaries that we draw – and ultimately into the fundamental boundary between life and death, and between eternity and time. Hermes, who crosses the boundaries from both directions, has a knowledge of both sides within him and is, therefore, beyond their opposition. So the god, uniquely, unifying life and death in his own story, offers to his worshippers a vision of life and death as a unity. This is also suggested in the Kerykeion or Caduceus that he carries as his symbol – the wand of intertwining snakes around a central pole. But first we have to understand Hermes' relation with death.

### Hermes Chthonios

*Chthonios* means literally "of the Nether World" or "Beneath the Earth," and the dead were called *Chthonioi*, the "Earth People." Yet this is no contradiction since Hermes, as *Agathos Daimon*, was inseparable from *Hermes Chthonios*, because in early Greece the very notion of fertility included the notion of death and rebirth, indeed was founded on it, as Jane Harrison explains in her discussion of the picture shown in Figure 5.4.[13]

A large *pithos* or jar is sunk into the earth as a grave. Hermes is holding a magic staff or wand, a *rhabdos*, in his right hand, and the *Kerykeion* – or, in Latin, *Caduceus* – in his left hand, and is both evoking and revoking the souls of the dead. (The *rhabdos* and the *kerykeion* are distinguished here, though they later merge into each other.) More precisely, the winged figures are called the *Keres* or *eidola*, little images, the shadow souls without strength, *menos*, because their

*Figure 5.4* Hermes Chthonios summoning the Keres out of the grave-pithos (or grave-jar). Lekythos. White figure vase. Fifth century BCE. University Museum of Jena. (From Jane Harrison, *Prolegomena to Greek Religion*, p. 43.)

107

life-spirit, *thumos*, has passed into the daimon of death and reincarnation, typically represented as a snake. The Keres have a different tonal emphasis to the Souls. Soul in Greek is *psuche* (becoming *psyche* in English), which means both soul *and* butterfly, a union of meanings that implicitly makes the idea of soul transparent to the graceful lightness of the butterfly, as well as to its miraculous nature of transformation. In the Ring of Nestor, two butterflies symbolize the souls of the two deceased persons at the end of their journey. *Ker* means "death," "fate," and "heart" – also a winged spirit – and sometimes death fates – the fate of death carried within as destiny and often thought to be given you with your daimon at birth and, in that sense, something chosen – ultimately, perhaps, an acceptance of mortality. So although the Ker of an ancestor is closer to a ghost than a soul, in many cases, the terms are interchangeable. It is as if Hermes guides the Souls but commands the *Keres*.

To understand this, we need to go to the Festival of the Anthesteria, which was both a Wine Festival to Dionysos and a Festival of All-Souls and the Blossoming of Plants – the annual feast of the great reincarnation cycle of Nature and human beings. It was held for three days at the end of February, when the Greek spring was about to begin.

The first day was called the *Pithoigia*, the Opening of the Pithoi – urns or jars that held food and wine and were also grave-jars, out of which the souls of the dead could come and go. Then there was a sacrifice of new wine to the Agathos Daimon to remove the taboo of the old year. The Scholiast on Aristophanes' *Frogs* writes of this sacrifice: "They have the custom of sacrificing at this feast, *not to any of the Olympian gods at all*, but to Hermes Chthonios . . . Those present appease Hermes on behalf of the dead."[14]

The second day was called the *Choes*, or Drinking Cups, when it was believed that the souls of the dead were released and rose up, and people chewed buckthorn and anointed their doors with pitch, both in respect and for protection. The souls of the Ancestors were revered but also feared.

The third day was called the *Chytroi*, or Pots, when a pot of grain and seeds of all kinds – *panspermia* – was boiled, but not tasted or eaten. It was for the souls to take the seeds down into the earth with them and send them back up in autumn as fruits, as *pankarpia*. This was a version of the *kathodos* and the *anodos* of Kore, Demeter's daughter, the "going down" of the seeds for the "coming up" as next year's growth – the immortal cycle of reincarnation. The dead were also called *Demetrioi*, Demeter's people; in the underworld, they became Kore, her children, as the participants in the Eleusinian Mysteries discovered. The *thumos* of the dead, their life and strength, passed into the daimon of life and reincarnation, the ancestral snake, a totem or symbol of the continuing life of the tribe. Thus the souls of the dead, like the seeds of the plants on which they have lived, are themselves sown as *panspermia* and reaped as *pankarpia* in the alternating cycle of life and death.

Significantly, the Pot of Seed was sacrificed to Hermes Chthonios alone, he who is explicitly described as *not* an Olympian, being instead the earlier spirit, the Agathos Daimon, the old god of fertility. Hermes may be closing the ritual in the vase painting shown in Figure 5.3. The Ker he is looking down on, poised directly beneath his raised wand, appears to be falling head first into the Pithos, as though being commanded back into the grave-jar, while one other Ker is just emerging – it seems as though the wings of the going down one and the coming up one form two parallel lines in opposite directions. Half of the jar is already in the earth. Two others flutter away upward. *"Out of the doors! You Keres; It is no longer Anthesteria!"* was said on the final day,[15] sending the souls back down with the seed and closing the ceremony.

### Hermes the Daimon

In the vase painting shown in Figure 5.5, the disjunctive angle of Hermes, which puts him outside the field of combat, suggests that he is an invisible presence beyond the warriors' awareness. Yet he holds the meaning and outcome of the fight, as he weighs the winged Keres, or *eidola*, the souls of the two combatants, probably Achilles and Memnon. Hermes may seem to be weighing the Keres against each other, but the dual image of combatant and man-shaped Ker suggests that the result, and the victory, will come from the characters of the combatants themselves, and specifically, perhaps, from their relation to their own daimon, represented by Hermes, the archetypal daimon. As Harrison comments, the Keres are images of men; therefore, "it is the lives rather than the fates that are weighed. So the notion shifts."[16]

This early fifth-century picture is the earliest image of *Kerostasia*, the weighing of the Keres. This ritual is also called *Psychostasia*, the weighing of the soul. The momentous shift of the idea here is toward an increasing inwardness, with the understanding that our character is our destiny. As Tom Singer suggests – extending the image of the Kerostasia – "it is as if the souls of the ancients are being weighed in the scales of history as the balance shifts to inwardness."[17] This shift of understanding prepares the way for the idea that, as Socrates was to demonstrate, humans were responsible not only for their own acts but also for their thoughts, how they related to their daimons and, through them, to the gods. Interestingly, in *The Iliad* (written around 200 years earlier than this picture of Hermes), the outcome of a similar Kerostasia appears still to come from an impersonal source. Zeus had become weary of the battle between Achilles and Hector, and so he "hung up his golden scales and placed in them two Keres, fates of death that lays men low." But it is Moira, goddess of fate, who decides: Hector's Ker then "sinks down," as being the "heaviest."[18] Heraclitus (535–475 BCE), who could conceivably have come across this vase, was the first to articulate that "the character of a human being is their destiny": *Ethos anthropou daimon.*[19] *Ethos* has the overtone of custom, the habitual bearing of a person that we call character. *Daimon* could mean both "destiny" and "daimon," although the daimon is defined as the intermediary between humans and gods, the figure who relates them to each other, making the threshold between them permeable, such that the soul of the person may be more open to the god.

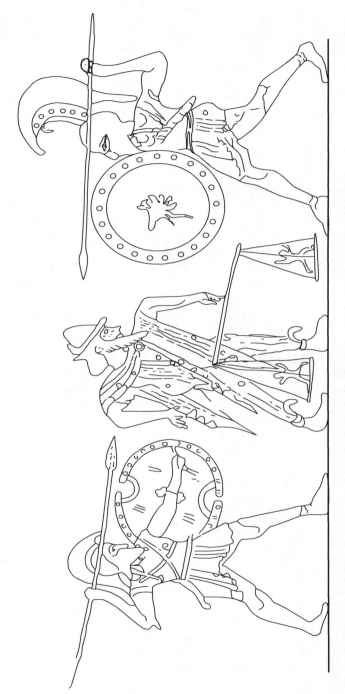

*Figure 5.5* Hermes weighing the souls of two combatants in battle. Black figure vase. 490–480 BCE. British Museum. (From Harrison, *Prolegomena*, p. 184.)

In Plato's *Symposium*, the priestess Diotima defines a daimon as that which goes between god and mortal, like an intermediary or a messenger:

> Everything that is daimonic is intermediate between god and mortal. Interpreting and conveying human things to the gods and divine things to humans; entreaties and sacrifices from below and ordinances and requitals from above; it stands between the two and fills the gap . . . god has no contact with human beings; only through the daimonic is there intercourse and conversation between humans and gods, whether in the waking state or during sleep. And a man who is an expert in such intercourse is a daimonic man.[20]

Socrates, being such a man, listened to Diotima, his *daimonion*, indeed attributed all his wisdom to her, even to choosing to die instead of living a restricted life, as his friends pleaded with him to do. Several centuries later, Plutarch warned that those who deny the daimons break the chain that unites the world to God.[21]

Here in Figure 5.6, Hermes, Paris, and the three goddesses – Hera, Athena, and Aphrodite – are all participating in a drama usually called the Judgment of Paris. But as Harrison declares,[22] this is not a picture of a vulgar beauty contest, but

*Figure 5.6* Hermes as Daimon with Paris and Hera, Athena, and Aphrodite. Black figure vase. Sixth century BCE. The Louvre. (Line drawing by the author, from Joseph Campbell, *Occidental Mythology*, p. 161.)

rather a man trying to escape his destiny and being compelled to make his choice by Hermes in his daimonic role. (The look on his face and his grasp of Paris' wrist appear to be saying: "Not so fast!") The root of daimon, from the Indo-European, is to "deal out." Paris may look as if he thinks his destiny is being dealt out *to* him but, as we saw, for Heraclitus, daimon and destiny are the same – what we deal out to ourselves by the *custom* (*ethos*) of ourselves, our character, and specifically in our "dealings" with the daimonic realm. W. B. Yeats explores this:

> I think it was Heraclitus who said: the Daimon is our destiny. When I think of life as a struggle with the Daimon who would ever set us to the hardest work among those not impossible, I understand why there is a deep enmity between a man and his destiny, and why a man loves nothing but his destiny . . . I am persuaded that the Daimon delivers and deceives us, and he wove the netting from the stars and threw the net from his shoulder.[23]

The personal daimon was intimately involved in all areas of life, as is suggested in the word for happiness, *eudaimoneia*, which means literally "to be well with your daimon," an idea that entered the debate between Plato and Aristotle. Plato argued that virtue – *arete* – was required for happiness or well being and further defined this as care for one's soul (the literal meaning of psychotherapy), whereas Aristotle thought that living well and doing well was sufficient – though *eu*, "well," lacks the depth and rigor of *arete*, "virtue."

As Ker also means "heart," we could compare the weighing of the souls in ancient Greece with beliefs in ancient Egypt which held that the heart of the deceased had to be weighed against the Feather of Maat, the goddess of truth and the moral order of the universe. If the heart was as light as the Feather of Truth, then the person was led into the presence of Osiris and so into eternal life. However, this was also a template of thought for daily life in time, showing a way of weighing up the truth of an action or an idea, just as it is now: *penser*, "to think" in French (from which we get "pensive"), comes from Latin *pensum*, which was the wool to be weighed out each day, thoughtfully weaving the pattern of the life to come.

### The Kerykeion or Caduceus

In Figure 5.7, the faces of the two sphinxes evocatively resemble the face of Hermes, as though they symbolize dimensions within him or phases of his coming into his own nature. If we read upward from the sphinxes' outstretched arms, which almost touch each other, then the flower on which Hermes stands, drawn as coming forth from between them, suggests itself as the blossoming of their coming together, the fruit of which is Hermes, who contains and transforms their opposition at the new level, which is himself.

Ker is also the root of the *kerukeion* – the staff, scepter, wand, or rod of intertwining snakes that Hermes holds as his emblem and symbol (the Greek *u* becomes *y* in English). It is also the root of *Kerberos* (*Cerberus* in Latin), the three-headed dog

*Figure 5.7* Hermes with his kerykeion, standing on a flower supported by two sphinxes facing each other, reconciling their opposition. Black figure vase. 600 BCE. British Museum. (©The Trustees of the British Museum.)

who guards the entrance to the underworld. *Kerux* means "herald," "messenger," or "envoy," and its derivation is uncertain. Is it from Indo-European *karu,* meaning "praise," or is it more likely related to the *ker* – the spirit, soul, or ghost – especially as it is spelled with an *e* not an *a*? Given Hermes' older title of Hermes Chthonios, we might wonder if Hermes in origin was a herald of death, the Daimon of the Ker, whose time had come to go down into the underworld or to come up into the light. In the *Orphic Hymns*, for instance (which are usually dated to between 300 BCE and 400 CE but are much earlier in feeling and sometimes said to be as early as 600 BCE), there are two separate hymns to Hermes: one to *Hermes Chthonios* and one simply to *Hermes*, significantly, in both cases, asking for a "good end" to a life of work.[24] In Aeschylus' *The Libation Bearers*, Electra calls on Hermes Chthonios to speak to the spirits:

> Almighty herald (kerux) of the world above, the world below:
> Hermes Chthonios, help me. Summon the spirits who live
> beneath the earth, who watch over my father's house,
> that they may hear.[25]

This *chthonic* meaning persists into the Latin *Caduceus* – now the more familiar term – which also comes etymologically from the verb *cadere,* "to fall" (the root of both "cadence" and "cadaver"). It was used originally to describe those who fell upon the ground in battle – "In Memory of the Fallen," as we still say. The last part of Caduceus – *ducius* – comes from *ducere* – "to lead," "guide," giving "guide of the dead," and "guide of souls" as the translation of the Greek *psychopompos*.

Yet, again, we have to remember that, in the old world, death was inseparable from rebirth, as we saw in the grave-jars of grain. So although, on an Etruscan mirror, Hermes is called "Hermes of Hades,"[26] the other name of Hades was *Pluto* (riches), as in coming back to life transformed, evoking the yearly celebration of Dionysos as spring. In the same vein, Heraclitus says, "Hades and Dionysos are the same"; "the way up and the way down are one and the same."[27]

Hermes goes back and forth, up and down, *between* life and death, not simply one way. The movement is always given as life-death-life. In *The Odyssey*, he leads the souls of the slain suitors to Hades with his "fair golden wand with which he lulls to sleep the eyes of whom he will, while others he wakens."[28] Hermes, Harrison says, is "a snake to begin with and, carrying always the snake-staff, is the very *daimon* of reincarnation."[29]

### Hermes as an old Moon God

In an earlier phase of thought, just as the Moon was seen to slough its shadow, so the snake was seen to shed its skin, and both were interpreted as being reborn. This created an identity between Moon and snake such that the snake was understood in the early world as the "Moon on Earth": in other words, what pertained to the one pertained to the other. In a later age, this way of thinking was named as the *Doctrine of Signatures* (persisting up to the seventeenth century in England): it held that if two things looked alike, or acted alike, then they *were* alike; they had the same "signature." Yet even without the hidden identity of snake and Moon, the lunar origins of Hermes are unmistakable.

He is born in a dark cave on the fourth of the month, the first day of the lighted crescent after the three days of dark. Maia's name is evocative of the Indo-European root of the three words for Moon in languages deriving from it – *me, ma, men* (as in *manas*, mother, moon, spirit, *men*, measure, Greek Moon god, and so on).[30] Hermes is called *nuxios*, "he of the night," *opopeter*, "he who sees in the night," and "companion of black night." He dallies with Herse, goddess of dew, the ambrosial liquid of the Moon, who was the daughter of Selene, the Moon goddess; and he is allied with Hekate, goddess of the dark phase of the Moon. In the dark of the New Moon, Hermes and Hekate received cakes in the place where three roads met, in the hope, perhaps, of a fortunate month.

In the history of humanity's divine images, the Moon held the image of the eternal before the Sun. Until the Moon's light was discovered to be reflected sunlight, the Moon, in its continuous process of life, death, and rebirth, carried the archetypal longings for transformation in this life and the next. The waxing and waning of the Moon, ending in three days of complete darkness, used to be understood as the life and death of the Moon. So when the Moon reemerged out of the dark as the new crescent, it carried the promise for the renewal of all life after death. Eternity continually gave birth to time, so that time, in Plato's phrase, was "a moving image of eternity,"[31] originally measured by the changing phases, or qualities, of the Moon. The Moon's modes of waxing and waning, death and rebirth, were then both eternal and temporal, as also were the lives of human beings. The Moon, in its waxing and waning, presented the first image of dualism as life in time, just as it showed the transformation of life in time through immersion in the eternal in the three nights of the dark phase, after which, miraculously, the cycle of light began again. The Yin/Yang symbol, for instance, began as a lunar image of waxing and waning, each containing within it the germ of its opposite. So a crucial distinction arose between the invisible eternal cycle and the visible temporal phase, which is echoed in the two Greek words for "life." *Zoe* is infinite life – the cycle – and *Bios* is finite, particular, biographical life – the phase – which lives and dies and is reborn from the eternal source. From the point of view of *Zoe*, the *bios* of life and the *bios* of death are both transformed in *Zoe*, the infinite life out of which they come and go.

The lunar origins of Hermes suggest that the kerykeion he holds as his symbol discloses the essence of who he is: He is himself the *Zoe*, the infinite life beyond and within the cycle of waxing and waning, the one beyond the boundaries of life and death, beyond the opposites of time and eternity, and, by extension, beyond "the opposites" of any situation. As the third term beyond the opposing two, yoking them together in equilibrium, he can reconcile their opposition – and this may be precisely why the kerykeion is transforming.

This would explain why of all the gods it is the bearded Hermes, playing on his pipe, who leads the dancing Horai, the Hours or Seasons, with the *Eniautos Daimon*, the Year Spirit, behind them (Figure 5.8) – bringing the Daimon of the Year out of darkness into light, transforming death into life. These Horai were originally the three visible phases of the Moon. Harrison writes: "The Moon is

*Figure 5.8* Hermes leading the Horai, the Seasons, and the *Eniautos Daimon*, the Spirit of the New Year. Marble relief. c. 600 BCE. Acropolis Museum, Athens. (© Acropolis Museum, photo: Socrates Mavrommatis.)

the true mother of the triple Horai, who are themselves Moirai, and the Moirai are the three parts or division of the Moon . . . and these Moirai or Horai are also Charities."[32]

This symbol of two serpents intertwined to create a new dimension of being is not, however, unique to Greece and was first recognized in the Cup of Gudea of the Sumerian god Ningishzida, where the two serpent dragons hold back two doors to disclose the god within: the third term, on the plane beyond, was the epiphany of the god. "Thrice-greatest" Thoth, the Egyptian Moon god of eternity, time, the calendar, writing, scribes, and almost *all previous thought* – imagined as an ibis, or a man with the head of an ibis, or, at other times, a baboon – holds two wands with a snake twisted round each of them in front of the pharaoh Seti I to awaken him in eternity, so he may "become Osiris." The caduceus, like the two waxing and waning crescents of the Moon placed back to back with *Zoe*, the reconciling third term between and beyond them, is an archetypal image of transformation.

All the stories of Hermes' golden wand are about the reconciliation of opposites, a transformation of a state of mind. Once Hermes sees two snakes fighting and puts his rod between them to bring peace. Or the seer, Tiresias, comes across a male and female snake in embrace and kills the female snake and is turned into a woman. Seven years later, he again sees two snakes mating and kills the male snake and turns back into a man. Asked by Zeus and Hera which sex has the most pleasure in love-making, Tiresias answers the female, whereupon Hera curses him with blindness and Zeus gives him the power of inner sight.

But his real sin may have been to disrupt the harmony of the two snakes together by polarizing them at that moment of their embrace. Perhaps the most compelling statement of this idea is given by Jesus in the Gnostic *Gospel of Thomas*:

> When you make the two one, and when you make the inner as the outer and the outer as the inner and the above as the below, and when you make the male and female into a single one, so that the male will not be male and the female not be female . . . then you shall enter the Kingdom.[33]

## II Reimagining Hermes in the Homeric *Hymn to Hermes*

In Figure 5.9, the one-day-old baby Hermes is lying in his cradle, having just stolen Apollo's cattle, and – as he intended – a furious Apollo has come into his cave to demand them back. The cows that Hermes denies knowing stand behind Apollo (with the lunar hare in the branches of the overhanging tree), while his mother Maia holds a white thread, like a weaving goddess of fate, and strands of this thread are picked out in Hermes' swaddling clothes. But who has the artist put behind her? The bearded figure, not present in the Hymn, may indeed be the older Hermes, standing as an eternal principle at his own new birth, in the same way that the Egyptian god Horus is present at his own begetting, standing, in many images of him, over the bier of his own conception, when his mother Isis hovers over his father Osiris as a hawk with breath-taking wings.

116

*Figure 5.9* Hermes in his liknon, with Apollo and his mother, Maia, in dispute above him. Black figure vase. 520 BCE. The Louvre, Paris. Hydrie de Caeré à figures noires / Peintre de l'aigle (6e siècle av J.-C.) (© RMN – Grand Palais (musée du Louvre) – © Hervé Lewandowski.) (See also Figure 5.1.)

Immediately, in the picture on the vase, we are faced with the startling discrepancy between the Hermes of old and this tiny baby of the same name. Starting from the older conception of the venerable and bearded Hermes, familiar to all, how would you, as it were, begin again and get back to where you were? How can Hermes be reimagined from the beginning and find his way, as he does in the *Hymn*, to being "the same" Guide of Souls who everyone already knows he always was? What is the question that the Olympian poet, or, in an oral tradition, poets, must have asked themselves?

In our age, we might ask, what is it to be a Guide of Souls? To go between life and death and back again to life, to be beyond the opposites of sleep and waking, eternity and time, life and death? To go, then, *beyond* the senses, beyond the dualism of life in time. We might wonder *what* is it in us, or *where* is it in us, that we might find ourselves not bound to the senses, freed from the restrictions of the rational mind and the polarizations of language, at home in endings as well as beginnings? Or, more cautiously, in what dimension of the psyche does the idea

117

of "guiding the soul" and "unifying opposites" have meaning? If we tentatively answered "Imagination," the Romantic poets would agree with us.

"Imagination," Samuel Coleridge writes in his *Biographia Literaria*, is a "synthetic and magical power": It "reveals itself in the balance or reconciliation of opposite or discordant qualities: of sameness, with difference; of the general, with the concrete; the idea, with the image; the individual with the temporal." So "the poet, described in ideal perfection, brings the whole soul of man into activity," since the Imagination is "the soul that is everywhere, and in each, and forms all into one graceful and intelligent whole."[34] It also reveals "the eternal in and through the temporal." All poets agree that Imagination seeks always to unify, to reconcile differences, to create new wholes. "Imagination," writes Yeats, "divides us from mortality by the immortality of beauty, and binds us to each other by opening the secret doors of all hearts."[35]

But, as the philosopher Owen Barfield has shown,[36] consciousness is continually evolving and so is not "the same" in different ages. It follows that when we look backward, we must not start uncritically from where we are now and project our contemporary point of view on the past as though we were outside history. In the infancy of the world, when, as Shelley says, everyone was a poet and language itself was poetry,[37] humankind seems to have lived in a relation of *Participation Mystique* with the universe. Barfield calls this "Original Participation," describing it, variously, as a state in which the soul of the human being and the soul of the world were one, or, again, as a time which "began as the unconscious identity of man with his Creator."[38] The long period of Original Participation (dating, from its sculptures and paintings, back to at least 35,000 BCE), is generally agreed to have been brought to an end in the Near East and Old Europe in the late Bronze Age, around 2000 BCE, with the entry of various nomadic animal-herding people who worshipped gods of Sun and Storm and took over the lands of the native agricultural peoples who worshipped goddesses of Earth and Moon.

Loosely, the direction in which consciousness subsequently evolved, from the Iron Age onward (c. 1250 BCE), is one where numinosity became gradually withdrawn from the universe and was relocated more and more within the human being. So what was once wholly outer – as goddess or god – becomes more inward. Barfield calls this stage in the evolution of consciousness "Withdrawal of Participation."

The same process of internalization can be seen in the difference between the *Vedas* (c. 1500–500 BC) and the *Aitereya Upanishad* (c. 500 BC) – roughly the same time period from the first mention of Hermes to the *Hymn*. In the *Vedas*, the divinities were wholly outer, in the sense that outer and inner were inherently unified, or, to put it another way, when the human soul was at one with the soul of the world. But by the time of the *Upanishads*, a thousand or so years later, the divinities were becoming more inward, closer to humanity. In the *Aitereya Upanishad*, Fire, Wind, Sun, Moon, and other divinities ask Atman to find them an abode where they can live. He brings them a Horse, then a Bull (whom they refuse), and finally a Person: "Verily," they say, "a Person is a thing well done."

Atman says to them: "Enter into your respective abodes." "Fire became speech, and entered the mouth, Wind became breath, and entered the nostrils, Sun became sight, and entered the eyes . . . Moon became mind, and entered the heart."[39]

The language of withdrawing projections does not do justice to the amazing change that must have taken place in the thousand or so years between the *Vedas* and the *Upanishads*, which also happens to be roughly the same period of time between the Mycenaean Linear B writing and the *Hymn to Hermes*. In this quotation, it is as though, with the loss of union with the soul of the world, humans did not stand *against* the once outer divinities with whom they were formerly identified, but, on the contrary, imagined them forming a new kind of union *within* the human heart. This "indwelling" allows them to be explored in a different way, becoming for the first time an aspect of humanity's potential understanding of itself and its mysterious world.

### *Inspiration and Imagination*

Generally speaking, we have been relatively unaware of this long process of internalization as it has happened in our own millennia of passage in the West since we have tended to read ourselves backward into history and failed to see that earlier people had an entirely different relation to the universe. We do this, most damagingly, as follows, when we bring a secular mind to an earlier sacred reality. For instance, Paleolithic straight lines in the paintings in Lascaux were initially interpreted as weapons, until microscopic analysis revealed them to be leafed branches, one, in particular, laid across the pregnant belly of a beautiful horse, not to slay the animal, but probably to encourage and identify with the miracle of renewal.

So it may come as rather a surprise that our modern sense of Imagination as a potential mode of knowing is astonishingly new, still almost in its infancy. Not until Shakespeare, and later the Romantic poets in the nineteenth and twentieth centuries, was Imagination formally given the dignity of bringing meaning and truth.[40] Before that, Imagination still retained its Latin meaning of *Imago,* which meant any kind of image, often closely allied to phantasy and fancy, images that have no real existence – only make-believe or memory. Hence, perhaps, the insistence of Blake and Coleridge that their vision of Imagination be distinguished from fancy or allegory, which they dismissed as merely images of memory or association – passively reflective not generative. Generally, up until the seventeenth century, Inspiration still carried its ancient Greek meaning when poets and prophets were understood as being the mouthpiece of the gods, daimons, or muses, who "breathed" into them divine thoughts that were not their own. The literal meaning of the word *Inspiration* from the Latin is "breathing in," though, in extreme cases, the inspired ones were themselves "breathed in" by the gods (though rarely out again). In *The Iliad*, when the gods have decided among themselves the fate of the warriors, the god "breathes *menos*" (strength, conviction, rage) into the man who is to win, and he charges across the field as if inspired, as indeed he was. Without *menos*, you lost. Similarly, in *The Odyssey*, Penelope says that some god "breathed" into her the idea of weaving at the loom.[41] Nearly two thousand years later, Dante still begins *The Divine Comedy* (c. 1321) with an invocation to the Muses, Genius, and Memory (in the sense of the Great Memory): "O Muses, O High Genius, aid me now, O Memory that engraved the things I saw . . ."[42]

But in the seventeenth century, once the center of gravity had shifted decisively from the cosmos to the human, a further process of "internalization" established itself in many of the ways of thinking about ourselves. The term *consciousness* was adopted by John Locke in 1632 as a "perception of what passes in a man's own mind,"[43] implicitly denying consciousness to Nature or anything beyond the human. "Inspiration" began to lose its *literal* and *external* meaning and acquired its modern and metaphorical meaning as something that arises from *within* human beings – "the breath of poesy" – or, as Wordsworth puts it: "Poetry is the breath and finer spirit of all knowledge."[44] Similarly, *genius* (the Latin translation of the Greek *daimon*, originally, in Roman myth, the tutelary spirit of a person, their own special angel) was until the seventeenth century understood as an ability given by the divine at birth – a gift, something you were "blessed with," something you *had*. But it now took on a radically new meaning: it was not only the creative spirit but also the person who possessed it; it became something you *were*: he *is* a genius, as we now say. So the new inflection of Inspiration as metaphor laid the way for the later Romantic idea of Imagination, which immediately absorbed all that had once belonged to the earlier literal Inspiration, with the new significance of it being recognizable to all as the fundamental *inner* reality of human beings. These two meanings, and the sea-change that had taken place between them, are present in Wordsworth's preface to *The Recluse*:

> Urania, I shall need
> Thy guidance, or a greater Muse, if such
> Descend to earth or dwell in highest heaven!
> For I must tread on shadowy ground, must sink
> Deep – and, aloft ascending, breathe in worlds
> To which the heaven of heavens is but a veil . . . [45]

So we could say that what was Inspiration to the Greeks of the sixth century BCE is what Imagination is for us now, with the difference that it is now located within us – though from depths that still remain mysterious, and so not, ultimately, so different as it might first have seemed. Whether we attribute Imagination to the depths of the mind, the gods within, or the collective unconscious, we characteristically experience it as *other* than ourselves, an image, feeling, or thought that *comes upon* us, beyond our rational mind and even against our will – often in a voice that is not entirely, and sometimes not at all, "our own."

Yet when we follow the story of Hermes, the playfully spontaneous and artful child of a god, we see a story of what we would *now* call Imagination. At every stage, he embodies the qualities of the imaginative mind that all the Romantic poets bring to life – especially Blake and Coleridge, perhaps, but also Shelley,

Keats, Byron, and, later, Yeats, Eliot, and Hughes. So it may be that the poet of the seventh century BCE *Hymn* tells what to us is a story of Imagination but ascribes it, necessarily, to the god, not to a human being.

For, as Cassirer, Jung, and others have shown, it is through the images of our gods and goddesses that we as human beings come to know ourselves.[46] "In the Collective Unconscious of the individual, history prepares itself," as Jung says.[47] So Hermes, as a god, embodies the Imagination that human beings are not yet ready for – that which could not yet be *imagined* as belonging to the human realm. In making visible the character and laws of Imagination, Hermes' story anticipates and prepares that way of thinking and being which will become an essential "dimension" of a future humanity.

The idea of Imagination as a mode of knowing would have to wait one-and-a-half thousand years until the late sixteenth century, when Shakespeare's subtle wit and irony allies it to madmen and lovers and then turns it into the vital force that "bodies forth the forms of things unknown."[48] Not until William Blake (1757–1827) and Coleridge (1772–1834) and the other Romantic poets would Imagination finally be accepted into consciousness as a unique mode of knowing, giving access to worlds that cannot be rationally known but only deeply imagined – the worlds of vision and dream that can truly be said to "guide a soul" and change a person's life. In the 1920s, in his hypothesis of the collective unconscious, Jung offered a rational framework for understanding this further dimension of the human mind.[49]

### *Hermes and Apollo*

If that is so, there is a further way that the *Hymn* can teach us about ourselves. For the poet to bring the new version of Hermes back to his original status now requires Apollo, the god who "works from afar," god of clarity and harmony, leader of the Muses, god of radiant form. In the terms of the *Hymn*, Hermes wants to get to Olympus, to become a god in his own right, and for that he needs Apollo to bring him to their father Zeus, king of the gods, who is the only one who can give Hermes a "local habitation and a name."[50] Then his intuitions and ideas can come to fruition – when they receive the sanction of the whole. The narrative drive of Hermes' actions is then to draw Apollo toward him by whatever means he can – thieving, teasing, mocking, enticing, beguiling, and finally disarming him. But it is not just any relationship with Apollo that he wants – or he could simply be "thrown down into Tartarus," as Apollo threatens – but one of mutual respect, and to this end he prepares with great care. First, he makes a lyre, so he has something to tempt and offer Apollo; then he steals Apollo's cattle to bring him to his house. But Hermes does this in such a way as to bemuse and intrigue him – driving the cows backward, making vast sandals of his own as he walks from side to side with them – all of which make it impossible for Apollo to work it out rationally, indeed mocks his earnest attempts to find a rational explanation. The idea is to make this fierce god less absolute, more permeable, and, most importantly, to baffle and confuse him, so that Apollo needs a further judgment, which means he will take Hermes to their father Zeus. Hermes does this most obviously by stealing his cattle, but also, more subtly, by having something unique that Apollo will want from him, something to trade. Hermes' design is to entrance Apollo with an object of desire, to instill in him an irresistible longing, so he can relate to this most demanding of gods on equal terms. The lyre and Hermes' magical playing of it serve this purpose, or, as we still say, do the trick.

This relationship between Hermes and Apollo tells us that the Imagination longs for form, and it is rendered in the *Hymn* through Zeus' laughter and his nod. Hermes has just lied on oath about stealing the cows, and then winked:

> But Zeus laughed out loud to see his mischievous child
> denying so well, so skillfully,
> that he knew anything about the cows.
> And he ordered both of them to be of one heart and mind
> and to search together for the cows,
> but he told Hermes the guide to lead the way
> and to reveal the place – without any further nonsense -
> where he had hidden the strong cattle.
>
> (ll. 389–94)

As Zeus says this, he nods his head as the ultimate sanction and ratification of the final authority:

> The Son of Kronos nodded his head
> and noble Hermes obeyed him.
> For the mind of Zeus who holds the aegis
> persuaded him easily.
>
> (ll. 395–6)

The *Hymn*'s ironic aside leaves us in no doubt that refusal was not an option: that, at heart, these two very different natures need and require each other to become whole. Nodding – *nouein* – is the root of "numinous" – the nod or wink of the god, the coming alive of divine presence, seeing through to the archetype. It is also the name of the New Moon – *noumenia.*

In Shakespeare's famous and prescient passage on Imagination, it first seems as though Theseus would conflate the lunatic, the lover, and the poet as of "Imagination all compact." But the distinction between them subtly emerges through the poet with his pen giving form to what his fine frenzied poet's eye has glimpsed:

> The lunatic, the lover and the poet
> Are of Imagination all compact.
> One sees more devils than vast hell can hold.
> That is the madman. The lover, all as frantic,
> Sees Helen's beauty in a brow of Egypt.

The poet's eye, in fine frenzy rolling,
Doth glance from heaven to earth, from earth to heaven,
And as Imagination bodies forth
The forms of things unknown, the poet's pen
Turns them to shapes and gives to airy nothing
A local habitation and a name.[51]

Here, the poet's eye and the poet's pen are shown to be so closely related as to belong to one continuous action. That is what makes the difference, it is implied, between fantasy and poetry, the realizing of the vision in human terms, giving it context and containment and closure – "a local habitation and a name." Jung also discovered, in his confrontation with the unconscious, that he could only sustain and withstand his visions by writing them down or painting them; without this he too thought he would go mad: "Had I left those images in the emotions, I might have been torn to pieces by them," he said.[52]

### III Hermes as imagination in the *Hymn to Hermes*

Following the nature of Hermes, then, we may learn something of the specific life and laws of Imagination. It will be instructive to compare the discoveries in the *Hymn* with the Romantic poets' evocations of the imaginative life, as well as with Jung's understanding of Imagination as "non-directed thinking," in which "we no longer compel our thoughts along a definite track, but let them float, sink or rise according to their specific gravity" – a gravity that is an expression of the unconscious mind.[53]

#### *Hermes the playful trickster*

In the *Hymn to Hermes*, Hermes is drawn initially as a playful, endearingly mischievous trickster, who gives the appearance of heedlessly playing his own games for his own fun, but gradually emerges as one whose activities at a deeper level are purposeful and intelligent, founded on a precise knowledge of the end he has in mind – played by "the child" as what he wants and who he wants it from. When, finally, he meets a limit, he accepts it gracefully. This already challenges the conventional polarizations of spontaneity and lawfulness, suggesting rather that spontaneity has its own law. The end is already implicit in his instincts: by following his instincts the end unfolds itself:

Maia gave birth to a son who was versatile
and full of tricks, a thief,
a cattle-rustler, a bringer of dreams,
a spy by night, a watcher at the gate,
one who was destined to bring wonderful things
to light among the immortal gods.

(ll. 12–16)

123

The adjective that follows Hermes around is *eriounos*, a word that is usually interpreted as *either* bringing luck *or* being fast and speedy, but it may be that both meanings illuminate each other. It is the sudden flash of an intuition that brings a *hermaion* – a gift of Hermes. If you don't catch it in the present moment, it's gone; you can't lay it aside to remember it later, because, like the dreams Hermes also brings, it won't be there. The same idea underlies the term *opportunity*, which comes from the Latin *porta*, "gate": if you take the opportunity, then you slip through the gate before it shuts, suggesting why Hermes is called *propolaios*, "the watcher at the gate." We still speak of a "lucky break," coming from the idea of a break in the weave – the pattern woven by the spinning goddesses of fate – which lets you out of what appears to be allotted to you. Similarly, as a "spy by night," Hermes sees into the dark beyond his senses: through intuition he *sees into* the depths hidden from the light of day, so he can *see through* the outer appearance to the possibility of energy and meaning within (hence the term *hermeneutics*, the art of interpretation). He is born in the dark, hidden in a shadowy cave, like the beginning of things that need to stay secret; he is at home in the twilight, the "wolf-light" that prowls among shapes not yet determinate, at ease with a radical uncertainty. By contrast, Apollo is born leaping into the light and is later identified with Helios, the Sun.

### Hermes and double vision

Hermes himself is always moving, never still: while he is doing this, he is thinking of that. Once he "sprang forth" from his mother's immortal womb he "did not lie still for long in his sacred cradle but jumped up to look for Apollo's cattle" (ll. 21–2). Then, climbing over the cave's roof and landing in the courtyard, he immediately comes upon a tortoise and is "the first to make the tortoise a singer" (l. 25):

> The son of Zeus who brings luck (eriounos)
> looked at it and laughed . . .
> "Already an omen
> of great luck for me,
> I won't turn it down!
> Hello, lovely creature,
> beating time to the dance,
> friend of the feasts,
> how exciting to meet you.
> Where did you get
> that beautiful toy from,
> that gleaming shell
> you wrap yourself up in,
> you, a tortoise living in the mountains . . .
> Alive you'd be a charm
> against vile witchcraft,
> but dead, you'll make
> such sweet song."

(ll. 29–39)

There are many parallels to draw here. The playful laughter with which Hermes greets his "omen of great luck" reminds us of Blake's verse, entitled "Eternity":

> He who binds to himself a joy
> Doth the winged life destroy
> He who kisses the joy as it flies
> Lives in eternity's sunrise.[54]

Similarly, Hermes' spontaneity is the opposite of effort and will, both antithetical to Imagination, and a warning that it is missing. "Effort is an objection," Nietzsche says, adding in a bracketed aside "(in my language: *light* feet are the first attribute of divinity)."[55] The "light feet" are evocative of the winged sandals of Hermes and Blake's "winged life," in his poem.

Hermes' seeing through the tortoise into what the lovely creature could become invokes Blake's central idea of "double vision," which he describes as looking not with but *through* the eye, when seeing and feeling become one:

> For double the vision my Eyes do see,
> And a double vision is always with me.
> With my inward Eye, 'tis an old Man grey,
> With my outward, a Thistle across my way.[56]

Double vision is to be contrasted to what Blake calls "Single Vision and Newton's sleep" (illustrating this by drawing Newton bent over a compass), which is the mind that measures and separates and polarizes. To a literal mind, "a Thistle" belongs to the vegetable world and the "old Man grey" to the human. They have to be one or the other; they can't both be there at the same time, so one must be fanciful, and it is not the thistle. To which Blake replies, "To a Man of Imagination, Nature is Imagination itself. As a Man is, so he sees."[57]

The *Hymn* plays with the difference between these two points of view. Hermes enrages Apollo, who understandably wants to know if Hermes did or did not steal his cows, whether he is telling a truth or a lie. Whereas Hermes, pretending to be the baby that he is on the grounds that, after all, he is only just born, makes fun of Apollo for coming after him in such a rage. Twinkling his eyes, glancing this way and that, and continuously whistling – as one who is denying what he is saying – happily lying through his teeth, as we might say – he effectively says to Apollo: "I didn't steal your cows; I'm only a baby – I don't even know what cows are any-way, except maybe I did but that's not the point and I can't tell you the point or the whole thing will be pointless." Hermes refuses to be trapped in Apollo's reasoned oppositions. So he tells a lie but tells the truth about lying: "I am telling you the truth but if you believe that you'll believe anything." He plays with the world of opposites that Apollo inhabits with such confidence, but stays outside them, elu-sively beyond them.

This invites us to see how the trickster has to play, tease, mock, steal, and lie his way into the established order, for how else to break through? "You rogue, you trickster, you crafty-minded cheat" (l. 282). Apollo returns, fully aware of Hermes' game but unable to deal with it. More seriously, the Fool in *King Lear*, who holds the wisdom that Lear has yet to find, can only guide him playfully, parodying his egocentricity through subtle hints, allusions, and ironies, as long as the truth for Lear is too shattering to accept. Single vision lays claim to what it sees as facts – even though, as Blake says, "Reason, or the ratio of what is already known, is not the same that it shall be when we know more," concluding that "He who sees the Infinite in all things sees God. He who sees the Ratio only, sees himself only."[58] The prevailing system, or current paradigm, militates against a new perspective, which has to rearrange or discard the limited facts in order to reach a higher truth, and is typically ruled out of court before it can speak. Later, Hermes also plays the trickster's double game with Zeus. He swears to his face "by these graceful porticoes of the immortals" that he didn't steal Apollo's cows (l. 383) – being only one day old and not strong enough for a cow anyway, whatever they are – and then winks. But Zeus, unlike Apollo, gets the joke and laughs out loud.

Hermes' act of truthfully indicating that he is lying reveals an irony that is not a simple reversal of literal meaning but a philosophical maintaining of conflicting values, refusing to give up one or the other in implicit allegiance to a more comprehensive whole. This is in the noble tradition of one of Shakespeare's Sonnets:

> When my love swears to me that she is true,
> I do believe her though I know she lies . . . [59]

### Hermes and the symbolic mind

The "gleaming" of the tortoise's shell shows Hermes the lyre it could become, or perhaps the lyre it essentially is. *Shining* is a beckoning into the symbolic world of essences where other things are possible than just what is given. Etymology teaches us that this is how gods "arise." In Indo-European, *Zeus* was not a name of a god but a participation in a "happening," an event – a verb not a noun. It meant "it lightens," *theos*, it shines, like a clapping of excitement and wonder; only later did Zeus become a god *of* light, lightning, and thunder. Similarly, in Coleridge's poem, *The Rime of the Ancient Mariner*, the mariner's change of heart begins when the water snakes in the sea suddenly shine at him and he feels their beauty. Then the winds come and the immobile ship that had imprisoned him – symbolic of his dejection at killing the albatross – starts to move.[60] Coleridge formulated these experiences in his idea of *translucence* – literally, "a shining through" – which became essential to his understanding of how Imagination works through symbols, bringing two worlds together as one:

> A symbol is characterized by a translucence of the special in the individual, or the General in the Especial, or the Universal in the General. Above all

by the translucence of the Eternal through and in the Temporal. It always partakes of the Reality which it renders intelligible; and, while it enunciates the whole, abides itself as a living part in that Unity of which it is the representative.[61]

A symbol, then, assumes an organic relation between the whole and the part, such that each part *potentially* contains and evokes the whole. When we are in the presence of an *actual* symbol, then the whole is translucent to the part, *shines through* the part, and so dissolves the distinction between them. A symbol implies a number of different planes of feeling, culminating in the greatest plane – the eternal or the spiritual world. Translucence and numinosity are the signature of the eternal, allowing us to intuit the world of ideal forms. This experience is only a rare visitation, though, Coleridge adds regretfully, quoting Plotinus: "It either appears to us or it does not appear. So that we ought . . . to watch in quiet till it suddenly shines upon us."[62]

So the *shining* makes possible the *seeing through*, the lighting up into a world of possibility. Coleridge also brings in the important idea that the Imagination works *as if*, and *leaves room* for what is to come:

> They and only they can acquire the philosophic imagination, the sacred power of self-intuition, who within themselves can interpret and understand the symbol that the wings of the air-sylph are forming within the skin of the caterpillar; these only who feel in their own spirits the same instinct which impels the chrysalis of the horned fly to leave room in its involucrum for antennae yet to come. They know and feel that the potential works in them, even as the actual works on them.[63]

The poet of the *Hymn* comments on how Hermes sees the "sweet song" that the tortoise could become, just like "quick thoughts" and "bright glances" spinning off the eyes:

> Just as when a quick thought darts through the heart
> of a man when cares crowd in on him
> and toss him about or when bright glances spin
> off the eyes – just like that –
> glorious Hermes devised word and deed together.
>
> (ll. 43–7)

### Hermes as slayer of the literal mind

Early in the *Hymn*, when Hermes, still just born, is diverting fifty of Apollo's cows off from the herd, he is called *Argeiphontes,* Slayer of Argos, suggesting that this quality is primary to his story and how it unfolds. This quality, or epithet, draws on

Olympian stories of the conflicts between Zeus and Hera outside the *Hymn* (though not written down until later), so that the principle it embodies is then inherent in the definition of who Hermes is.

*Argos Panoptes*, literally, "All Seeing" Argos, or he who is "all eyes," is the giant usually given a hundred eyes, two of which never shut – a parodic image of the over-conscious mind that has to stay always in control and can never "suspend disbelief for the moment," which is Coleridge's advice for encountering a poetic vision and the chance for an imaginative life.[64] At the request of Zeus, Hermes charms Argos to sleep with his pipe, so breaking the "spell" of the alert and watchful mind with which Argos guards the Moon Cow Io at the command of Hera. Once he is asleep, Hermes slays Argos with the very sickle sword that Gaia gave to Chronos (Time) to harvest the genitals of Ouranos (who was lying so heavy upon her that she could not give birth), thereby separating the original parents of the world and so setting life, and time, moving again. The sickle sword evokes, appropriately for an old Moon god, the original curved crescent of the Moon – "thinned to an air-sharpened blade," as Philip Larkin puts it[65] – an image at once of the creative and destructive consequence of Time (*chronos* was the word for time as well as for the god). This is the same sword that Hermes later gives Perseus to slay the petrifying Gorgon – the image of fear that petrifies Imagination. This sword, then, is resonant of freeing the creative life in whatever form it manifests.

The slaying of Argos is arrestingly harsh for Hermes, the "gentle god," who is "friendliest of gods to humans," and it was an epithet often used instead of his own name, almost as though, until Argos is slain, Hermes will not be present. The mind that cannot stop keeping an eye on things may be diligently watchful but cannot dream, wonder, create; the vision is single – literal, rational, well-lit – not symbolic, questioning, not "the blue and the dim and the half-light," of Yeats's embroidered cloths of heaven.[66] John Keats defines what he calls "negative capability" as "the ability to rest in doubts, uncertainties, mysteries, without any irritable reaching after fact and reason."[67] Where a large giant with ever-open eyes can hardly be overlooked, Hermes, by contrast, wears a cap of invisibility, given him by Hades, so no one can see him unless he lets them. If you look for him willfully you will not find him. If you try to tie him down, as Apollo does, the ropes will fall away from him, rooting in the earth and growing where they like. If you come at him with "positive capability," being, as politicians are wont to say, "very clear" about something, then the passing thought, the flash of intuition, the beguiling image and lingering dream, will promptly vanish. What Hermes kills is the literal mind as a condition for his being there at all.

### Hermes as the wind-spirit

Here, again, is the god beyond all boundaries, the god of journeyers, the once solid Herm now flying at speed through insubstantial air. Unusually, wings sprout from his legs above his feet, his leading foot stepping out of the rim of the vase (Figure 5.10), the wing of the other foot brushing the top of the clouds. This flurry

*Figure 5.10* Hermes flying. Red figure vase. 495 BCE. British Museum. (©The Trustees of the British Museum.)

of wings and feet gives the impression that they are in front of him as well as behind him, so fast is he moving. Facing away from the direction in which he seems to be going, his body turned against the thrust of his motion, he holds his lyre close to his wind-filled robes like a feathered wing. Only the Caduceus points forward, as though intuiting the way ahead.

After Hermes has slain and burnt two of Apollo's cows and made due sacrifice to the gods, he returns to his cave "sliding in sideways through the keyhole, passing into the hall like a breeze in autumn, like a mist" (146–7). He climbs back into his cradle, lying there like a helpless baby, covering his lyre with his left hand, but in no way deceiving his goddess mother Maia who scolds him severely.

This intimation of the older magical Hermes, now depicted with winged sandals flying through the air, recalls the ancient association between birds and the dimension of life beyond the human realm. The bird who flies out of the vast unfathomable distance was once thought to bring the weather and before that to make the weather, as well as the spring, babies, and anything new. The great cranes trumpeting across the sky let the rains fall so planting could begin, and the black and white stork carried the babies from the black and white Moon. The Egyptian Moon god Thoth, god of eternity and time, god of inspiration and scribes, was portrayed as an ibis or a man with an ibis-head. In Ancient Greece priests would cut out (*temnein*) a circle on the ground, creating a *temenos*, a sacred space, to study the birds who flew above it, reading the auspices (Latin, *avis*, bird, *specere*, to look).

The primary metaphors of Inspiration, which Imagination later inherits, are those of wind, breath, breath of life, soul, spirit, all themselves etymologically related in Greek and Latin, deriving from their original Indo-European. Greek *anemos*, wind, becomes *anima*, soul, in Latin (from which we get animal) and *animus*, spirit; Greek *pneuma*, breath, wind, and spirit, becomes in Latin *spiritus*, spirit, but without the "outer meanings" of wind and breath. *Hagion Pneuma*, the Holy Spirit, a neuter word that originally meant wind, breath, *and* spirit, was also reduced and oversimplified in Latin to refer to the inner world alone – *Spiritus Sanctus* – a masculine noun, losing Nature's breathing wind yet still embodied in the image of Aphrodite's winged and feathered dove. Plato's "winged and feathered" soul, who grows ever more feathers from the "unaccustomed warmth" at the sight of beauty, belongs to this tradition; though, Plato adds, pointing, perhaps wryly, still further back, "in former times the soul was feathered all over."[68]

When Inspiration merges into Imagination and is sought for within the human being, the closely allied images of flight come into focus, with their related images of lightness, movement, and speed, for these attributes, natural to the bird, may now be seen as mirroring a specific kind of "flight of the mind," freed from earth-bound restrictions of logic and argument and criteria of relevance. Hermes in the *Hymn* returns to his cradle by going through the keyhole – magically shape-changing into his essential nature, always in motion like wings on the wind. In *The Iliad*, he already wears "his winged and golden sandals," with which "he could fly like the wind over land and sea."[69] As As Karl Kerenyi, puts it, in his seminal book, *Hermes: Guide of Souls*, Hermes "volatizes" himself.[70] It is the movement, the adventure, which fascinates him, not the possession of ground, which belongs to Zeus.

But once "the breeze" has arrived it can go anywhere, as it does in Coleridge's poem, *The Eolian Harp*, where the poet's pen gives habitation and name to the poet's eye as a poem – *poiesis*, the thing made:

> And what if all of animated nature
> Be but organic Harps diversely fram'd,
> That tremble into thought, as o'er them sweeps
> Plastic and vast, one intellectual Breeze,
> At once the Soul of each and God of all?[71]

### Apollo

Just as Hermes hailed from 1500 BCE Crete, so did Apollo under his original name of Paean, which was also the name of any hymn sung to him, and a hymn was found in Mycenaean Pylos, the city of Old Nestor in *The Iliad*. The paean was a magic song, believed, just in the singing of it, to banish disease. Yet, in *The Iliad*, Apollo sends a plague to the Mycenaean Greeks, though he can just as quickly release it. He is the one who "works from afar," "shooting his arrows from far away," and, apart from his dealings with Hermes, he always gets his way.

Apollo also is reimagined in the late sixth century BCE, around the same time as the *Hymn to Hermes*. He, too, is adopted into the Olympian cosmology, becoming a son of Zeus and Leto and the twin sister of Artemis (the Mycenaean *Eleutha*), who, in archaic statues, found in Delos and elsewhere, appears as the ancient goddess of the Moon and the animals. Leto was the daughter of Coeus and Phoebe (whose name means "radiant," "bright," "pure"), the Titans of Sun and Moon. Apollo inherited the epithet of his grandmother, Phoebe in "Phoebus Apollo," and the fierce nature of the flaming Greek sun from his grandfather. Apollo was always a figure of great potency, for good or ill, and this ambivalence is reflected in the stories about him.

In the *Homeric Hymns*, there are three hymns to Apollo, and a further one to the Muses and Apollo. He is conceived in different ways in each of them – all, however, linked by the lyre. In the *Hymn* of his birth, the *Delian Apollo*, all the islands of the Cyclades (the circle of islands that floated around Delos) were afraid to give his mother a place to give birth, and only Delos, the tiny island in their center, was shamed into accepting him because she was barren. As soon as he was born he "leapt into the light and all the goddesses screamed." His golden cords could not hold him and came loose, so he declared: "May the lyre and curved bow be dear to me, and I shall reveal to immortals the infallible will of Zeus," upon which he left. The story went that when he was born on Delos, the island stopped floating and became still – an image of rooted orientation and singular perspective that makes possible a "point of view." But when he entered the house of Zeus, all the gods trembled.[72]

The intensity of Apollo's vision is conveyed in a sculpture from Delphi, called "the Charioteer," undoubtedly an image of Apollo himself, the figure who directs the horses one-pointedly and unflinchingly, bringing order to unruly instincts, harmony to the team.

In another hymn, *Hymn to the Pythian Apollo*, the story is told of his coming into Greece to find a place to build his temple, in the course of which he slays the Typhaon (Hera's dragon child), given into the care of the Delphic Python (Gaia's dragon child), who was guardian of Delphi (the two dragons are sometimes conflated). Apollo slays them both and seizes for himself the oracles that belonged to the Pythian serpent, mouthpiece of Themis and Gaia. He also hurls rocks into the stream Telphusa to lay the foundations for his temple, which was later to bear the inscriptions "Know thyself" and "Nothing in excess." Here, he is the relentless god whose ideal of purity destroys what is misshapen or unintelligible. But when he wants priests to take care of his temple he, as it were, goes back to his origins, to Crete, where there was a cult of *Apollo Delphinios*. Transforming himself into a dolphin (*Delphi* means both dolphin and womb), he springs into a ship of Cretans,

*Figure 5.11* Apollo, holding a bough of laurel which crowns him, is seated beside the
Delphic *omphalos* (believed to be the navel of the universe) with the mantic
raven on top, offering a libation dish to a warrior who has come to consult the
oracle. Etruscan cistra. (From Jane Harrison, *Themis*, fig. 128, p. 428.)

directing them to Krisa, the land of vines. Then he "leapt from the ship like a star
at mid-day," and when they have feasted he forbids them to go back to woody
Knossos and leads them in the dance, "striding with high and beautiful steps, holding a lyre in his hands [Figure 5.12] and playing it beautifully":

> So the Cretans followed him to Pytho,
> stamping the earth in the dance
> and chanting the Paean
> like the paean-singers of Crete,
> those in whose hearts the divine Muse
> has put sweet-voiced song.[73]

The *Hymn to the Muses and Apollo* places him as the leader of the Muses and the
leader of the dance:

It is because
of the Muses
and the archer Apollo

that there exist on the earth
people who sing songs
and play the lyre.

Kings come from Zeus.[74]

But the most evocative hymn, called simply *To Apollo*, celebrates him as the god
of poets:

Phoebus,
it is of you
the swan sings clearly,

his wings beating,

swooping down to the shore
of the whirling river Peneios.

And it is of you
the poet sings,

speaking sweetly
to his clear-voiced lyre.

At the beginning
and at the end

it is always of you . . . [75]

The precise parallels drawn in the poem between the singing of the swan and the
poet on his lyre speak of an innate harmony intrinsic to the meaning of the god. He
is here the beautiful god of radiant form, evocative of Rilke's words: "Beauty is
nothing but the beginning of Terror we are still just able to bear, and why we adore
it so is because it serenely disdains to destroy us."[76]

### *Hermes and Apollo unified*

Hermes knows, then, precisely what would move Apollo – that god not known for
his deep feeling or empathy – and this is the lyre, which becomes a symbol of all
that relates the two brothers. For Imagination needs Form to embody the "forms
of things unknown," but Form also needs Imagination to revitalize its tendency to

*Figure 5.12* Apollo playing the lyre. Red figure vase. (From John Boardman, *Athenian Red Figure Vases: Archaic Period*, London, Thames & Hudson, 1975, no. 197.)

fixedness, to ordering but not feeling life's infinite variety. Both need each other to become whole. "Concepts without intuitions are empty, intuitions without concepts are blind" is how Kant puts it.[77]

Another way of understanding this is through the Greek distinction between *Gnosis* and *Episteme* as two ways of knowing. *Gnosis* is knowledge won through participation, relationship, and love, knowledge that changes you or that you have to change to know: the way we know a person, an animal, a tree, a garden – gradually and mutually – and also how we come to know a poem, painting, story, or myth. *Gnosis* engages the individual's whole personality and exacts a total commitment, in contrast to *Episteme*, which is knowledge *about* something, and does not require participation between the knowing subject and the so-called object – idea, argument, logic, theorem, or mathematics, and so on – whatever would be known through thinking rather than feeling (though all of these could be known gnostically too). This is one meaning of "far-worker" to describe Apollo: his arrows do not feel the pain of their target, they slay from too far away. Indeed, epistemological knowledge values the separation of the knower from the known, on the assumption that subjective and objective points of view need to be distinguished so the knowledge can be rationally tested and verified. "If you have to be there it isn't science," might be a contemporary statement of this position. Essential as this was in the earlier struggle to wrest freedom of thought from the overweening Church, epistemological knowledge has now to reckon with the findings of psychoanalysis that such distinctions are not always reliable, as well as with Heisenberg's principle that the observer is implicated in the observed.

From a gnostic point of view, epistemological knowledge depends on a divorce between thinking and being, and this is of value only *after* an initial relationship with who or what we want to know. If gnostic knowing comes first and stays first (as it does if we do not override it), then we do not name things, people, events, ideas, which we have not related to and thereby jeopardize any future relationship we might wish to have with them. As Rudolf Steiner would say, begin with intuition and think about it afterward.[78] If Imagination is a way of being, then what we know is limited, or expanded, by who we are. Coleridge takes this further:

> Grant me a nature having two contrary forces, the one of which tends to expand infinitely, while the other strives to apprehend or find itself in this infinity, and I will cause the whole world of intelligences . . . to rise up before you.[79]

Significantly, in the light of this, Apollo's rulership of Delphi had to be shared with Dionysos, the great dissolver of forms, who took over in the winter when Apollo went north to dance with the Hyperborean maidens in the land beyond the North Wind where the sun never sets. Otherwise, it is implied, form becomes rigid, fixed in the past, refusing to change and so stifling the life it had helped to create. Then Dionysos is needed to break it apart. This was how Nietzsche conceived Tragedy, as the perpetual dance of Apollo and Dionysos, the creation and destruction of form: the Apollonian radiance of *principio individuationis* and the Dionysian communal abyss, both necessary to each other and to the whole that they manifest.[80]

After Hermes has shown Apollo where his cows are and thrown off the willow ropes with which Apollo tied him up, he needs to soothe Apollo's pride very quickly, so he takes out his lyre and plays. Apollo laughs in delight, "for the lovely throbbing of the ineffable music went directly to his heart and sweet longing seized his soul as he listened." Hermes then sings of the origins of the world – of the immortal gods and the black earth – praising first Mnemosune, mother of the Muses (for "he was a follower of hers"), telling the story of all the gods, "singing how each one was born, relating all things in order, playing the lyre upon his arm":

And Apollo felt a deep and irresistible longing
lay hold on his heart and he cried out,
uttering winged words:
"You scheming cattle-killer,
you busy little friend of the feast,
this song of yours is worth fifty cows!
I think our differences will soon be settled peacefully.
Come now, tell me this,
you ingenious son of Maia,
were you born with a talent
for this marvellous thing,
or did some deathless god
or human being give you
this great gift
and teach you divine song?
For I hear a wonderful voice
with a fresh sound
which I vow no one else
ever before has known how to make,
no man and no god
who has his home on Olympos,
no one but you, you thief,
son of Zeus and Maia.
What art is this,
what muse for inconsolable sorrows,
what skill?
Surely there are three things
to choose from and they are all here
at the same time:
joy and love and sweet sleep.
And though I'm a follower
of the Olympian Muses
who love dance
and the stately strains of song,
the swelling chant
and the thrilling tones of flutes,
never before and by nothing else
has my heart been so moved,
not even by displays of skill
at the young men's feasts.
I am filled with wonder, son of Zeus,
at the lovely way you play the lyre! . . .
I will make you the famous
and blessed guide among the gods,

and I will give you glorious gifts,
and right up to the end
I will not deceive you."
                    (ll. 420–64; Apollo's speech, ll. 434–54)

The gift Hermes wants most of all, it is now disclosed, is to have a share in the "arts of prophecy and the divine utterances," which Apollo has from Zeus. In return, he pledges to give him his lyre, together with some uninvited advice on how to play it light-heartedly – "for it shuns laborious drudgery" – and, in return for that, he proposes to be keeper of the cattle. Apollo accepts the lyre and delights in playing it himself, upon which they go back to Zeus together:

Wise Zeus was glad and made them both friends.
And Hermes loved the son of Leto continually,
even as he does now, from the proof that he gave
the lovely lyre to the Archer and taught him,
and Apollo played it skilfully upon his arm.
                    (ll. 506–10)

Hermes, lacking his lyre, then invents the pipes for himself to play. But Apollo is still concerned that Hermes is so full of tricks that he might steal the lyre back from him, and his own curved bow at the same time, so he asks him to swear an oath – one, we note, that can now be trusted. Then they both nod their heads: Hermes that he will not steal anything from Apollo, and Apollo that never would there be anyone among the immortals whom he would love more than Hermes – evidence, if any were needed, of the change in Apollo that Hermes has wrought.

Only now that they are truly of one heart and mind, does Apollo offer – and withhold – his gifts to Hermes: he will make him a "perfect symbol" and give him: "a marvellous wand of blessing and fortune, a golden one, with three branches, which will protect you and keep you unharmed as it accomplishes all the decrees that I claim to know through the voice of Zeus" (ll. 526–32). But Apollo denies Hermes knowledge of the art of prophecy as being unlawful, against the oath he swore to Zeus, for only he may know the profound will of Zeus, and "the divine secrets which far-seeing Zeus contemplates" (l. 540).

So, returning to the perspective of the older Hermes here reconfigured, the mar-velous golden wand is none other than the kerykeion or caduceus, which is, as it were, returned to him by Apollo as a gift of friendship, suggesting that Imagination given form creates something new that transcends the opposites. It is as though, in an unexpected twist of meaning, the two snakes intertwined symbolize Hermes and Apollo in their union of heart and mind, and this is what creates the third term – the vision that transcends anything either of them could create on their own. Such was the "wisdom" of Zeus in bringing about their union.

But, significantly, the change from Inspiration to Imagination – from the mind of Zeus to the mind of Hermes – brings with it the awareness that absolute knowledge is no longer possible. With increasing interiority, embodied in Hermes, the friendliest god to humans, comes a realization that Imagination, becoming more accessible to humanity, loses its earlier identification with the ultimate source of knowledge, whether called Zeus or the Self. Human fallibility has entered into the new idea of Imagination, where before, in the idea of Inspiration, it was initiated by the god, muse, or daimon who had access to superior knowledge denied to human beings. This had the disadvantage that when it "went wrong," it could be bypassed as the deception or unwillingness of the god or muse whose breath it was, or at least attributed to the opacity of gods in their relation with humans. This interpretation did not offer a chance to learn or grow. Instead of the art of prophecy, Apollo gives Hermes the bee-maidens who taught him divination as a boy. But, again, the bees need the golden honey to inspire them, and if they have not had enough they swarm to and fro and tell you lies not truths, and who, it is implied, can be sure that they have had enough? Hermes has then to tolerate, and even embrace, a radical uncertainty, as do all those who open themselves to the claims Imagination makes upon them.

Interestingly, Hermes does not speak back after he has sworn his oath to Apollo. The final restoration of his former role is given by Zeus, who decrees that Hermes should be lord of the animals – over "flashing lions," "gleaming boars," dogs and sheep – and that he should be "the only consecrated messenger to Hades" – just as, in the figure of Hermes Chthonios, he once was. Zeus, who earlier called him "the guide," now "gives him grace as well." Hermes is called "messenger of the gods" at the beginning of the *Hymn*, but this new Olympian role is only formally given to him by Zeus at the very end of the *Hymn* in the context of his being "messenger to Hades." This gift is named a "consecration," reminiscent of the original sacred role of the older Hermes Chthonios, and perhaps also of the holy awe surrounding death in any age. This "gift" also brings the ideas of messenger and psychopomp together in a mutually illuminating way, suggesting that all souls need an intermediary to listen and accept the guidance that comes from the dimension of being deepest within us, farthest from us: "Always I hearken," writes Rilke, "Give but a small sign. I am quite near."[81] Although "messenger" might seem at first a poor substitute for Hermes's ancient roles, on closer study it reveals itself to hold all the earlier attributes of the god of death, the good spirit of fertility, journeys of the mind, the "luck" that brings a change of heart, a rebirth. For only Imagination, moving between the realms of the gods and human beings, the unknown and the known – between, in our terms, unconscious and conscious and back – can bring "messages" from one to the other, exploring their permeability to each other in order to bring them into dynamic relationship. Translucence, numinosity – these are the thresholds between the worlds that open one to the other. Whether seen as daimon or messenger, Imagination carries something of both worlds and relates them. In this sense, there is a deeper meaning to the Caduceus that the Olympian Hermes now shares with his pre-Olympian namesake: it expresses the essence of the soul's guidance as an imaginative synthesis of hitherto antithetical modes of being, which makes possible transformation.

Yet the *Hymn* closes on a thoughtful ambivalence. As "messenger of the gods," when he is instructed by Zeus – that is, in our terms, when Imagination is in harmony with the Self – Hermes will reveal truths and be a true Guide of Souls to that soul who has earned guidance and revelation – "a few he helps" – if only by deeply longing for it; otherwise the "message" would not be understood. As gnostic knowledge, the relationship remains primary between the knower and what would be known: we cannot – and should not – know beyond ourselves, which includes our responsibility to render that knowledge into life by giving it form.

However, when Hermes is independent of the gods, acting autonomously, maybe indiscriminately, not necessarily in harmony with the source – "mingling with everyone, mortal and immortal alike," there is a warning: "A few he helps, but he endlessly beguiles the race of human beings in the darkness of the night" (ll. 576–79). If this seems unduly and rather abruptly harsh, then we might remember, in this juggling of ages and ideas, that the crucial distinction between Imagination and Fancy (that is, fantasy) has not yet been fully explored or named, nor yet the parallel distinction between Symbol and Allegory, which had to await the Romantic poets to be doggedly pursued into the consciousness of the time. Shakespeare's famous passage, already quoted from *A Midsummer Night's Dream*, is followed by Theseus's own reservation:

Such tricks hath strong imagination,
That if it would but apprehend some joy,
It comprehends some bringer of that joy;
Or in the night, imagining some fear,
How easy is a bush supposed a bear![82]

In that sense, it seems right that the poet of the *Hymn* understands that Hermes could not know the mind of Zeus, reminding us that human beings should likewise be aware that we also cannot always tell where the images that come to us are coming from. In general, images of Fancy are flat, repetitive, interchangeable, collective, allegorical; images of Imagination are complex, baffling, opaque, individual, and often incomprehensible, but always numinous, symbolic. Yet an image energized by a complex may initially present itself with an urgency that mimes the imperative of a signal from the Self. We have to become aware that the ego, the center of consciousness, can be "fooled" or misled by images from the unconscious, especially when the ego is out of harmony with the Self, the center of the whole psyche. We might ask whether an image represents the whole psyche or only a part, why it has arrived, what does it want of us, what is its purpose, how does it relate to images in our dreams, and, if still lacking any conclusive answer, consider more comprehensively whether the conscious is in complete, or sufficient, or "good enough" harmony with the unconscious? Hence, the importance of taking our images seriously and learning their "language," the language of feeling, and, on occasion, submitting them to the logical arguments of the rational mind. Otherwise, we, too, could be "endlessly beguiled in the darkness of the night."

Yet when Hermes plays his proper role as Daimon, then he is "the compelling image," as Rilke puts it in his poem to the poet Hölderlin:

> To you, o majestic poet, to you the compelling image,
> O caster of spells, was a life entire; when you uttered it,
> a line snapped shut like fate, there was a death
> even in the mildest, and you walked straight into it;
> but the god who preceded you led you out and beyond it . . . [83]

That is perhaps why there has to be a learning of the Imagination, as all the poets recommend, so that we may strengthen the ability to know the difference between the daimonic image and the self-serving one, and all the variations in between.

## Conclusion

Returning to Jung's idea that "[i]n the Collective Unconscious of the individual history prepares itself,"[84] we should perhaps ask ourselves Jung's question: what is "history" preparing for itself now in the collective unconscious of individuals that will shape future generations? Beginning with a diagnosis of our own collective psychopathology in the West, dominated by two thousand years of Judeo-Christian thinking, we might turn initially to the loss of any collective culture of the image. It is arguable that the replacing of the Greek *daimon* with Christian *demon*, as well as the edict against the autonomy of images in sacred discourse, seriously diminished the language of the psyche. Doctrinal Christianity did not and, strictly, does not recognize the morality of the image, nor the *temenos* of Imagination within which such explorations take place.

The question of how to weigh images, test them, compare them, let them speak to us, follow them, or not – in other words, how to value them and distinguish between them – is itself an art still waiting to be refined, as James Hillman has many times said.[85] With so many random and unchosen images flooding indiscriminately into our homes and communities from television and the Internet, engaging our unconscious as well as conscious minds – especially in advertising – we need more than ever an instinctive apprehension of the difference between those images that harm and those that inform, teach, and inspire – images of Imagination not Fancy, in Coleridge's terms. And without the true images to lead and guide us, we have also lost the balance, and mutual fruition, between intuition and concept, feeling and thinking – between *Gnosis* and *Episteme*, between *mythos* and *logos* – on which the imaginative life depends and, in turn, fosters and creates.

We have lost the friendship of Hermes and Apollo. They are no longer each other's equal. We are far from Yeats's understanding that images are living souls, carrying within them their own histories and destinies. In "The philosophy of Shelley's poetry" he says: "an image that has transcended particular time and place becomes a symbol, passes beyond death, as it were, and becomes a living soul."[86] The "dwelling-house of symbols"[87] was for him the Great Memory. In his essay on magic he writes that "whatever the passions of man have gathered about, becomes a symbol in the Great Memory . . . "[88] At the beginning of this essay he defines the Great Memory as "the memory of Nature herself,"[89] and at the end he urges: "and surely, at whatever risk, we must cry out that imagination is always seeking to remake the world according to the impulses and the patterns in that Great Mind and that Great Memory?"[90]

And finally, we might turn to the hierarchical models of reality that we have inherited through the doctrines (but not the art) of Judeo-Christianity, which has now become, as Jung says, a psychological attitude of adaptation to the world without and within, and will not simply fade away through any number of intellectual denials.[91] To take one example: In the West, from Plotinus onward, metaphors of the soul of the world have been hierarchical, implicitly placing Nature as the furthest from the source and so inferior. This, we might suppose, is a consequence of the hierarchical model that is assumed to be the inevitable and only way of seeing what it sees: a "fallen" world created by a transcendent god. It does not address the possibility of the divine becoming immanent *as* creation while being transcendent *to* creation, such that the created universe participates in the divinity of the creative source. In orthodox Christian doctrine, immanence is sacrificed to transcendence, in contrast to the metaphor, say, of *Indra's Net*, from the Mahayana Buddhist tradition, where transcendence and immanence are not opposed to each other and become a unity. There the universe is seen as an infinite net, and wherever the threads cross there is a clear shining pearl that reflects and is itself reflected in every other pearl in an infinite pattern of reflection. Each pearl is an individual consciousness – whether of a human being, an animal, a plant, a cell, or an atom – so a change in one pearl, however small, makes a change in all the other pearls, each one both singular and responsive to the whole.[92]

Locating Imagination within the human psyche brings with it, inevitably, a moral responsibility for the way we think and what world our thinking contributes to creating. Are we entitled to hope that in the collective unconscious of many individuals the future history of a unified universe has long been preparing itself, and will tell a new story in which all of creation is sacred and for which we are all responsible? If a new vision were to break through, it would surely begin, as in the Homeric *Hymn to Hermes,* with the poets. For, as Shelley concludes his *Defence of Poetry:* "Poets are the hierophants of an unapprehended inspiration, the mirrors of the gigantic shadows which futurity casts upon the present . . . Poets are the unacknowledged legislators of the world."[93] So if, returning to Blake, "everything that lives is holy," then it would follow that "if the doors of perception were cleansed, man would see everything as it is, infinite."[94]

*Figure 5.13* Apollo seated on the omphalos, the navel of the earth, at Delphi, holding a laurel branch and the lyre. Line drawing by the author of a red-figured vase painting. (From Jane Harrison, *Themis*, fig. 123, p. 411, Close-up of Apollo.)

## Notes

1  For a discussion on the dating of the *Hymn*, see Norman O. Brown, *Hermes the Thief: The Evolution of a Myth*, Great Barrington, MA, Lindisfarne Press, pp. 102–32.

### *I The older pre-Olympian Hermes*

2  The *Hymn to Hermes,* in Jules Cashford (trans.), *The Homeric Hymns*, London, Penguin Classics, 2003, pp. 55–84, lines (ll.) 17–20. (Line numbers will be included in the text for subsequent quotations.)

3  John Chadwick, *The Decipherment of Linear B*, Cambridge, Cambridge University Press, 1958.

4  See Joseph Campbell, *Occidental Mythology, The Masks of God*, Harmondsworth, Middlesex, Penguin Books, 1964, pp. 141–85.

5  See Anne Baring and Jules Cashford, *The Myth of the Goddess: Evolution of an Image*, London, Penguin, 1993, chapters 3, 7, 8, and 9.

6 Walter Burkert, *Greek Religion: Archaic and Classical*, Cambridge, MA, Harvard University Press, 1985, pp. 43–6.

7 Jane Harrison, *Themis: A Study of the Social Origins of Greek Religion*, London, Merlin Press, 1963, pp. 277–97.

8 Ibid., p. 296.

9 Plotinus, *Enneads, III, vi, 19*. Quoted by Edgar Wind, *Pagan Mysteries in the Renaissance*, London, Penguin Books, Peregrine Edition, 1967, p. 27n3.

10 Rainer Maria Rilke, *The Selected Poetry of Rainer Maria Rilke*, ed. and trans. Stephen Mitchell, London, Picador Classics, 1987, p. 157.

11 John Keats, *Poems by John Keats*, London, Bell & Hyman, Ltd., 1979, p. 324.

12 William Wordsworth, *The Prelude*, Oxford and New York, Oxford University Press, 1970, Book XII, p. 222, ll. 145–52.

13 Jane Harrison, *Prolegomena to the Study of Greek Religion*, London, The Merlin Press, 1980, pp. 32–52. See Harrison, *Themis*, fig. 77.

14 Harrison, *Prolegomena*, pp. 36–7.

15 Ibid., p. 35.

16 Ibid., p. 184.

17 Tom Singer, editor, private conversation.

18 Homer, *The Iliad, II*, trans. A. T. Murray, Loeb Classical Library, Cambridge, MA and London, Harvard University Press and William Heinemann, 1925, Book 22, p. 471, ll. 209–13.

19 Heraclitus, *Fragments: The Collected Wisdom of Heraclitus*, trans. Brooks Haxton, New York and London, Viking, 2001, Logion 74, p. 82.

20 Plato, *The Symposium*, 202 d–e, in Edith Hamilton and Huntingdon Cairns (eds), *The Collected Dialogues of Plato*, Bollingen Series LXXXI, Princeton, Princeton University Press, 1961, p. 555.

21 Plutarch, *De Defectu Oraculorum*, in F. C. Babbitt (trans.), *Moralia, V*, Loeb Classical Library 416, Cambridge, MA and London, Harvard University Press and William Heinemann Ltd., 1936, section 13, E, pp. 387–9.

22 Harrison, *Prolegomena*, pp. 292–5.

23 W. B. Yeats, *Mythologies*, London, The Macmillan Press, 1959, p. 336.

24 Apostolos N. Athanassakis (trans.), *Orphic Hymns*, Atlanta, Scholars Press for the Society of Biblical Literature, 1977, Numbers 28 and 57, pp. 41 and 77.

25 Aeschylus, *The Libation Bearers*, in David Grene and Richmond Lattimore (eds), *Greek Tragedies*, Vol. 2, Chicago and London, The University of Chicago Press, Phoenix Books, 1960, p. 9, ll. 123–6.

26 Karl Kerenyi, *Hermes: Guide of Souls*, trans. Murray Stein, Zurich, Spring Publications, 1976, p. 80.

27 Heraclitus, *Fragments*, Logion 15, p. 60.

28 Homer, *The Odyssey II*, trans. A. T. Murray, Loeb Classical Library, Cambridge, MA and London, Harvard University Press and William Heinemann Ltd., 1919, Book 24, ll. 1–4.

29 Harrison, *Themis*, p. 295.

30 See Jules Cashford, *The Moon: Myth and Image*, London, Cassell Illustrated, 2003, chapters 1 and 5.

31 Plato, *The Timaeus*, 37, C, D, *The Collected Dialogues of Plato*, p. 1167.

32 Harrison, *Themis*, pp. 186–91.

33 *The Gospel According to Thomas*, Coptic Text established and translated by A. Guillaumont et al., Leiden, E. J. Brill, 1976, Logion 77.

## II Reimagining Hermes in the Homeric Hymn to Hermes

34  Samuel Taylor Coleridge, *Biographia Literaria*, London, J. M. Dent & Sons Ltd., 1975, pp. 167–74.

35  W. B. Yeats, *Essays and Introductions*, London, The Macmillan Press, 1961, pp. 161–2.

36  Owen Barfield, *Saving the Appearances: A Study in Idolatry*, rev. ed., Hanover, NH, Wesleyan University Press, 1989, passim.

37  Percy Bysshe Shelley, "A defence of poetry," in *Poems and Prose*, London, J. M. Dent, 1995, p. 250.

38  Barfield, *Saving the Appearances*, pp. 123, 168, and passim.

39  Quoted in Cashford, *The Moon: Myth and Image*, chapter 5, "The Moon and Mind," p. 118.

40  Barfield, *History in English Words*, Edinburgh, Floris Classics, 1985, pp. 201–20.

41  *The Odyssey*, 19, ll. 138ff.

42  Dante Alighieri, *The Divine Comedy*, 1: Inferno, Canto II, ll. 7–8. Italian text with translation and commentary by John D. Sinclair, Oxford, Oxford University Press, 1961, p. 35.

43  John Locke, quoted in Barfield, *History in English Words*, p. 170.

44  Wordsworth, Preface to *The Lyrical Ballads*, 1802, in Charles W. Eliot (ed.), *Prefaces and Prologues*, Vol. XXXIX, The Harvard Classics, New York, P. F. Collier & Son, 1909–14, p. 20.

45  Wordsworth, *The Recluse*, London, Macmillan, 1888, p. 51.

46  Ernst Cassirer, *The Philosophy of Symbolic Forms*, New Haven, CT, Yale University Press, Inc., 1957, vol. 3, passim.

47  C. G. Jung, "The philosophical tree," *Alchemical Studies, The Collected Works of C. G. Jung*, Vol. 13, Princeton, Princeton University Press, 1968, ¶371. (Hereafter references to *The Collected Works* appear as CW and volume number.)

48  William Shakespeare, *A Midsummer Night's Dream*, in *The Riverside Shakespeare*, Boston, Houghton Mifflin Company, 1974, V, i, p. 242, ll. 7–17.

49  Jung, passim, especially CW 7, 8, and 9, i and ii.

50  Shakespeare, *A Midsummer Night's Dream*, V, i, p. 242, l. 17.

51  Ibid., ll. 7–17.

52  C. G. Jung, *Memories, Dreams, Reflections*, London, Flamingo Paperbacks, Random House, 1983, p. 201. See the whole of chapter 5, "Confrontation with the unconscious," pp. 194–225.

## III Hermes as imagination in the Hymn to Hermes

53  C. G. Jung, *Symbols of Transformation*, CW 5, ¶¶17–21.

54  William Blake, *Blake: Complete Poetry and Prose*, ed. Geoffrey Keynes, London, Nonesuch Press, 1961, p. 99.

55  Frederick Nietzsche, *Twilight of the Idols*, Harmondsworth, Penguin Books, 1968, p. 48.

56  Blake, *Blake: Complete Poetry and Prose*, p. 860.

57  Ibid., p. 835.

58  Ibid. 148. See also Kerenyi, *Hermes: Guide of Souls*, p. 26ff.

59  Shakespeare, "Sonnet 138," *Riverside Shakespeare*, p. 1774.

60  Samuel Taylor Coleridge, *The Rime of the Ancient Mariner*, in *Samuel Taylor Coleridge: Selected Poems*, London, Penguin Books, 1994, p. XX.
61  Samuel Taylor Coleridge, *The Statesman's Manual: Critical Theory since Plato*, ed. Hazard Adams, New York, Harcourt Brace Jovanovich, 1971, p. 476.
62  Plotinus, *Enneads* 5.5.7, trans. A. H. Armstrong, Loeb Classical Library, 444, Cambridge, MA, Harvard University Press, p. 179.
63  Coleridge, *Biographia Literaria*, ch. XIV, p. 173.
64  Ibid., p. 169.
65  Philip Larkin, "Vers de société," *Collected Poems*, London, Faber & Faber, 2003, p. 181.
66  W. B. Yeats, "He wishes for the cloths of heaven," *Collected Poems*, London, Macmillan & Co Ltd., 1965, p. 81.
67  John Keats, *The Letters of John Keats*, ed. M. B. Forman, Oxford, Oxford University Press, 1952, p. 71.
68  Plato, *Phaedrus*, 251, b–c, *The Collected Dialogues of Plato*, pp. 497–8.
69  Homer, *The Iliad*, Book 24, p. 587, ll. 340–2.
70  Kerenyi, *Hermes: Guide of Souls*, p. 13ff.
71  Coleridge, "The Eolian harp," *Selected Poems*, p. 37.
72  Cashford, *Hymn to Delian Apollo*, in *The Homeric Hymns*, pp. 27–37.
73  Ibid., *Hymn to Pythian Apollo*, pp. 38–54, ll. 515–19.
74  Ibid., *Hymn to the Muses and Apollo*, p. 130, ll. 2–4.
75  Ibid., *To Apollo*, p. 126, ll. 1–4.
76  Rainer Marie Rilke, *Duino Elegies*, trans. J. B. Leishman and Stephen Spender, London, Chatto & Windus, 1975, p. 25.
77  Immanuel Kant, *Critique of Pure Reason*, trans. Norman Kemp Smith, New York, St. Martins, 1965, A 51/B 75.
78  Rudolf Steiner, *Intuitive Thinking as a Higher Path*, trans. Gertrude Reif Hughes, New York, Anthroposophic Press, 1995, passim.
79  Coleridge, *Biographia Literaria*, ch. 13, p. 162.
80  R. W. Corrigan, *Tragedy: Vision and Form*, San Francisco, Chandler Publishing Company, 1965, p. 15.
81  Rainer Marie Rilke, *Poems from the Book of Hours*, trans. Babette Deutsche, New York, New Directions Books, 1975, p. 13.
82  Shakespeare, *A Midsummer Night's Dream*, V, i, ll. 18–22.
83  Rilke, "To Hölderlin," *The Selected Poetry*, p. 141.
84  C. G. Jung, "The Tavistock lectures," *The Symbolic Life*, CW 18, ¶371.
85  James Hillman, "The pandemonium of images," In *Healing Fiction*, Barrytown, New York, Station Hill Press, 1983, pp. 53–81.
86  Yeats, Essays and Introductions, p. 80.
87  Ibid., p. 79.
88  Ibid., p. 50.
89  Ibid., p. 28.
90  Ibid., p. 52.
91  C. G. Jung, *Psychological Types*, CW 6, ¶313.
92  Jules Cashford, "Gaia and the Anima Mundi," in Llewellyn Vaughan-Lee (ed.), *Spiritual Ecology: The Cry of the Earth*, California, Golden Sufi Center, 2013, pp. 172–82.
93  Shelley, "A defence of poetry," p. 279.
94  Blake, Blake: *Complete Poetry and Prose*, p. 187.

# 6

# PENELOPE SCAPES

*Melina Centomani Rutter*

In September 2012, Ben Ferris screened his film *Penelopa*, based on the Homeric myth of Odysseus' waiting wife, at the second *Ancient Greece, Modern Psyche* conference on Santorini. Ferris, an award-winning filmmaker and artistic director of the Sydney Film School, is also a classicist. His relationship with *The Odyssey*, as well as his travels in coastal Croatia, eventually coalesced in this provocative film, which aims to evoke Penelope's world through image, sound, and careful pacing, rather than dialogue. *Penelopa*, however, is not a pure retelling of the myth. Ferris is "interested in the tension between the woman and the archetype, and the pressure that living up to that archetype places on the human being."[1] In kind, the film examines Penelope and her predicament in fearless, sensual scenes that ultimately dismantle the patriarchal values inherent in Homer's myth.

## I "Her hands are so cold." – the maidens[2]

Penelope's maidens wait in lines, in the dark, by candlelight. They wait, armed with axes, to the sound of the sea. They wait.

In line with the maidens, we move through the chambers of Ben Ferris's *Penelopa*: from a fresco depicting the goddess Artemis shooting Actaeon, to the unmade beds and translucent dresses of Penelope's girls, bluish lights casting shadows through their open windows.

Indeed, in our first glimpse of Penelope, she is gazing out her window as if seeing into unknown worlds. When she stands, a slow, intimate kind of pain resonates in her movements; her environment has absorbed the grief of her waiting. The bend of the branches on the tree outside her window carry the same careful burden as her slender fingers fastening her heavy black hair behind her ear before she leaves her room.

## II "I don't expect you to wait for me." – Odysseus[3]

If readers of *The Odyssey* consider it as a text that instructs on values of "moral virtue," they soon distinguish between the classical model of male and female excellence.[4] Whereas Odysseus is exalted as a hero for his cunning, bravery, physical strength, and loyalty to his homeland, his wife Penelope is praised above all for her patience.

Throughout Homer's epic, Penelope is described as loyal, patient, constant, and clever, though it is understood that her cleverness is recognized only as it is applied to her faithfulness to her husband: she picks apart her weaving each evening in order to put off the day when she will have to choose to marry one of the suitors who have invaded her home.

As Eumaeus, Odysseus' trusted swineherd, attests to his master, "[Penelope] stays with steadfast heart in your halls and always sorrowfully for her the nights and days wane as she weeps."[5] Her whole being is consumed by her waiting, her loss. She has not chosen her predicament. In this way, it is her helplessness that defines her excellence – and her womanhood.

The pace and texture of Ferris's film reveal the weight of such womanhood. Shot in Brezovica castle outside of Zagreb, Croatia, the film's echoing, overgrown location is Penelope's landscape of abandonment. In her rooms and on her grounds, she moves with excruciating static, as if each step, each breath, each strand of hair pushed into place, each piano key pressed into song, drives her further into the absence of her husband and the siege of her home.

In a dream as real as any of her waking moments, Penelope walks trance-like to the river to visit her beloved geese. The sky darkens and the rumblings of war are heard overhead. White feathers rain. Penelope cradles a dead, bleeding goose in her arms.

Upon his return in *The Odyssey*, a disguised Odysseus misinterprets this dream when he asserts to his wife that the geese symbolize the wild, lecherous suitors – soon to be destroyed. The white, gliding dream-geese, however, in every way incarnate Penelope's maidens. In Odysseus' absence, they are her companions, her mirrors, her comforts, her loves. Most importantly, they are the innocents, left unprotected as their hero-men go off to the wars.

Both the Croatian landscape and the spare words exchanged in Serbo-Croatian give the slaughtered geese a dark relevance. Scores of properties like Brezovica were destroyed during the country's involvement in the region's civil war in the 1990s. Many that still stand are battered with bullet marks, carrying the absences of those they used to shelter.

Likewise, words in the film – maiden to maiden, man to man – in whispers and in yells that texturize its stillness, remind the viewer that the female predicament of waiting, and that of war, is recent, audible, and within reach.

When he appears in a sunlit memory, we can smell Odysseus' cigarette smoke. We know the pattern on his fatigues.

He says to his wife, "I don't expect you to wait for me."

To which Penelope, at the piano, her back turned to her husband, replies, "When will you be back?"[6] That is: what choice do I have?

## III "There is no place for me in this world." – Penelope[7]

Artemis, patron goddess of maidens, is the deity to whom Penelope prays for relief from her nightmares – both waking and sleeping. Although Penelope expresses her paralyzing grief with a wish that Artemis grant her death, thus reuniting her with Odysseus, her prayer extends beyond the personal.

Penelope confides to Artemis that the world has changed beyond her recognition. As the suitors' drunken revelry grows ever more raucous, Penelope retreats further into the upper stories of her house, hostess cum prisoner in the space she was to rule alongside her husband. In his absence, however, Penelope relegates herself to "a room of [her] own in the women's quarters."[8] Penelope and her maidens hold fort in near silence in a purely female space. In Ferris's film, this space is not only physical – Penelope's room looks out over the sea, protected from the rest of the house only by the bedroom of her maidens, which she moves through like a spirit to descend the stairs – but also relational. There is a palpable physical intimacy between the women in the film. They comfort each other with embraces, collude in whispers with hands on shoulders, mouths pressed to ears.

When they find their mistress lying nude in the leaves after a particularly wakeful dream, the maidens take on a distinctly Greek chorus-like quality, moving together as one sea-green-draped entity to protect and revive her. To Penelope, the maidens are tender and worshipping. They cover her, lift her aloft, bathe her with utmost care.

In Homer's *Odyssey*, Penelope's closest maiden companions are found to be duplicitous and disloyal. Homer has them sleeping willingly with the invading suitors and mocking the disguised Odysseus. The most specific example is Penelope's young maid, the "fair-cheeked" Melantho, "whom Penelope had reared and cherished as her own child, and gave her playthings to her heart's desire. Yet even so she had at heart no sorrow for Penelope . . . "[9] In contrast, Ferris's maidens are, though giggly and gossipy, firmly on Penelope's side. For as she is their queen and mother, the maidens are to Penelope, as Margaret Atwood's version confides, "my most trusted eyes and ears."[10] In Ferris's film, the maidens make up a female collective, a vulnerable stronghold who remain, despite all horrors, lively and resilient. In Atwood's story, they affirm, "If we were pretty children our lives were worse. But we wanted to sing and dance too, we wanted to be happy too. We laughed together in our attics, in our nights. We snatched what we could."[11] The camera lingers on their hair, twined with vines, their full mouths, their bare shoulders.

In their physical beauty as well as their confinement, the maidens echo Penelope's predicament of the waiting woman. Their presence, rustling through Croatian woods, contains a further reaching suggestion: a world full of female communities that war continuously corrupts and attempts to annihilate.

It is for the community that Penelope is afraid. She prays: "Dear Artemis. Please. Not my geese."[12] She has seen the future in her dream.

## IV "The best way to rape a sheep is – " – the suitors[13]

Although Homer's *Odyssey* spares no detail in describing how Penelope's lecherous suitors disrespected their hostess's hospitality and "wasted [her] house," it is nevertheless surprising to be confronted with Ferris's suitors in *Penelopa*.[14] Drunk, frenzied, and slobbering, the suitors of Ferris's film sport faces smeared with wine the color of blood, their shouts carrying up to the women's quarters of the palace like a warning. Alternately tearing meat from bone and snoring into their plates, the men banter about sexual conquests in a chaotic show of one-upmanship. As the film progresses, their behavior escalates, growing ever more grotesque and animalistic. As Atwood's Penelope describes, "They were like vultures when they spot a dead cow: one drops, then another, until finally every vulture for miles around is tearing up the carcass."[15]

The suitors are the inverse of the upstairs, female collective: the invaders below, eating their way to the ultimate prize – Penelope – louder and louder they become, closing in.

These suitors are surprising not because their violence is unfamiliar, but because there is no effort on the part of the production to glamorize them or or make them comic. Unlike so much contemporary myth-derived film and television, such as HBO's *Game of Thrones*, where sadism and misogyny on the part of powerful male characters are excused as typical to its imagined world, and worse, fetishized for its graphic depictions and excused as "real" by viewers, Ferris's film exposes the suitors for the predators they are. This exposition becomes essential in the wider implication of the film as it pertains to rape as a war crime – one that often goes unpunished. In Ferris's hands, however, the ancient tradition of rape as a right of conquerors is laid bare, and he blames the perpetrators instead of, as in *The Odyssey* and plenty of contemporary examples, the victims.

Following the rescue of their mistress from the woods, the maidens descend to the dining room at the bidding of one of their own: "Girls," she says. "Don't you hear how loud the suitors are? I think it's best to go downstairs. To calm them down. Together."[16]

In the darkness of the dining room, the suitors close in around the huddle of girls. "Where is Penelope?" they demand, pronouncing ironically, "We have waited long enough," before yanking girls by hair and elbow, forcing grapes into their mouths.[17] The scene escalates rapidly as the suitors throw the girls on tables and hold them in the air, ripping off their clothes and raping them to a relentless score of braying, screaming, and howling. It's a scene undeniably redolent of the mass rapes of women and girls that we know occurred throughout the war in Croatia and Bosnia in the 1990s.

Upstairs, Penelope wakes in a puddle of blood from between her legs. The clamor of the rape below mixes with the ever-present sea wind, rising into a storm.

She opens the door to her room to find her maidens' sheets blown like death-shrouds around their sleeping chamber. Their beds, of course, are empty. Penelope's blood stains her own bed, a reminder not only of her fertility/vulnerability – the woman-hood that renders her prey – but also of her archetypal connection to her maidens. Their suffering is physically manifested in Penelope's body, an echo of her earlier prayer to the goddess Artemis. Penelope is a vessel, and she carries the violence of her surroundings as well as their unbearable calm.

Upon finding her girls lying silent and abandoned in the dining hall, her geese nightmare come to life, Penelope torches the shroud she has been so carefully weav-ing and unweaving. This destruction is another major plot departure from the original myth, and one that bears mentioning in line with the film's thoughtful subversion of the female helplessness that classical culture encourages women to emulate.

As morning brightens Penelope's weaving room, and the storm of last night disappears, Penelope rushes outside to the chatter of her maidens. Covered in fresh, new frocks, they are hanging laundry on the line, cheerful and alive.

It's as if nothing has happened.

Penelope, however, carries the memory for them. "Thank god you're alive," she says. "I had a terrible dream. You were all dead."[18]

Then a strange thing happens. The girl Penelope embraces dissolves into hys-terical laughter, a laughter that is echoed and accompanied by that of the other girls. It is an uncontrollable reaction, directly in contrast to the horror Penelope and the viewer have just witnessed. Here, then, do we have Homer's "shameful" maids, as fickle as Penelope is constant?[19]

We know, because we have *seen* their brutal rape, that Odysseus' eventual accu-sations in Homer's epic – the maidens have been enjoying the sexual advances of the suitors – are untrue in the film.[20] The laughter that bursts from the girls in the wake of their rape is not a laugh of joy or insolence, but one of hysteria in the face of trauma. The chilling laughter of the maidens proves not only a denial of what has happened to them (as can occur directly following trauma) but also an implica-tion of the depth of their injury. They have been drawn irrevocably into the war that has infiltrated Penelope's home. Their laughter shows how intrinsically the rape has transformed them.

## V "To him I give my life." – Penelope[21]

A single maid prefigures the climax of the film when she wakes Penelope from where she is dreaming of Odysseus outside in the leaves. "Don't you think it's time?" the girl asks. "We are ready to do it." To whom Penelope replies, "That's something that I have to do."[22]

A viewer who knows the myth assumes the task of which they speak is the inevitable one: Penelope must finally choose a husband from among the suitors. In Ferris's remaking, however, a new inevitability emerges.

Penelope enters the raucous dining room elevated on a dais. She holds Odysseus' mythic bow and wears a quiver of arrows on her back. Her maidens, armed with

151

axes as in the opening scene, guard her in their line. The suitors continue their uproar as she addresses them, declaring a contest of the bow: "Whoever can bend and string it, and send an arrow straight through the twelve axes . . . to him I give my life."[23]

Upon finishing her avowal, Penelope pulls the first arrow from her quiver and shoots the suitors expertly, one by one. They fall dead at their plates, bleeding from thighs, necks, and heads. Her shooting posture mirrors that of Artemis, whom we saw enfrescoed, frozen in action during the opening credits. Penelope's prayer to the goddess, "I can feel you inside of me," is actualized. For Artemis is the patron not only of maidens, but also of the hunt. In the penultimate scene in the dining room, Penelope embodies Artemis, avenging the maidens she is meant to protect by hunting and killing the beasts who threaten the balance and tranquility of her world.

The rape of the maidens, likewise, has transformed them from ordinary girls to warriors: their innocence traded for axes, their gossip for action. Unlike in Homer's version, where the maidens are executed for their treachery – "the women held their heads in a row, and round the necks of all nooses were laid, that they might die most piteously. And they writhed a little while with their feet, but not for long" – Ferris's maids are survivors, and ultimately defenders.[24]

It is not until the dining room is silent, and Penelope stands alone with her bow on the dais, that a figure enters from behind the dead: Odysseus. He is dirty and disheveled. Penelope steps down from her platform to lead him by the arm out of the dining room and up to their bedroom, as if he is a stranger in her house.

For now that Penelope has avenged herself, her home, and her maidens, the events of the story take on a new causal relationship. Contrary to the classical tale, Penelope is in control. She is the hunter, the master, the decision-maker. She is the hero. Thus, when Odysseus appears suddenly, in the wake of her massacre, it is as if she has conjured him there herself. He is not disguised as a beggar, as in Homer's epic, still full of tests and deceits for his subjects – who include his wife. Instead, he has *become* the beggar: his roughed-up face and ragged coat are no costume, but the true garments of a man who has failed to live up to his task. Failed, indeed, to claim his masculine excellence. His wife has assumed this excellence for him.

In the last scene of the movie, Odysseus lies prone on their bed in his boots and fatigues. Penelope has dropped her bow, removed her quiver. She curls next to him. He is too exhausted to move. His pea coat is open to expose his heavy armor: useless now, except as a headrest for Penelope.

What Ferris has done in *Penelopa* is a pulling-apart, a true examination that we see too seldom in contemporary film and television. He has questioned authority. He has shown terrors for what they are. He has pulled the *human* Penelope apart from her archetype-self and into modern consciousness. Penelope is transformed into a woman who will not be oppressed. As she develops beyond her myth, a new archetype is emerging, one that speaks to twenty-first-century women.

Ferris's *Penelopa* raises questions of accountability that address our present culture. Why are women held accountable for loyalty in marriage while their husbands are not? Why are men allowed to rape women and never held accountable? Why is womanhood synonymous with victimhood?

But *Penelopa* is not a film that relies on dialogue to achieve its impact. The answers are contained in its characters, male and female, and its slow unfolding. Wordlessly, the film calls our ancient heroes into question and, in doing so, reveals thorns in our contemporary truths.

# Notes

1 Simon Foster, "Penelope: Ben Ferris interview," Film/Movie News and Features, SBS, 24 June 2011, available: <www.sbs.com.au>.
2 *Penelopa*, directed by Ben Ferris, Croatia, Artemis Projects, Focus Media, 2009.
3 Ibid.
4 Harold Bloom, *Homer's Odyssey, Bloom's Notes*, New York, Chelsea House Publishers, 1996, pp. 5–6.
5 Homer, *The Odyssey*, Books 13–24, The Loeb Classic Library, trans. A. T. Murray, ed. William F. Wyatt, Cambridge, MA and London, Harvard University Press, 1995, XIV.36.
6 *Penelopa*.
7 Ibid.
8 Margaret Atwood, *The Penelopiad*, New York, Canongate, 2005, p. 109.
9 Homer, *The Odyssey*, XVIII.321, 323.
10 Atwood, *The Penelopiad*, p. 114.
11 Ibid, p. 14.
12 *Penelopa*.
13 Ibid.
14 Homer, *The Odyssey*, XXII.37.
15 Atwood, *The Penelopiad*, p. 103.
16 *Penelopa*.
17 Ibid.
18 Ibid.
19 Homer, *The Odyssey*, XXII.430.
20 Ibid., XXII.444.
21 *Penelopa*.
22 Ibid.
23 Ibid.
24 Homer, *The Odyssey*, XXII.471.

# 7

# DREAMING IN PLACE
## Santorini, Greece

### Robin van Löben Sels

### Dream gathering

During several years of dream gathering in different countries, I've come up with a map of our dreaming-mind-psyche that shows how I imagine human consciousness to be at work without exactly declaring itself (see Figure 7.1, page 156).[1] I think of this map as the Pillar of Isis,[2] and I'll use it here to illustrate how I think about the process of dreaming, how I imagine that dream images and dream experience enter our consciousness, and what we do with those images. I will also use it to illustrate how the shared experience of Dreaming in Santorini was imaged.

Like a hexagram from the *I Ching*, I read the Pillar of Isis from the bottom up.[3] The image is reminiscent of the Egyptian *djed* pillar or the Tree of Life, but, for me, it is more than a tree and other than Osiris' *djed* pillar of death and resurrection. In Egypt, says the old myth, Isis helped to raise the sun. But like many others, this old myth serves us too. Like the First Woman of the Navaho Emergence story, Isis still serves our consciousness as it rises from the dark night of our own beginnings – thus, my "Pillar of Isis."

The vertical stack resembles the human backbone, but note that I add depth and weight to the cubes to suggest full embodied being, not just bony vertebrae. I want to avoid the imposition of a mind-body schema like the chakras on this "torso." And there are five cubes (although once I dreamed of three), so perhaps some will find the number five relevant: to alchemists, five represents the quintessence.[4] Dreaming is one among several of the body's languages, but the psyche's grammar is subtler.

I have also referred to this chart as "Sounding the chord of having a dream."[5] Granted that the human body remains the psyche's first and final metaphor as well as the soul's home, perceiving a dream as a "whole body experience" calls for more than a grasp of symbolic metaphor; it demands a differentiated, sensate

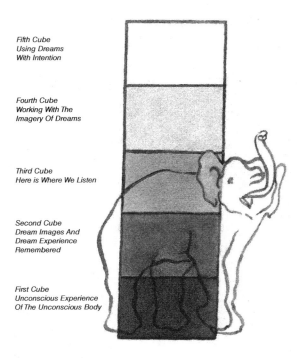

Fifth Cube
Using Dreams
With Intention

Fourth Cube
Working With The
Imagery Of Dreams

Third Cube
Here is Where We Listen

Second Cube
Dream Images And
Dream Experience
Remembered

First Cube
Unconscious Experience
Of The Unconscious Body

THE PILLAR OF ISIS

*Figure 7.1* Pillar of Isis.

perception similar to the perceptive listening we use to distinguish musical tones. At times, I imagine we can listen to dreams as if we were listening to music, aware that dreams, like music, continually form themselves *and their meaning* in our feeling-saturated senses and imagination. Listening for the "sound" of a dream, then, can be likened to listening to the notes of a chord or imaginatively feeling a dream's texture. Sensate, perceptive activities help us sense and perceive the psyche's grammar.

When we imagine that dreams sound "chords of Being," deeper imagination germinates: does this particular dream sound a major or a minor chord? Is the dream soft, drifting through my sensibilities, or is it loud, demanding my attention? Does my dream rhyme? Does it provide narrative? Did this dream arrive in rhythmic syncopation with others, or is it the first I've had in a long time? Does this dream have a backbeat? Does it punctuate my life or enlarge my imagination? Is this dream harmonious with my life as a whole? Or is it discordant?

In dreams, we find metaphor without cuteness or irony. We notice chiaroscuro. What is the texture of this dream? Does it come across as a quick sketch or a laborious masterpiece? Do my dreams seem to create space, or do they crowd out my sense of self? Does this series of dreams assemble a supporting structure for my life? Can the overall fabric of my dreams breathe, or is it tightly woven? Do my dreams interact with the environment? Is this dream a random snapshot in time, while another is static and poised like a deliberate portrait? How important to my dreams are my associations?

Another way to think about a dream is to understand it as a *Holon*,[6] which means "whole in and of itself." For example, in relation to a dream image, a dream (as a whole) is autonomous and self-reliant. But a dream is also dependent, emerging from the psyche and the world in which the individual psyche lives or feels "placed." Individual awareness differentiates these factors, for only awareness has access to our fully sensate experience, whether in dreams or in life. Consciousness, awareness, and attention – we need these three factors for conscious access to the fullness of our experience, the texture of which may range from simple presence to something globally rich – whereas the unconscious, bodily process of dreaming immerses us in a "just-so" experience that is simultaneously and inexplicably resonant with other whole, ongoing, "just-so" experience whether "we" happen to be above or below the threshold of consciousness. But even with consciousness, attention, and awareness wide open and available to us, full human experience – dream experience included – is difficult to illustrate.

We seem to have been pondering dreams from the beginning of time. Perhaps one thing dreaming does for us is it increases our available stock of conscious reality. Attention to one's dreams over time can become an important life resource, for attention and awareness are gateways to the mind. Youth can be ignorant of not only the mind but also the Deep (mythopoetic) Imagination: for example, although I was always interested in the imagery of dreams and found dreams aesthetically appealing, in my twenties I felt that dreams were somewhat irrelevant to how I lived. Perhaps my attitude toward dreams mirrored my generalized (conventional) approach to life: "Row, row, row your boat, gently down the stream. Merrily, merrily, merrily, merrily – life is but a dream."

I remember when this attitude changed. When I became no longer able to swallow what was served up by convention, I reached for something else to hold on to, something close to soul. After several sobering experiences, my rapidly developing dream-life became a depended-upon Reality Consultant. I became conscious of this change in attitude when I overheard myself mutter an amendment to a friend's similarly facile, carefree description of life: "Yes," I murmured *sotto voce*, "Life *is* like a dream – *more real than it may seem.*"

It seems to me that we are culturally in need of increasingly greater vocabularies for both subjective and objective experiences of our inner and outer worlds; cultivation of the Deep Imagination has become crucial. Dreams are both a source and a representation of our collective, increasingly psychological turn toward the exploration of subjective experience as interiority. I believe that because our dreams draw from such depths of soul and our world at large, they offer access to new images seeping not only into our personal awareness but also into the collective unconscious and from there into collective, social awareness. Long ago, because they believed that those individuals who experienced waking thoughts as visions must be able to dream in a waking state, our ancestors turned to tribal shamans for help with inexplicable illness and alienation. Today, we depend less on other people – or even scientific institutions – to investigate the unconscious for us. For a little over a century, our burgeoning psychological awareness is indicative of a turn to the shamanic capacities of the psyche itself. So when we attend to our personal imagery now, or listen to psyche in our dreams – what do we find?

Like metaphor itself, the images of our dreams are transparent windows and sliding doors. We discover that dreams can be recognized as "inner locations," close kin to "thin places" in the outer world through which our experience of what is subjective and objective and what is inner and outer meet, collide, penetrate, and receive each other. Dreams can become an inner personal grounding field, a place of feeling-brought-to-earth. Dreams offer individual, multidimensional experience of an earthy incarnation during which we come to understand in our bodies how metaphorical, psychological, emotional, and conceptual opposites live and move and have their being, by which I mean we *experience* how opposites become each other.[7] We find this when we attend to personal dream imagery. We will make other discoveries as we read the Pillar of Isis from the bottom up, because entire ecologies of self and culture have emerged from the profundities of human experience that we regularly relegate to dreams.

When we as Jungian analysts speak of "depth" we don't mean dark inaccessibility or complete unavailability. We're talking about experience that differs from thinking or conscious understanding or analysis, or knowledge, or even intuition. The Logos of the psyche is quite different from the Logos of conscious life, and the Logos of the unconscious is even more profound. Those of us who work with the unconscious cannot simplify a dream into a puzzle that lacks a solution. Rather, just as our kin of earlier cultures assumed, we expect our dreams will *lead us* somewhere. We know well enough that myth deploys the faculties of conscious imagination, but we may lose sight of the fact that the *roots* of myth, those taproots and tendrils of Deep (mythic) Imagination, swim into our dreams out of a biocosmic depth, as portrayed in the First Cube, Cube 1 of the Pillar of Isis.[8] *How* we use dream images (addressed in the Fourth and Fifth Cubes), as well as *that* we use dream images, play major roles in what we understand to be the healing properties of dreams.

This brings up another quality of experience offered by attention to dreams. In daylight hours, our species wants to *know*. Our very name – *Homo sapiens sapiens* – defines us this way. (Whether this definition adequately defines us is open to question, but that is the name we've selected.) Psychological experience, however, informs us that all too often, *knowing* – while it feeds our interest and put us at ease – *simultaneously closes us off from fullness of experience in ways that we barely understand.*

Fortunately, we thirst also for something that seems to be the opposite of knowing. We feel some fidelity to an ungraspable "other" and beyond, that lies at the root of biological existence and all that we experience as beauty and mystery.

*Dreams open us to this counter-thirst to knowing* because dreams work not on what we *know* but on what we *don't know* about ourselves and our world. For all that we know dreams may even proceed from this counter-thirst.

Attention to dreams hones individual attentiveness to whatever is deeply felt and individually grasped, embraced, and intuited, even when barely perceived. The Imagination of the World works through us as we dream, and the individual attention we are willing to pay to whatever is hidden and uncertain generates an energy that surprises us, even as it enlarges and deepens our lives.

For example, dreams are often saturated with unconscious feeling. Clues and trails to feeling hide in the images themselves as well as in the associations the images bring forth. (Whether unconscious affect was lost or split off or never experienced to begin with, we may not know.) Some of us who work as therapists may probe for affect first. Others may feel that whatever is emotionally important will emerge in its own time. But however we acknowledge the presence of unconscious feeling, we hold in mind that dreams represent a full-body experience of *both* therapist and patient, an experience in which images – some familiar, some not – are not being perceived as something on a horizon, say, in the way we think about images in a myth, but perceived as a contextual dimension of space-time that is emerging in the form of *events that happened to or are continuing to happen to the dreaming person in time.*

As I take you through the Pillar of Isis, I will use a dream image of my own that I gleaned from the dream-gathering experience in Santorini to illustrate the different levels or cubes of the Pillar of Isis. I will demonstrate how this relatively simple dream image was enriched by my experience of the gathering as well as the *place* of Santorini, and by subsequent places and events in my life. My dream, comments on it, and my ongoing experience of the image over the following years will appear in italics. *My dream from Thursday morning: I see a baby black woolly mammoth about the size of a small elephant, who is joyously waving its trunk at me.*

Now let's look at the Pillar of Isis, one cube at a time.

## First Cube (Cube 1): unconscious experience of the unconscious body

The First Cube (or Cube 1) is the most important. Were I to further illustrate this bottom cube I would draw – in back and along the sides – dark caves and dirt and soil – the chemicals and elements of earth – and plants and insects. Here, what consciously we call "a dream" is an event of deeply visceral, often emotional human experience. At bottom, the invisible psyche breathes itself in and out of being, night by night, day by day, and dream by dream, whether or not we remember our dreams. Dreams are as deeply rooted in our human flesh and blood as any imaginative image or idea; thus, when we say *depth*, as in *depth psychology*, we point to a realm of *relatively unconscious feeling experience* that is as different from our conscious experience as in physics the quantum world differs from Einstein's $E = mc^2$.

159

Here is where the animal sleeps. *(Perhaps my little mammoth slept in a cave in ice or earth before it came to me.)* The dreams we have in Cube 1 are full of darkness and probably bones, for the Deep Imagination excavates the earth itself and peoples it with images of ourselves. Our unconscious sense memories brim with nostalgia that points us toward a Deep Past – the past of one's self, one's tribe, and one's species. The Imagination of the World weaves itself, our earth, and even psyche as we dream.

Here, for example, we experience diurnal rhythm. Our particularly human eco-niche is webbed with trust in the ancient rhythms of day and night, as well as a shared deeper trust in the functioning of bodily reality: we trust that our hearts will pump blood, our lungs will breathe, and our physical wounds can scar over without our noticing. Similarly, we digest early infant experience without noticing. Much of life that we simply take for granted goes on below or beyond noticeable thresholds. I suspect that primordial human experience will forever remain nameless and without form, yet eventually we *do* come to know that we have it.

In Cube 1 we experience sleep and solitude as privacies, yet also we sense the faint presence of other evolutionary experiments in becoming human. Apparently *Homo erectus* and the Neanderthals were as capable of love, hate, tenderness, and violence as we are. They had composite tools, art, ritual, and religious beliefs, as well as grave goods and infant dependence. Although Neanderthals lacked our particular abilities of speech and our kind of language, they possessed skills to communicate social needs. Despite wide differences in mind and culture, these now-extinct peoples were our physical and emotional kin. *(I presume they hunted woolly mammoths and had memories of sighting them – across open plains? – along the edge of giant glaciers?)*

Dreams offer our conscious minds access to memories and imaginings of ancestral (archetypal) experience that is rooted in our earliest beginnings as a species. They are an instinctive avenue toward "visiting the ancestors." We have to assume that any inkling of personal trust we experience toward our individual bodies, whether we are awake or asleep, unthinkingly extends an instinctive trust that has changed little over 600,000 years.[9] We still speak of "bodily wisdom" and "bodily strength" or of "bodily weakness" or instinct. In our genetic ponderings, we take this level of psyche for granted. We speak of a "body of knowledge" because our very thoughts construct themselves in a world of material objects and sensual presence in time. The body that each of us inhabits is still the only body in which all that we can possibly imagine as "knowledge" dwells.

Cube 1 is where thinkers like D. W. Winnicott and Masud Khan point when they tell us that *having* a dream is more important than remembering a dream.[10] This means that at times a dream's importance is not that it harbors unconscious *meaning* but that it out-pictures unconscious experience. Perhaps someone has lost the innate ability to dream, or perhaps his or her ability to dream never developed. In Cube 1, the ability to dream represents a therapeutic achievement developed over time. It marks a capacity to *have* the dream from which we may gain (or with help, regain) irreplaceable dimensions of personal experience that we may have repressed, denied, split off, or traumatically forgotten.

Sometimes we don't remember a dream or forget it once we are awake, and we can't possibly expect to be conscious of everything that happens to us all the time. But if a dream hovers around or behind my attention, or some image sticks in my mind like a burr, as uncomfortable as a pebble in my shoe (the "soul" of my shoe?), what then? Clearly I have been "at home" (present) not only to dream the dream, but to continue dream experience into a waking experience of hovering discomfort. Dreaming offers me a link between night and day, consciousness and unconsciousness, mind and body – an imaginatively *embodied* link that I may experience as perceptual alarm, say, or as sensate discomfort (something indigestible), or as acute, unexplainable anxiety.

## Second Cube (Cube 2): dream images and dream experience remembered

This dimension reveals itself whether we wake up with our minds overtaken and a hammering heart, or simply shake loose a drowsy image as we brew the morning coffee. Sometimes simple, effortless movement helps the mind snag wisps of dream-life as we go about our day. Or – more intentionally – one man I knew discovered he could remember his dreams when he went swimming at the gym. It was as if his dreams had taken up residence in his muscles until he could swim them into mind. Another person, a woman, took up running and began to weep, not knowing why. It was as if unconscious feeling suddenly poured itself into her flesh and entered personal time. Her lungs breathed deep breaths they had forgotten to breathe, her sobs wrenched previously unshed tears into her startled heart (and mine) until – a miracle, actually – her breathing became in-spirited before our eyes.

I once saw an oriental print that depicted a robed sage leaning against a tiger. Both were sound asleep. Perhaps that's the only time consciousness and the unconscious peacefully coexist, suggested my then-analyst. But Buddhists tell us of a storehouse consciousness, an infinite junk shop of the mind that holds not only everything we have forgotten but also everything our ancestors (including our Neanderthal kin) have forgotten: the sight of primordial creatures, large and small, the taste of the original oceans still run in our blood. Perhaps my sleeping sage and his sleeping tiger were peacefully browsing that great compendium together.

You and I coexist with dreams night after night, and although it may be *most* important that we have a dream in the first place, clearly unconscious dreaming isn't all there is to it. In paying attention to Cube 2, we begin to cultivate an awareness of how the psyche permeates the Pillar of Isis around the edges. We glimpse dim images as they seep toward the light of consciousness (*just as my black baby mammoth seeped into my dream*).

Sometimes we don't remember dreaming, but when we enter therapy we start dreaming up a storm. An active dream-life often ensues whenever an important relationship takes hold, and that is why we believe a therapeutic relationship

161

constellates the interpersonally related *lived time* that is necessary to begin to let us *have* a dream-life. On an inward note, a sense of time as well as a sense of identity seems to begin with personal memory, and we place memory at the very beginnings of human thought and culture.[11]

In Cube 2, an active dream-life grants us access to what I call *episodic-emerging-from-implicit memory*, the memory that we suppose infants or young children or animals experience – those momentary archipelagos of consciousness that we too may remember from before we suppose our capacity for narrative memory begins. Current neurobiological studies demonstrate that what we call "implicit memory" *stays* implicit and nonconscious throughout our lives, composing what Alan Schore calls our "affective and relational unconscious."[12] Even when we are adults, early, barely conscious memories remain embedded in implicit context and are only episodic. A *first* memory, whether of a perceived image or a felt sensation (or a felt image or a perceived sensation) will be forever a momentary event that usually tugs at our awareness only if and when we're asked about it, whereas *before* and *after* remain shrouded and gone.

As surely as neurobiologically encoded implicit memory forms our most basic albeit nonconscious sense of "self-being-with another," when we remember early episodic-emerging-from-implicit memories they have a dream-like relevance to our nascent conscious identity. Like Chinese signature stamps, each memory indicates a psychic "mark" of who we are. Sometimes in therapy we treat a patient's earliest memory "as if" it were a dream. Jung's earliest memory was of lying in a pram, looking into the sky through tree-dappled sunlight with an indescribable feeling of happiness. Other writers made different uses of Jung's early memory.[13]

Evidence of symbolism as well as symbolic perception extends beyond our species. Whales and dolphins dream, for example, for dreams seem to be the province of mammals (and so is play). Some scientists speculate that we experience neither dream nor play for entertainment but from need, which probably means these mammalian activities have to do with survival as well as enjoyment.[14] That other creatures clearly experience the same swerve into the connecting mind of likeness as we do suggests that other mammals experience not only perception but also metaphor – not metaphor as a figure of speech, perhaps, but *metaphor as an event in time, as sensate happening*. Perhaps our early memories share this nature of metaphor as an event in time, a sensate happening; this helps explain why often the best we can do to *reach back then* is to *enact* early experience metaphorically, as happens in transference situations (or life itself). How else would we haul the depth of implicit early experience into consciousness? The idea of the leap between water welling forth as springs from the earth to the origins of human thought and human creativity and originality has its roots somewhere around *here*, as do the roots of sentience.

Like William James (one of our earlier and most masterful psychological writers), I am defining sentience as "what it *feels like* to be *here*" – what it feels like to be here now or wherever a dream may take us.[15] This sensual experience borders on feeling, and it is not conceptual. Like language itself, dreaming begins in the facts of our physical life and seeps upward with creative strategies of tension. With a grammar internal to themselves, our dreams interweave delicate, intricate patterns and complex systems of mind and body, and within seconds, these strategies blossom into attachments soaked with emotion. (Please note that attachment happens in seconds, whereas love emerges only over longer-lived, even personal, time.) Perhaps, at this stage, we can think of what I call a *creative strategy of tension* within the psyche as kin to molecular bonding that is as utterly impersonal as gravity.

I think of Cube 2 as the place where the *voice* of a dream becomes evident, and by *voice*, I mean the design of a dream, a sense of lived inhabitance, neither subject nor activity. I find that the body language of dreams gives voice to our *underlying personal style of being*, a style that is continuous, idiosyncratic, recognizable, and replete with information. The voice of a dream can be ironic, fantastic, concise, funny, serious, irreverent, philosophical, or compassionate. It can be argumentative or formal, or linear, or emotional. By its very nature, the voice of a dream conveys attachment and engagement – with life, with the dreamer's self, and sometimes with me. In dream seminars, I may forget a participant's name, but usually I can track who dreams what because as I recognize the *voice* or style of a dream I match it to the person. To me, the voice of a dream sounds the dreamer's identity.

The deep, sensate, perceptual roots of our symbolic and image-based language are as elemental to the psyche as the sea is elemental to our blood. These roots are of our own substance, so any grasp we have of the workings of the human imagination and creative understanding remains elusive and mysterious. We have to struggle to comprehend how it is that we dream in an already-inexpressible presence of image and language, and how it is that the entangled presence of image and language form such an impenetrable threshold of consciousness – a threshold in which subject and object are still one. Our conceptual minds remain in abeyance even as a new wideness of being leads us both toward a self and away.

This second dimension (Cube 2) feels a long way from our modern sense of perspective. From this place, a dream can seem flat, as in early medieval paintings, or it can feel the way those repeating handprints feel when you stand in the dark caves of Lascaux; noticing how those hands pattern the walls below big colorful drawings of imposing animals. Those hands were signing sensation and perception, not even images. They are a long way from concepts.

Yet dream images aren't really flat, like those we see on paper or screens. Rather, in Cube 2, I think we experience a dream image as if it were an icon hanging on the wall of an Orthodox church. Icons are felt to penetrate viewers with presence by actively pouring into the perceiver a feeling of timelessness. Religious icons re-turn (we would say "mirror") the gaze we turn upon them. In a similar fashion, therapists find that a dream (a facet of the "face" of the unconscious) mirrors to consciousness the attitude with which it is being perceived.[16] This is why we feel a dream image speaks to what is happening to us *now*, is gazing upon us *now*, even as we feel how the energy portrayed by the image is being held *in potentia*.

In other words, at Cube 2, we access iconic energy by description. Here, we hope only to describe a dream; we can't explain it further because the "depth" of dream experience beggars explanation. I suggest that between Cubes 2 and 3 an important *quality* of consciousness (which I see in spatial terms) has the potential to *emerge in our minds, as well as to be blocked*. Somewhere between the iconicity I'm struggling to describe in Cube 2 and the formation of narrativity in Cube 3, there seems to be an intersection in the psyche where – particularly in someone who has experienced early trauma – concepts can be misperceived as perceptions, or perceptions can be misconceived as concepts. These misperceptions and misconceptions (if they occur) seem to prevent images from naturally evolving or emerging toward the feeling of presence to metaphor and narration that I will describe in Cube 3. When this happens, the psyche stutters, or stammers, or blocks, or blanks out.

In Cube 2, there is a hinge, a joint, an intersection, a place where an image can freeze in time, where an image can be squashed, made static, or shattered, if not altogether turned off and done away with. I remember a man who early on in analysis dreamed in marks, like sketch lines, that he called sticks and twigs. Months went by before the sticks and twigs of dreams formed anything at all, even as outline. I had to imagine that this man's mind and psyche were dwelling in Cube 2 until he (and the psyche) could move along.

## Third Cube (Cube 3): here is where we listen

This cube marks where I imagine our dream images begin to take on words. As we tell each other dreams or write them down, or turn and re-turn them with self-reflection, nascent consciousness begins to clothe images in words, even though some dreams may contain words before we get here. Once I dreamed of the title of a book in Chinese. I have never studied Chinese, so I could not read the title; I struggled consciously (with a lot of help) to make the title understandable. That I needed help with this dream was appropriate, as Cube 3 implies the presence of someone else, or relatedness.

A relationship can form with a therapist or a friend. Sometimes the necessary "other" is a blank page, as some of us know from beginning a diary or journal. (*For my dream of a black baby woolly mammoth, this "other" is you, my reader.*) The importance of Cube 3 is that psyche enters the picture as something that emerges from *between*. In the early days of therapy, the psyche may be seen as a simple byproduct of the therapeutic process. Cube 3 is the dimension from which I drew the raw dream imagery some of us shared on Santorini, the dreams I lightly tended or "pruned" into the read-aloud version of *Dreaming in Santorini* (not included in this chapter).

In this third dimension, iconic dream imagery morphs into the possibility of narrative. Here images not only come alive, they come *to* life, differently. Something in the psyche transforms itself into an equation that tips in the balance like a seesaw, and images appear no longer static and transparent. In Cube 3, we relate dream experience to a place outside of and other than the place of one's own skin, by which I mean the dream speaks to an actual physical place and time: last night, we say, or suddenly, or yesterday, or this morning. Here dream images begin to form story. Whereas iconic imagery beggars even simple description, here – where "morning breaks" or "light begins to dawn" – or whatever image consciousness uses to conjure up beginning-warmth-feeling-movement, personal associations feel relevant. Images become context-related and story begins.

Iconic images have teleological coherence. Even though iconic coherence limits us to describing what happens in the present, we need it to anchor us firmly *in* the present, in a world of objects and facts that exist today, here, and now. Stories, however, relate *within* themselves, so they can *relate us to other dimensions* – to place in time. Stories have what I call *practical* coherence. Narrated events lead us toward a goal of some kind, good or bad.

*The iconic coherence of my dream would be: I see a black baby woolly mammoth waving its trunk (Cube 2). But in Cube 3, the "story" cube, my small dream begins to fill out. On waking, I remember, I associated a memory from twenty or thirty years ago: in a magazine called* Science News, *I came across an article about Russian scientists (working in Siberian glaciers) who had uncovered the frozen remains of a small black woolly mammoth. The scientists hoped to salvage enough viable genetic material to bring the creature alive again and were proposing to try.*

*I told this story to my analyst and commented, "Lordy, can you imagine how lonely it would feel to be brought to life again and discover that you were the only one alive of your own kind?"*

*I remember she made note of my response.*

*This time in Santorini, however, I muse, a baby mammoth joyfully waves at me and I'm full of joy to see it. No frozen remains here, only lively delight on both sides. Not much actual story around the image of this little mammoth, either, except my story of an early association. Another memory, this one tactile: how like a stiff little toothbrush the back of a real baby elephant felt to my fingers (once on a trip to the African jungle) when I stroked it, even though it looked soft.*

Big collective stories, by which I mean our big myths, combine the iconicity of Cube 2 and the narrative of Cube 3. Despite being set in the past, myths refer us to the present, to something happening now. Apparently, even before psychology, myth did not dwell in the past for its own sake. Myth exists to shed light on whatever present it inhabits (note how I borrowed from the mythic dimension to name the Pillar of Isis, for example; and the mythic figure of Poseidon appeared among dreams gathered in Santorini). In part, this makes it possible to use mythic figures psychologically: now, as in the past, myth is explanatory. Mythic thinking both establishes and encloses a psychological arena in which human experience and actions can be oriented because myths attribute meaning to human reality.

Stories, too, occur in the past, but a story also anchors us firmly in "before." And we create stories more consciously. Telling a story, we say, "when I was a child," or "last night I dreamed," or "I heard that such-and-so," or "it so happened," or simply, "I remember."[17] An old saying suggests that the gods created human beings because they love stories. We love stories too, for they weave our inner and outer realities together.

Articulating our own narrative can help us make sense of life. But some of us need help from someone else to do this. I asked a young woman in her early thirties to write an *anamnesis,* a brief history of her life. Despite her enthusiasm, she got no further than age 12. Not until then did she become *painfully* self-aware, conscious of the fact that by the time she was 12 years old her life had become so confused and scrambled that even years later she literally could not string together cohesively certain memories of a particular time. Narratologists tell us that a guided revision of our personal story helps us heal, and that was true for her. Her ability to narrate a fuller, more cohesive story of her life depended on therapeutic relationships with several people who knew how to listen. It also depended on dreams that brought her an ongoing story from another realm, unspooling itself to her waking mind in a series that bundled together images and feelings hauled up from the depths of each nightly excursion.

Here, in Cube 3, we begin to suspect our lives may have a plot. The simple appearance of images may begin a thaw – *is this what happened with my joyful woolly mammoth?*

Now I caution you analysts who are already clambering up to the Fourth and Fifth Cubes (Cubes 4 and 5) and analyzing this image (frozen instinct, early trauma, and so on) against premature translation "upward" into the mind and rational meaning. It's important to stay on the Cube 3 level of simple narration and associative richness for as long as possible, so the living psyche feels made room for instead of being colonized into a "mind object." It is also better for the patient. Leaping to Cube 5 may defend against the messiness of Cube 3, but staying with narrative helps both patient and therapist loosen and relax interwoven feeling that is as unconsciously tangled and densely knotted as the seaweed of Sedna's hair.[18] Like the shamans of Sedna's story, we must feel our way toward a manner of approach that combs through and gently releases those knots and tangles, rather than seeking to net them in understanding. In this place, feelings are metaphor. It is too early for meaning.

Along with an ability to string our dream images together comes a capacity to revise a sense of a personal role in our own story. This is particularly true if we've spent years embedded in other people's stories – those of our parents, our friends, our ancestors – or other people's stories of ourselves (particularly the stories our parents told themselves about us) – or if we've spent our childhoods overwhelmed by myriad pressures of a particular environment or culture. If we've never been able to sense what having a private myth might feel like, it is certain we've never had a story of our own.

Recent neuroscience supports the idea that retrieving specific personal words is essential to an individual sense of self because no one person can tell another person's story from the inside out. And it is the same with personal feeling and with the images from our dreams. That I tell my personal story in ways that reflect my personal idiosyncrasies is to be expected. But we tell our unconscious stories through collective avenues of expression we hold in common: through body language (posture and gesture) and physical symptoms (illnesses), or facial expressions and emotions. However we tell our stories, all of us *find* the stories that we can tell as we go along; we can't think them up beforehand. That our bodies sleep slowly, over hours and hours and night after night, enables dreaming to add to our lives not only the lived time it takes for the psyche to re-imagine elements of our personal story *but also the lived time it takes to re-imagine Being.*

Sleeping, we keep pace with our donkey self, close to the earth and close to the seasons, plodding along. Led as we are to words by the psyche's parade of images, we are also led to a wordless experience of ourselves that can gradually fill in a sense of "*here* I am, now, in *this* place." Literally, we are trying to re-locate ourselves in time and space. The *quantity of time* matters because only a sequence of images (sequences take time, they can't be intuited or thought out) paves the way for a core experience wherein we feel ourselves, and feel *for* ourselves, most simply, "I am who I am."[19]

In Santorini, sitting on an island formed from the molten magma of a volcano, I found the mythic image of the Greek Goddess Hestia.[20] Hestia is, I think, the goddess of warmth – not volcanic warmth, necessarily, but earthy warmth and the warmth of place – a "place of fire," meaning fire built and tended by human beings, fire lit by human significance.[21] Hestia marks the sacred space symbolized by hearth fire and temple flame. I will use my musings on Hestia and the Bronze Age peoples who disappeared in the fiery eruption of Akrotiri some 4000 years ago to illustrate how my mind meanders and creates mythic resonance at the level of Cube 3.

I found Santorini extraordinary. I had read about ancient Thera and modern Santorini, and I've had a book of beautiful reproductions of the Akrotiri murals in my library for years. I rejoiced to be there and finally see them for myself. I had also read historic accounts of the volcanic eruptions and the disappearance of the Akrotiri civilization. Unlike the people of Pompeii, Akrotirians were not found buried in the ruins of Thera. Apparently the Akrotirians left before the big eruption.[22] I like to imagine how *they* imagined (accurately, it seems) what was going to happen, for archaeologists think that the people of Akrotiri moved out after an earthquake some years earlier. Clearly, when their mountain spoke, these people listened. Might that be how they survived the fiery destruction that brought Thera, their impressively civilized early city, to an end?

*Probably woolly mammoths were extinct before the Akrotirians arrived, or at least by the time they left. Generally speaking, woolly mammoths were highly plastic mammals capable of surviving great shifts in climate and environmental variation. Looking to Wikipedia, I find that a small band of woolly mammoths survived on Wrangel Island until 4000 years ago. Where is Wrangel Island? Can I wrangle more meaning? Maybe mammoths did roam Thera. The ecology must have been different then – not many sedges and grasses on this stony island now.*[23]

167

Colorful murals found at Akrotiri and painstakingly reconstructed depict a graceful, sea-going people moving among lovely plants, exotic animals, and the peaceful activities of everyday life. Surely Hestia was known here, but probably not by name, for our mythic Hestia is a classical Greek goddess. Even in Greece Hestia was rarely depicted as a woman; more, she was *essential* presence. Known as the fire of hearth and home, Hestia was everywhere hidden, with few shrines. Without Hestia neither dark nor light was warm.

In Ancient Greece (and in Thera, I imagine), Hestia centered not only hearth and home but also *heart* and home, the inner and outer warmth that makes human life possible. Aliveness at the center is still the source of our most transforming knowledge, so I imagine Hestia's realm as the warmth of centered feeling. I imagine Hestia blessed and warmed the conference center that we inhabited as we told our dreams and stories, turning it into sacred space. Hestia allows life to *be*.

Nevertheless, at the most basic level, fire is fire, and fiery. Remember Jung saying "the body's carbon is simply carbon – hence 'at bottom,' psyche is simply 'world'"?[24] That's the level at which I mean "fire is fire." Goddesses are not simply sources of comfort. In pondering Hestia's more complex nature, let's imagine we can experience Hestia's nature in warmth that ranges from the gentle glow of embers on a hearth that lights our faces and heats our food to the warmth of the living body. Hestia is in the lingering glow we feel when we find ourselves at the center of someone's gentle attention. She's in the warmth of affection we exchange, or even in the delicious feel of morning sunlight on our skin after a cold night. Because Hestia has to do with heat at the heart of matter, she has to do with heat at the heart of the earth, more to do with the earth's molten core than with the heat of the sun. Here, perhaps, is Hestia's hidden link with the fiery magma of Akrotiri's volcano.

Hestia's hidden nature, even her relative absence from our collective imagination, lends both substance and necessity to my personal feeling for darkness and shadow. Perhaps my awareness of Hestia's presence helps me turn and deepen a quick, collective take on darkness as simply the absence of light. Hestia's centering warmth works to transform my collective fear of the dark and all that is nameless. She helps me ignite a cautious appreciation for all that prefers to remain hidden and unexamined, unnoticed and unseen. (Perhaps Hestia qualifies as a Patron Goddess of Depth Psychology.)

*Wrangel Island is in the Arctic Ocean between the Chukchi Sea and East Siberian Sea, on the 180-degree meridian. It belongs to Russia. My little black dream mammoth wasn't frozen like the one the Russians found. Maybe Santorini's Hestinian warmth thawed it out. Mammoths were warm-blooded creatures, although they were at home in the cold. (I suppose adaptability is what scientists mean by "plastic.") Mammoths lived in the Arctic, in Siberia. Today their image brings to mind survival, hunger, and curiosity . . . and loneliness, solitude, and the alchemical nigredo. But my little mammoth was glad to see me. And I was glad to see it. At first I was intensely curious, wondering at seeing such a creature, then I responded to the joy and greeting – did I smile, in my dream? I don't remember, but I smile now, recalling it.*

Aliveness at the center shifts a dark, foolish, unseeing ignorance toward a wise memory of hidden, cooling shade, and necessary shelter. Aliveness at the center transforms a prison into a sanctuary. Homer sings of Hestia[25] in one of the *Homeric Hymns*. And Plato had Socrates say that *the essence of things* is called Hestia.

Musing on Hestia, I remember that any revelation of spirit happens to us in the material world, and that because spiritual life is uniquely ours, it is also completely up to us. Hestia's abiding warmth reminds me that any experience of eternity happens to us in time, and that *here* is where we are. *Here* is where we live. Each of us as individuals may know only the space of a single body, for we are each bounded by an individual skin, yet skin is immensely responsive to whatever surrounds it, remaining as permeable as it was in the womb. And as we were each once both in and of a single human womb, we are now – each one of us – both in and of the earth. At this moment in time, here is home and home is here, even in Thera on the lip of the caldera. Wide awake and deep asleep, we *Are*. *This world* is our Human Place. And out of this world we dream.

## Fourth Cube (Cube 4): working with the imagery of dreams

Poets weave dream images and visions into poems. We ladle out whatever we need from Cube 4, pouring our efforts into and out of form. Literature and the arts, all our creative efforts, shape our collective memory by giving to ever-so transitory ephemera "a local habitation and a name."[26] This is how art is born from instinct. And even if instinct has been badly wounded, the psyche moves as if to keep channels of energy open – open for healing, open for expression, open for life, for this is what a dream is – a channel of psychic energy.

We help shape our collective memory when we dance our dreams or paint them or do active imagination. Here we do not deal with raw dream imagery, as we did in Cube 3, because more ego effort is involved. The body dreams on, and we, on waking, harness the psyche's creative energy and meld it with personal desire so it may be channeled toward collective ends. Dreams crop up as the substance with which we think and the face of what we will become. But *we* have to provide the creative attention.[27] Might life as a whole have a plot?

Perception is not whimsical, but fatal, Ralph Waldo Emerson tells us, because perception is also thinking (of another kind), for re-cognition (perception) depends on grasping both place and function within overall patterns.[28] For those of us who spend time and attention "working on ourselves" and the imagery of our dreams, the half-opened-door or half-closed-window nature of dreams lends living another dimension, completing and filling out our 360-degree experience of being alive. Our ability to perceive dream activity changes over time, so given a dream's elusive nature our dreams may come to represent transformation within the psyche. Yet marked changes in overall cultural patterns represent transformation of the Deep Imagination, not necessarily transformation within our human perceptual system.[29] I am talking about mythic change. Unless we are too ill to do so, we will always look for meaning because we are meaning-making animals, so meaning remains of paramount importance. But one glorious thing about an image – whether in myth, imagination, or dream – *is that, by nature, image always has more than one meaning.*

That is why, among a plethora of meanings, an image itself can appear to remain stable. If I tell someone to imagine a white elephant, he or she pictures a white elephant. If I say "white elephant" in Spanish or French, people from different cultures probably see in their mind's eye a white elephant. In this way, image (as we find it in iconic Cube 2, at least) doesn't change. This stability of image is what lends stability to our notion that image is the language of the psyche, as well as the language of the soul. Images reveal themselves to us or we discover them by feeling our way into them, or we perceive an image, as in a dream: *we don't "make up" images by "thinking" images into being.* In the presence of image, we re-connect with our senses and imagination, our bodies and emotion.[30]

On the other hand we can't detach image from larger meaning either, for *as* the language of the soul, image is also a universal language of spirit. Each of us may differ in his or her meaning of a single image, and all are probably true. This is because even if an image is singular – *like my black baby woolly mammoth* – the inherent generosity of image is vast enough to hold all readings.

Until recently we did not imagine cultural transformation in terms of events experienced within the time frame of single, individual lives. Cultural change happens faster these days, and I wonder if one factor in this generalized speed-up of time isn't the increase in the attentive exercise of Deep Imagination on the part of so many of us.[31] What if *intentional* focused attention on the Deep Imagination on the part of *many* proves to be as important as any singular meaning found by any single person in our cultural myths or individual dreams? Here I'm looping back to my earlier comment: *that* we use images, as well as *how* we use them, plays a large part in the healing function of dreams, as well as in the cohesive containing power we experience in the emerging, ongoing myths we engage in spinning now.[32]

*Animals. Animals. What does it mean, to dream of animals? Instinct, of course. A vague memory of Barbara Hannah in Zurich, years ago – dogs, cats, horses, and Jim Hillman, lots of talk about animals; and Jung's comment on how animals can't help but remain true to their nature but we do not. An Irish woman's wry comment: "Every four-legged creature is a saint."*

*We are the only creatures I know of who concern themselves with spirit in any manifestation. But spirit doesn't define our species as much as our capacity for ordinary consciousness does, I think, whether our capacity for consciousness is fully developed or not. Perhaps I add to my personal definition of what it means to be human a capacity to deepen and expand imagination. Imagination is more important than knowledge. Another personal association: remember the children's game, "What kind of animal would you be?" Once in my early teens I replied, "Huh. I have trouble enough being the animal I am; I need help being 'this' animal." Others felt that my answer spoiled the game – I wasn't playing fair. But I meant what I said.*

Throughout his writing, British object-relations thinker D. W. Winnicott suggests that observation is also invention; that as infants, for example, we both discover reality and create it in what Winnicott calls the "transitional space" that exists between two parties involved in any relationship beginning with that of mother and child.[33] The Buddhists remind us that a similar two-sided process of discovery and creation takes place throughout our lives (Winnicott says so, too): that when we meet the incidental events of our lives (including the incidental imagery of dreams) with the same intense gaze that we bring to the *chosen* objects of our attention (focused attention, again), *we enter a gate to original thought that opens us to creativity.*

All art springs from heightening, deepening, and widening our capacity for attention, along with a sense of craft, a lot of waiting, and a tremendous amount of hard work. Every image in a poem, for example, portrays possible states of soul. No matter the circuitous route psyche takes, personal creativity springs directly from instinct, and Cube 4 marks the dimension of our dreaming-mind psyche where we experience personal access to creativity.

Cube 4 marks where intentional, attentive work with dreams offers something extraordinary. Even if our instincts have been injured, we've seldom been injured so badly (though some of us have) that we don't begin to dream again; and the psyche's creative energies may flow most freely through our deepest wounds. Representing the psyche's healing process, dreams open and reopen channels of instinctively creative energy. We learn from each other to experience dreams as fully as possible, how to read and track them, and how to trace the energy patterns dreams express. Then the energy-channels that dreams are, and the energies of dream-progression, and the energies native to the directions pointed to by images, all blossom into inherently creative living. And all of us inherit the possibility of living a creative life.

Merlin Donald, a Canadian psychologist, suggests that the progress of our human minds can only be adequately described in terms of cultural achievements. Donald is not talking about a "group mind," for he imagines our individual minds remain sealed in their individual biological containers. But as culture-creating creatures, says Donald, we do very little alone. In his view, we depend on culture for virtually everything that is unique to our world, including language and thinking.[34] Donald speaks for the collective psyche and what he says is surely so, yet in his view the collective is more paramount than it is for many of us who practice individual clinical work.

For those of us who work long and hard with the psyche, words cannot be the meaning of anything in itself. This is to say that words do not "capture" moments as much as communicate them. Importantly and paradoxically, words do bridge our human isolation and loneliness, but they do so by breaking them without eradicating them. Think of an early experience of reading a poignant poem, for example; perhaps you, too, suddenly felt in your bones, "Oh, someone else is lonely, too?" A new relationship of an unknown-but-felt *kinship* with someone else, alive or dead, may seem unimaginably fragile, but relationships of this kind are real to us, too; they warm us, they culture us, and we expand.[35]

We think of culture as consisting of sets of shared habits, languages, or customs that define populations of people. Culture is also a gigantic cognitive web that defines and constrains the parameters of our memories and our dreams, our knowledge and our thoughts. Deeper still, *all cultural forms, including dreams, manifest, provide, and define human relatedness.* Hence, cultural aspects of our lives dwell under the aegis of the Greek god Eros.[36]

Nevertheless, we *experience* personal experience as if it were our own (rather than collective) – as if physical eyesight were insight. So when open awareness of the world's effortless expression happens to summon us, we cannot help but answer. Then the voice of nature and the voice of dream meet in a duet that we find ourselves as helpless to refuse (or refute) as one loon exchanging calls with another over the lake. By the time this amazed surrender happens, we've been moved through gravity, through tension, through attachment, and on through affection into what we in our present culture – not in imaginal Greek memory – called Eros, too – for why else does song arise from deep within us, if not for love?

## Fifth Cube (Cube 5): using our dreams with intention

Here we think about dreams and analyze dream images. Whereas Cube 4 opened us to instinctive creativity and the possibility of experience as well as expression of soul, in Cube 5, we find dreams meaningful and take them to heart. This deepens and matures our spiritual sensibilities. Cube 5 is where we lend psychological energy toward developing what we think of as *ego strength* – a sense of ourselves that is supple enough to embrace psychological, biological, spontaneous self-experience; that is flexible enough to *hold* (contain? embrace? – delay through necessary transformation and then *express*) the instinctive push of creative energy set loose in Cube 4 because pure un-ego-mediated instinct is not what we mean by art or culture.

When dreams become relevant to our personal lives, we become our own shamans. This involves an odd "ego dance": when I stop trying to understand a dream (e.g., make it *mean* something that feels as if it would *fit* – what? left-brain understanding? a cultural format?), the dream loosens, mirroring my relaxing ego; the image comes "alive" (we can say "shamanic") and the dream becomes *symbolic experience that I undergo.* When a dream doesn't have to mean anything other than what it is, a dream becomes the shaman that the psyche offers by nature[37] – a wounding/healing symbolic experience. Some will say that we "extract" meaning, and others will say that we "make" it. However we imagine that it happens, here we sense strongly the ongoing process in the psyche; and here we are pulled into narrative and find extended story. When we glimpse the possibility that *we* may be partial images too, we come into focus in our personal lives.

*Words bridge loneliness, but so do images. The joyfully waving trunk of my woolly mammoth bridges – what – its isolation in time – my isolation in time – that lonely feeling, as if I were "one" of a kind alone in the world – my isolation in sleep, in life? Loneliness itself hailing me past my puny considerations of time and kin – both of us feeling, "Hello! I'm glad to see you! I'm so glad you've come!"*

*Were I of a more Freudian persuasion, would I decide my black woolly mammoth is simply a stand-in for my unborn twin and leave it at that? That I dream of my "other self," some part who lived briefly but didn't fully make it into life and remains "frozen in the past" – an "Other" who is also me, hence, my unknown Beloved? Any strict translation of one thing into another – "this means that" – can seize me or any of us when we're into our own material, dreams or otherwise. "Reaching for signs" lives in the psyche's world, the world of complexes, more than it does in the symbolizing mind.*

*Beyond personal meanings, the image of my black woolly mammoth opens me to broader musings. Every person and every creature alive expresses a miracle of biocosmic development and evolution. How often do we think like that? How often do I really open myself to the extraordinary gift of existence? How often do I fully experience my life, allowing myself to feel how each moment exists only once in the vastness of time?*

At this level, a series of dreams begins to make sense. Our ability to read a series of dreams becomes like an ability to read music. We feel how to grasp the turn and re-turn of rhythm and theme. We discover mythic motifs. We become psychologically thin-skinned, able to read emotional manifestations with a new sensitivity. And we begin to find our selves, literally and figuratively, in the midst of ongoing narrative. Because we *live* in narrative, this new narrative will hold more weight than our logical sensibilities. In other words, although logically we can't know the full outlines of the story we are living, for now, at least, we *know* and *feel* that we can't; we *know* and *feel* how the bigger picture in which we dwell is always beyond our ability to imagine.

I call Cube 5 the place of the head-ego. It is also the place of more defined relationship with our dreams as well as others outside ourselves, and with alchemy: analyst and patient, alchemist and *soror*. If dreams increase our available stock of reality, then here you and I trade on our dream experience both individually and together: here we become *translators* of the Real. Although to think that the transcendent materializes in day-to-day events may be a simple category mistake, an *embodied experience* of the transcendent materializing, whether we experience it in dreams or while we are awake, resonates with reports from mystics since time began. Such psychological experience often heralds the release and integration of hitherto unconscious feelings (that have been dissociated or defensively held at bay), and life becomes fuller. The simple sentience we experienced in Cube 2 – "What it feels like to be *here*" – becomes in Cube 5, "*What it feels like to be Evolution.*"[38]

In this dimension, we yearn for ego strength necessary to resist the continuing temptation to make ourselves the center of the world. We try to stretch beyond that innate capacity beautifully expressed by William Blake – to "hold infinity in the palm of a hand"[39] – and further broaden our gaze. Perhaps we become able to contemplate the possibility of tragedy for the whole of humanity. Where formerly we would have habitually rushed to symbolic understanding when a dream (our own or a patient's) pictured disaster or apocalypse, from the perspective of Cube 5 – if we can hold the dream here, deepen ourselves, and let *it* happen – even a little dream becomes creative.

*How can I perceive an image of a living creature that – in my "real" life – is extinct? My woolly mammoth belonged to a tribe, a species that was probably hunted to death for food by my own kind around the end of the last Ice Age. Or at least hunted for its ivory, say some – even then.[40]*

*Does this dream greet me across eons of time and space to remind me that extinction is not the end of all life? Or that extinction could happen to my species, too?[41] Is it supposed to help me contemplate the not-too-remote possibility of extinction so that I grieve?*

*Well, that thought isn't new. What is new is that I say it out loud. I fight despair and struggle to keep it private. Perhaps this dream nudges me to risk being heard as a doomsayer, a Cassandra.*

*My despair seems seeded by my self-referential species: we seem unredeemingly self-referential! To my left lies a book called* The Sixth Extinction: An Unnatural History.[42] *To my right, the latest issue of* Science[43] *features an article titled "Exploring Martian Habitability." Will this be the legacy of our species? Like St. Paul's imagination of redemption, the idea of extinction applies to ALL of creation – to other creatures, plants, trees, and oceans – not just to us. Do we imagine we will cope with extinction by moving to Mars?*

*Is this a shadow aspect of human consciousness? Most of us feel that a capacity for consciousness is one of the defining gifts of our kind. As analysts we ponder whether consciousness creates our observer-dependent reality. We strive to "become conscious." We wonder what the word really means; we say consciousness only comes about in relationship; and some of us remember Jung's warning that "the world hangs by a thin thread . . . "[44] Do we remember that Jung stressed the importance of the psyche at the end of his life, not the importance of consciousness?*

*Our little planet, so trivial in galactic immensities, is all we have to live on. Our self-referential treatment of it, if not destroying the planet, is destroying aspects of the earth that we find livable, that we call home. Not to mention other species and plants. "In wildness is the preservation of the world," wrote Thoreau;[45] but not this kind of wildness,* our *kind of wildness: what I seem to see is flight behavior, something gone terribly wrong. Perhaps our world will not be preserved.*

*(And I'm not going near the issue of how savagely we treat each other, in a manner and with behavior possessed by no other species known. I remember Jung suggesting we would do well to possess some "imagination for evil," for only fools permanently disregard the conditions of their own nature.[46])*

In Cube 5, we have to realize that even the workings of chance can reveal the self. As creatures of contingency, we are inseparable from all that happens and from everything we touch.[47] Yet our brief lives don't just *happen;* they require a modicum of space and time. We *dream in place* because our lives *take place.* Our lives take *up* place, and they are more than metaphorical events. Our dreams *and* our lives take place in the physical world, in a current of lived events, and within shared awareness of interconnected being. The more that particularity and feeling, individual perception and emotion join hands, the more aliveness permeates us all.

One notion we hold of the psyche is religious[48] and allows for spiritual experience. By "spiritual experience," I mean a quality of discernment and relatedness to our lives. Other notions of the psyche also help rejoin us to ourselves, to each other, and to the world. The creativity of the psyche – not necessarily spirit – sends us images that link and couple; the creativity of the psyche (not necessarily spirit) fashions those song lines of images and soul that lead us home.

Sometimes I imagine that as our nights circle the globe and country after country falls dark, we all lie down to sleep beneath night's shadow, bending like grasses in a great dark wind. The wind encircles the globe and I hear the psyche breathe. Psyche's great lungs open and close, her huge soft wings moving like the great dark wings of *The Angel of History*,[49] her deep breaths as rhythmic as the movement of the tides.

We are asked to bring presence to our individual lives, and presence is relational. How we access what is, and how we offer ourselves to what is, has to do with presence. It seems to me we need presence in order to willingly inhabit our lives both from the bottom up and from the top down. Presence is what we draw on when we are asked to experience fully every uncertain transport and every suffering that makes up a personal fate.

We know from individual experience as well as from clinical work that one's inability to be present to life – to inhabit his or her life fully – indicates a psyche in travail, a psyche laboring under the impact of traumatic experience whose earlier existence deforms a capacity for full presence in the moment. Formed by early trauma, psychological defenses[50] prevent us from fully metabolizing personal experience. We also know that when we can't bring full presence to our lives, someone else's presence, therapist or friend, can help us move the psyche on. We need these links and linking. We need human mediation. We need help from each other. And we need the dreaming psyche to jump-start and nourish the Deep Imagination so that blocked and suppressed powers of memory re-emerge and merge again with personal desire.[51]

So in addition to wrapping our imaginations around images of a musical chord and a *Holon*, let's imagine the Pillar of Isis as five dimensions of conscious presence available to us as we are able to avail ourselves of them. Because full presence in our lives is required, we know, and yet must question our knowing; we feel, and yet must question our feeling; this, lest we forget that "we are such stuff as dreams are made on," as Shakespeare's Prospero tells us, and that each "little life/ is rounded with a sleep."[52]

And, although our times feel perilous, we still *have* our little lives, and so we tend them and care for each other. We tend our dreams and we question them. Somehow we've got to agree together to wander (together and apart) for most of our lives lost in the dark, just as we are, where every journey of the soul begins again.

## Black baby woolly mammoth reanimated

*It's now the end of September 2012: Don and I fly home from Santorini to resume our summer life in Calf's Nose, our house built on a point of land that extends into the Atlantic Ocean off the coast of Trinity East, Newfoundland. My little black woolly mammoth comes with me.*

*In December during the long drive home from Canada to Albuquerque, New Mexico, meeting with family and friends over the holidays and moving back into the other half of our lives, the image of a black woolly mammoth begins to appear everywhere.*

*Reclining in the dentist's chair while my teeth are being repaired, I watch a cartoon story of a woolly mammoth that carries a small human boy-child to safety on top of its head through glacial country. The mammoth finds cave drawings depicting the death of its ancestors by hunters carrying spears. As the mammoth grieves, the little boy clasps the mammoth's trunk and hugs it. Mammoth and child resume their journey.*

*The December 2012* New Yorker *magazine runs an article on "Repopulating a Pleistocene National Preserve in the Netherlands" with species similar to prehistoric animals and a short story about someone who steals a baby mammoth-like creature from a zoo and tries to keep it at home until it escapes.*

*We are eerily connected to collective consciousness, not only to Jung's collective unconscious, and – to both – not only through our dreams.*

*I continue to read current news: "Regenesis" (a TED talk in February 2013) tells about a current genome assembly of extinct species like passenger pigeons. Someone characterizes our time – here and now – as an "era of the deliberate and successful re-creation of extinct ecosystems," and as the "dawn of de-extinction."*

*A conversation ensues:* Atlantic Monthly, *TED, and* Science *are publishing articles on reanimation, that is, bringing to life extinct species. "Can We Do It" merges with "Should We Do It" in interesting ways.* Scientific American*'s Board of Editors publishes Opinion and Analysis that concludes we ought not "reanimate," that all projects to revive long-gone species are sideshows to the real extinction crisis.*[53]

*I learn that "re-wilding" (to these scientists) means the clearing of forests so forestlands become biodiverse meadows able to support different (often older) populations of wild life. (What, I wonder, about our need for the trees of those dwindling forests? Aren't they the lungs of the earth, as we know them?) Really, re-wilding seems to mean large-scale restoration of complex natural ecosystems and restoration of lost natural food chains that once surrounded us.*

*Why was my mammoth so young? Is this small creature my inner beast? Ravenous? Not often now – except for understanding. Concerned with survival? Yes . . . O yes . . . and tribal, as many creatures are tribal. Lonely? Maybe not as lonely as it was before it was dreamed. Now that I know it roams the heartlands of my inner world, I'm not as lonely either . . . or sad. Small, dear, funny beast.*

*Not sad? Actually this woolly mammoth was not at all sad. Nor was I, in the dream. The true feeling of this dream was joyous mutual meeting and recognition. A phrase comes to my mind, written by a twelfth-century Beguine whose joy in life returned full flood when she found herself able to live "without a why."*[54] *Maybe living without a "why" is how my baby mammoth and I feel when fears for survival don't utterly destroy that greater feeling of gratitude, a simple ability to rejoice in being alive.*

*Browsing through the Albuquerque Museum before we leave, I read that there were mammoths in the Rio Grande Valley 12,000 years ago (when there were perhaps fifty human beings in this area, total.) That's close to home.*

*In Albuquerque, still preparing for our long migration to our northern home, I worry as always about Pooks, our beloved Maine Coon Cat, who detests car travel. "I think she'll be OK" Don says. "She'll survive. I mean, she's an animal." "So," I hear myself reply, "are we."*

# Notes

1 First published as "Sounding the chord of having a dream," in Robin van Löben Sels, "Dreaming in Gersau, Switzerland," in Stacy Wirth, Isabelle Meier, and John Hill (eds), *Jungian Odyssey 2010, Trust and Betrayal: Dawnings of Consciousness,* pp. 153–62, Jungian Odyssey Series, Vol. 111, New Orleans, LA, Spring Journal Books, 2011, p. 159. Republished with acknowledgement and thanks to Spring Journal Books.

2 This essay is a modified version of a talk presented at the *Ancient Greece, Modern Psyche* Conference in Santorini, Greece, September 2012.

3 This "bottom-up" mode of "reading" the Pillar of Isis helps me focus on the full experience of other sources of imagery too. Habitual reliance on words as well as images from the "top-down" privileges a habit of looking for meaning over more visceral sensation and feeling.

4 See Sallie Nichols, *Jung and Tarot: An Archetypal Journey*, York Beach, ME, Red Wheel/Weiser, 1980.

5 In van Löben Sels, "Dreaming in Gersau, Switzerland," p. 159.

6 Arthur Koestler first used the term *Holon* in *The Ghost in the Machine*, New York, Macmillan, 1968, p. 48.

7 Jung looked first to *unconscious* material for emerging evidence of the transcendent function. Opposites become a foundation for each other, seeding each other, a *complexio oppositorum*, paradoxical and antinomic. Jung alluded to this condition in *Seven Sermons to the Dead*, when he said that the pairs of opposites do not exist because they cancel each other out. C. G. Jung, *The Red Book: Liber Novus*, ed. Sonu Shamdasani, London, W. W. Norton & Company, 2009, pp. 347–8.

8 In a time when consciousness was weather, I imagine that great swirls of myth emerged like stationary psychological "storms" out of the geo-eco-psychological experience of particular peoples in particular places at particular times: think of Zeus and his Pantheon, Thor and his Fellow Gods, perhaps even Yahweh. Connected with the people and places of their emergence, these great stories are never simply interchangeable. They come together around universal human commonalities; when the point of a myth is to explain death, say, it doesn't matter whether the context is Babylonian or Native American. The presence of mythic figures in dreams and the emergence of "mythic thinking," belong in Cube 2 of the Pillar of Isis.

9 It also explains why someone who has experienced a diagnosis of cancer remains shaken even if the cancer is cured. Trust in the integrity of the body has been betrayed and does not forget.

10  D. W. Winnicott, *Playing and Reality*, London, Routledge, 2005; and Masud Khan, *The Hidden Selves: Between Theory and Practice in Psychoanalysis*, London, Karnac Books, 1983, are contemporary British object relations writers.

11  Here memory is associated with early experience that bestows a sense of personal identity. This kind of memory is not deliberate: we remember something or we do not; experience internalizes itself within us, or it does not.

12  A. N. Schore, *Affect Dysregulation and Disorders of the Self*, New York, Norton, 2003.

13  I think of D. W. Winnicott's review of Jung's *Memories, Dreams, Reflections*. D. W. Winnicott, "Review of *Memories, Dreams, Reflections*," in C. Winnicott, R. Shepherd, and M. Davis (eds), *Psychoanalytic Explorations*, Cambridge, MA, Harvard University Press, 1989, pp. 482–92.

14  We inoculate ourselves through dream and play. The way inoculations work; we let a little bit of the energy into us: too little, and fear still holds sway; too much, and we feel swamped.

15  William James, *The Varieties of Religious Experience: A Study in Human Nature*, New York, Modern Library, 1905.

16  Generally, this attitude is felt to portray Jung's attitude vis-à-vis unconscious material. Freud postulated "dreamwork" that consisted of unconscious operations like censorship, displacement, and condensation, which mirrors his "hermeneutics of suspicion" that unconscious material does not state what it means but needs translation. See Carlo Strenger, "The classic and the romantic vision in psychoanalysis," *International Journal of Psychoanalysis*, 1989, vol. 70, p. 593.

17  In dreams, as in life, a story or scenario may be oddly repetitive and lack a progressive narrative. Early unremembered trauma tends to set up shockingly repetitive psychological situations in life as well as in dreams.

18  Sedna, a mythic figure from Inuit culture, dwells at the bottom of the ocean under the ice. Betrayed by her father, Sedna is pushed into the ocean. When she tries to climb back into the boat, her father cuts off her fingers. Sedna's fingers become the seals, walruses, and other creatures of the sea, circling around her in the depths. During times of hunger, shamans of the northern tribes descend to the depths to comb through Sedna's seaweed hair, hoping to persuade her to release seals and fish to the surface of the water (even below the ice) for the hunters so that the people will not starve.

19  In the same way I emphasize *Place*, I emphasize *Here*. When called by God in the Garden, Adam steps forth with "*Here* I am." Turning aside from the Burning Bush, Moses hears God's call and responds with "*Here* I am, Lord;" Abraham, too. When asked His name, Yahweh replies differently: "I Am Who I Am." Even if we question that there is such a thing as a "whole self," (counterintuitively, all of life's present situations are seamless and sufficient), a personal response to any summons from the Self toward healing and wholeness feels essential. Marion Woodman refers to this as a mythic experience of the Feminine, an experience of The Virgin (as in "virgin forest," meaning uncorrupted, full of innate possibility), a mythic dimension of experience that becomes a resource in men as well as women. See, for example, Woodman's *Sitting by the Well: Bringing the Feminine to Consciousness through Language, Dreams, and Metaphor*, Sounds True Audio Learning Course, 2007.

20  For information about Hestia I consulted Jean Boland's books, *Goddesses in Everywoman: Powerful Archetypes in Women's Lives*, San Francisco, Harper & Row, 1984; and *Goddesses in Older Women: Archetypes in Women Over Fifty*, New York, HarperCollins, 2001. Thank you, Jean.

21  This spring at a brass foundry I watched a "pour" of molten metal. Feeling immense heat penetrate skin and bone despite the shielding distance, I remembered Hestia in terms of a Zen koan: "In the center of the cosmos, between heaven and earth, there is a treasure hidden in the body." Warmth, I answered; Hestia is warmth, the treasure hidden in the body.

22  In a letter to her Unknown Master, the poet Emily Dickinson wrote about not "hearing the mountain": "Vesuvius dont talk" she writes, "– Etna – dont – (Thy) one of them – said a syllable – a thousand years ago, and Pompeii heard it, and hid forever." Dickinson goes on to describe Pompeii: "She could'nt look the world in the face, afterward – I suppose – Bashfull Pompeii!" quoted in Mary Ruefle, *Madness, Rack, and Honey: Collected Lectures*, Seattle and New York, Wave Books, 2012, p. 213.

23  According to Wikipedia, woolly mammoths lived across eastern Eurasia during the early Pliocene some 200,000 years ago. Their closest relative is the Asian elephant. Europeans knew mammoths in the 1600s. A newborn mammoth weighed about 90 kilograms, or 200 pounds. They were covered in fur; adults had long curved tusks; and they could live to the age of 60. Mammoths did coexist with early humans, but they disappeared from the mainland range around 10,000 years ago, probably hunted to extinction.

24  C. G. Jung, "The stages of life," *The Structure and Dynamics of the Psyche*, in *The Collected Works of C. G. Jung*, Vol. 8, Princeton, Princeton University Press, ¶752. (Subsequent references to Jung's *Collected Works* are referred to by CW and volume number.)

25  Paired with Hermes.

26  William Shakespeare, *A Midsummer Night's Dream*, New York, Dover Publications, V, i, ll. 12–17.

27  A Zen teacher suggested that attention is love. Attention is also a Hestia form of warmth.

28  Ralph Waldo Emerson, in "Self-reliance," in *Essays: First and Second Series*, New York, Vintage Books, 1990, p. 5.

29  I think that perceptual evolution and change occur, and the psyche evolves over time, but these ideas are not my focus here.

30  James Hillman called image the language of the soul, and in early writings Jung characterized image as psyche itself. Early psychoanalytic pioneers (who called themselves "alienists") approached images from the top-down, in contrast to how we read the Pillar of Isis from the bottom-up, as I imagine images emerge from the dreaming-mind-psyche into consciousness. Jung's increasing sensitivity to image *qua* image (for example, as displayed in *The Red Book*), along with personal experience of what he later conceptualized as "developing one's psychological typology" helped him in his headlong descent out of a "primary" thinking function into the depths of imagination, a feeling life, and a painful recognition of neglect of psyche and soul. The idea of "the unconscious mind" serves as a starting point for descent out of current concepts of mind toward rediscovery of a world ensouled with ensouled selves. The psyche bridges this descent for us, and dream images form crucial links.

31  The instant culture we live in, where petroleum and dynamite allow us to move beyond space and time at an accelerated rate, allows us to believe that we do not have to follow natural laws or patterns. In the name of progress and science we pollute waterways and oceans, change the face of the planet, exploit natural mineral deposits, and create a consumer-based society that cannot be sustained, thereby putting thousands of species, including our own, in peril.

32 Anthropologists call our ability to pass on knowledge from one individual to another, or one generation to another, until someone comes along with an idea for an improvement, "cultural ratcheting." "It's not how smart you are . . . It's how well connected you are." In Heather Pringle, "Human evolution: The origins of creativity," *Scientific American*, March 2013, p. 43.

33 D W. Winnicott pursues this idea throughout his work, see especially *Playing and Reality*.

34 Merlin Donald, *A Mind So Rare: The Evolution of Human Consciousness*, New York, W. W. Norton & Company, 2001, pp. xiii–xiv.

35 Ruefle, *Madness, Rack, and Honey*, p. 95.

36 Ideas and feelings about Eros live in our Western culture under various guises (attachment, love, connection, "we are all one," interconnection, interbeing, and so on – even "the psyche"), a major one being the idea of *ubuntu* ("I am, because of you") from South Africa.

37 Usually clinicians imagine that the image of the wounded/healer (the shaman) is embodied in themselves or another person. I emphasize that as an archetypal figure, the image of the shaman inhabits a complex activated often in therapy between two people and that the psyche "shamans" a wounding/healing situation.

38 See Terrence W. Deacon, *Incomplete Nature: How Mind Emerged from Matter*, New York, W. W. Norton & Company, 2012. The extraordinarily important idea of evolution lends a trans-historical frame to Jung's idea of synchronicity. Using the experience of the psyche and the idea of evolution in a binocular fashion makes us visionary: everything we discover about the past and imagine about the future we simultaneously learn about ourselves.

39 This capacity is innate; we hone and deepen it by integrating mind and body, heart and head, sense and sensibility and perception.

40 "Siberians rarely ate mammoths: Stone Age folk mainly killed for ivory, fossils suggest." This is the title of an article by Bruce Bower, *Science News*, 13 July 2013, p. 10.

41 See Chris Stringer, *Lone Survivors: How We Came to Be the Only Humans on Earth*, New York, New York Times Books, 2012. See also Jeremy Rifkin, *The Empathic Civilization: The Race to Global Consciousness in a World in Crisis*, New York, Tarcher/Penguin, 2009. Rifkin argues that the core of the human story is a paradoxical relationship between empathy and entropy.

42 Elizabeth Kolbert, *The Sixth Extinction: An Unnatural History*, New York, Henry Holt and Company, 2014.

43 "Exploring Martian habitability," *Science*, 24 January 2014.

44 Jung continues " . . . and that thread is the psyche of man." See the YouTube video of excerpts from *Face to Face,* the filmed interview in which John Freeman talks with Carl Jung for the BBC in 1959 shortly before Jung's death. Available: <http://www.youtube.com/watch?v=FPGMWF7kU_8>.

45 From Henry David Thoreau's essay, "Walking," in *Walden & Other Writings of Henry David Thoreau*, ed. Brooks Atkinson, New York, Random House, 1965.

46 C. G. Jung, "The undiscovered self," in *Civilization in Transition*, CW 10, p. 299. Jung wrote this essay under the shadow of World War II. Before the war, Eglantyne Jebb (1876–1928), founder of Save the Children, wrote more hopefully, touching on what I characterize here as Deepening the Imagination: "We have to devise means of making known the facts in such a way as to touch the Imagination of the World" (capitalization

mine). "The world is not ungenerous, but unimaginative, and very busy." Quoted in Jasmine Whitbread, "Features: 'Inspiring women,'" *Intelligent Life*, September/October 2013.

47  Given our dawning recognition of the disastrous impact we have on the environment, we might grieve with old King Midas: granted his wish that everything he touched be turned to gold, Midas wept helplessly as his young daughter ran into his arms and became a golden, lifeless statue. See Howard Moss's poem, "King Midas," which ends "Dear Dionysus, give me back again/ ten fingertips that leave the world alone." In *The Oxford Book of American Poetry*, ed. David Lehman, Oxford, Oxford University Press, 2006, p. 677.

48  The word *religion* comes from the Latin word *religio,* which has a meaning influenced by the verb *religare* that means to bind, in the sense of "place an obligation on" (*World Book Dictionary*).

49  In 1921, Walter Benjamin purchased from Paul Klee a cherished drawing called *Angelus Novus*. Inspired to call the figure *The Angel of History*, Benjamin used the drawing to illustrate his meditations on war, later published in *Tikkun* in November 1998 in an article titled "Walter Benjamin's vision of hope and despair."

50  Donald Kalsched explicates this in Trauma and the Soul: A Psychospiritual Approach to *Human Development and Its Interruption*, London & New York, Routledge, 2013.

51  Here *memory* is an immanent power that follows its own rules, a force that hinders recall (as in forgetting) or blocks recall (as in suppression) but a force that can also be steered by insight and desire or ignited by the new requirements entailed in a therapeutic relationship.

52  William Shakespeare, *The Tempest*, Shakespeare Online, available: <http://www.shakespeare-online.com/plays/tempscenes.html>, IV, i, lines 156–8.

53  In Science Agenda: Opinion and Analysis from *Scientific American's* Board of Editors, "Do not reanimate," *Scientific American*, June 2013, p. 12.

54  Hadewijch of Brabant. See Robin van Löben Sels, *A Dream in the World: Poetics of Soul in Two Woman, Modern and Medieval*, London, Routledge, 2003.

# CLOSING TRAVELLING ARIADNE

## A romance

*Craig San Roque*

*The story[1] was recited for the closing of the* Ancient Greece, Modern Psyche *Conference at sunset, overlooking the volcanic bay of ancient Thira.*

### Ariadne at Naxos

*. . . for when I look at you even a moment*
*I cannot speak at all. My tongue is frozen, and on that instant*
*A subtle fire runs underneath my skin, with my eyes I see nothing and in my ears*
*I hear a roaring. Sweat runs down all over my body. I am paler than grass in summer*
*And I feel myself close to the edge of death.*

(From Sappho of Lesbos)[2]

### A woman alone

A woman is sleeping; she is sleeping in the sand, no blanket,
Ariadne, the woman of string, sleeping on the sand; the black sail of his ship
sailing away; sailing away to his black cliff; a crow wing cutting the water.

In her dream she saw the black sail and crow's wing throwing an old man
down into the sea; down from the cliff; and in the sand of Naxos she saw her
promised husband leaving her; she dreamed herself alone.

(Why do young men forget their fathers, young men without thought, drunken;
forgetting the promise made, forgetting the future; throwing old men and old
stars into the back of broken trucks, letting them die with no blanket?)

Ariadne asleep on the sand, dreaming of him sailing in, Dioniso in his dolphin
ship, sails of panther, sailing in; sails of wine, ropes of vine; she dreamed him
up, she dreamed him in, her husband, the new one, in his dolphin panther ship.

He came to her in the night at Naxos, the one who loosens, being bound by love, holding her, dancing and rolling; snake on the water, returning; she, asleep in the sand, dreaming; the great singer, the great wave, intoxication carried her.

## Ariadne mapping

She dreamed out the line of their travels, she mapped the way on the dusty holes of his empty heart and broken skin; the countries to travel she drew in the sand; she went ahead in her dream body; her dream ship on the waves of the inner world. She entered the countries of her sisters, she knocked at their gates and marked the walls of cities; on the sand at Naxos she did these things, laying out the track to follow, remembering Semele's baby, remembering Demeter's baby; he in her arms now on the beach at Naxos, collecting for him the lost pieces: the torn and broken infant. He who, regathered, becomes Dioniso the loosener, the vine, the indestructible life.

Ariadne the woman of string, sleeping on the sand; sometimes she follows her own thread, begun from the beginning of women in caves; the unbroken thread, right down from the beginning of time. Lose not the thread.

This is the story I tell you, the mysteries from all our beginnings, this thread began us and this track will complete us; in the sand and the blue nights, the wind on the water.

## Travelling Ariadne

Ariadne stands; she begins her travelling, she goes to the gate of the evening star; she takes the road the women travel, she passes the place of the Seven Sisters, they travel together. Ariadne gathered herself with her seven sisters, they took up their sticks and their billy cans, they took up their bedrolls and they started walking; they started walking and they started singing; they picked fruit as they travelled, they picked sweet fruit, they picked up seeds, they rolled and sorted and ground them, they carried the grinding stone, they started walking and they started singing; they did this a long time ago and they did it their way.

Sisters travel like this today, "we sing, we pick sweet fruit, we walk and we remember; today we drive in motor cars, we hit the road, driving the thread . . . we remember."

## Ariadne's thread

From Naxos, east through Anatolia, she crosses into Kybele's country, the beehive and the tambourine; she crosses into Kybele's country; south toward Egypt.

She travelled down the coast of Phoenicia, she travelled in a ship and she landed on the beach of Byblos; she met Ishtar in the room of the evening star and the dancing steps of the evening star, she and seven sisters wove into patterns.

She went down into Canaan, she travelled on a donkey, she marked the histories of the women of Israel and she learned their storyteller's art; she walked on the coast of Galilee and found the footsteps of three Marys, three women waiting for a body to fill their hands; and it was done; and after it was done they sailed for France; and she watched them go with Sarah, the black madonna weaving the gypsy path; she watched them go in a small ship drifting west, three Marys and Sarah and Lazarus alive.

And she went down into Egypt. She went down into Isis country; she learned the gathering dance and how to tie the knot of Isis, gathering pieces of Osiris scattered in the mud of the long river.

She travelled into Africa. She marked the beginnings of her people and the paintings in the caves of Tassili. The old stories and the walls alive . . .

Ariadne the woman of string, following threads, she gathered her sisters and turning northeast toward Sumeria; they followed the morning star. Ariadne with the seven sisters, flying like finches, swallows, hawks . . .

On the early morning breeze; they went northeast into the mouth of Inanna's country, into the river, the reeds and the cave; and down with her to the hook hanging on the wall; Ariadne recited the list of powers and drank beer with Ereshkigal, Inanna and faithful Geshtinanna; there the seven sisters learned the crafts and all the powers; walking through high river reeds and over long mud flats, on stilts, singing the song of the morning star.

They kept moving through Persia; they saw the smoke of the Phoenix on the horizon, a column of smoke in the spinifex or an oil well on fire in Basra; their hearts turned over as they saw Homa the Simurgh, the bird heart of Zoroaster, raising his fiery wings.

Blessing him they passed by, preferring to keep to their own way and their own quiet fire, gathering themselves together.

185

By now, with silver earrings and silver rings around her ankles, Ariadne and the seven sisters sat in silence for seven years and; catching the scent of Rahda and Parvati, stood up and walked into Kashmir with nothing.

They asked directions to Mount Meru;[3]

What do you want, said the taxi-driver, a smile on his face; in his hand, cigarette smoke looping through the window of the black battered taxi. We want Shiva, they said. Shiva's on holiday, he said, but I know where he is. OK said the girls, take us there; and turn on your meter.

Over in the shadow of a hut they saw Parvati, Rahda, Draupadi and Kali, all sitting, rolling bread; rolling the stuff of the universe, rolling flour on a tin plate. Over in the shadow of a tree, the men lying about; Krishna, Arjun, Ram, Shiva and Dioniso playing cards for motor cars. The stakes were high; Ariadne didn't interrupt.

The four women made a place for the travelling women; seven sisters and Ariadne sat down; they rolled bread, they put fingers into each other's mouths, passing on bread and stories, tongue to tongue. Tongue to tongue.

## The meeting with Shiva

She walked into his room; it was 7 o'clock in the morning, he was sitting on an old iron bed, his body was black like polished stone, he did not speak; his hands moved in beautiful gestures; like swallows at a water hole, she thought; he smiled at her.

Ariadne unravelled a thread from Crete to Mount Meru, from her father's door to this, her other father's door, from the labyrinth of Knossos to the ear of Shiva, she unravelled a thread.

What beautiful women, he thought; what wonderful women; what remarkable women who travel the world . . . She spoke to him; she spoke quietly, her head bowed, her memory telling him where she had been, what she had seen; she gathered together everything she had found, everything she had seen. He listened; he held the secret string to her heart in his hand and tugged; a little tug and she came apart in his hand.

He did not move, the trees moved, the wind moved, but he did not move, he waited; he listened and waited till she came together in her new and wondrous form; in her new and wondrous form she stood up, she could feel her feet cool on the stone floor; she saw him sitting there on the old iron bed, his hands like swallows swooping at a rockhole, she thought; how could such an extraordinary being be sitting there like that and so much happen and hardly a moment had passed.

The sisters were sitting with their backs along the stone wall of the little room, half in shadow, watching and waiting till the meeting was over; they began to sing and the seven sisters sang the only song in the world worth singing; the song of the human heart.

## Traditional dances

These gestures recall the map of where the seven sisters travelled; the gathering gesture with the hands like this; the weaving gesture with arms thrown back like this; this; and all the moves of the hand and the moves of the feet are remembered in the circling dances of the seven sisters. Some are marked on the walls of caves, some on the dancing grounds of Crete.

And so the soul of the buried woman is freed; the woman hanging above the bed is released; the woman locked in the cave is freed; the woman whose tongue was cut begins to speak; the one whose children were taken away; she finds what is lost.

The women whose hearts are split find strings to string across the split. The seven sisters sing something that makes sense to all the women, at last. Spinning the thread of women unravelling; from the blue steps of Knossos to the lime-washed steps of Kali, Rahda, Sita, Parvati, Draupadi . . . unrolling meetings with remarkable women.

What is the point of all this travelling?

The point of all this is simple, the point of all this is that, after you travel so far with women like this you can take anything anyone throws at you and you don't go up in flames. Ariadne and her seven sisters went travelling; they went and they created themselves; they found what lies beneath, they found what lies above; they learned to hold their liquor; they saw themselves in the face, they did not go up in flames; they went away; they came home; they came back with presents for all their friends.

This is the story of travelling Ariadne. End.

## Dedication

To the many remarkable women who helped compose and enact the *Sugarman/ Dionysos* performances at Intjartnama and Alice Springs 1996–99 – and to Francis Brabazon.

# Notes

1 "Travelling Ariadne" is an extract from the performance text of the *Travels of Dionysos*, the third part of the *Sugarman* events, presented over six weeks in 1997, at the Araluen Cultural Centre, in Alice Springs, Australia. The *Travels of Dionysos* are based on legends, referred to specifically in the opening scene of Euripides' *Bacchae* (and elsewhere), suggesting that Dionysos travelled east to India and returned to Thebes, his birthplace of tragedy, and there in his hometown, declared his divinity (whatever that may actually mean). In my version, the Dionysos and Ariadne journeys are figured as a reintegrative romance and a cultural linking road-story. This extract begins on Naxos after Ariadne's abandonment by Theseus and ends at the mythical Mt. Meru (aka Mt. Kailash), seat of Shiva/Parvati.

On Naxos, Dionysos comes to Ariadne. This, as I construct it, is at the end of Dionysos' season of derangement. Ariadne maps out a "honeymoon" of divine "family visits" and a voyage of recollection for the previously dismembered Dionysos. After the legendary wedding, Dionysos and Ariadne, in this version, travel south and east, sometimes together, sometimes separately. And according to poetic license, Dionysos, Ariadne, and the Seven Sisters visit, in mythic time, their ancestral siblings – Isis, Osiris, Inanna, Mary of Nazareth, her son, the Phoenix, Zoroastrian Ahura Mazda, the Persian Simurgh – each meeting a step back along the treks of Avataric time, each a re-memberment of a deranged god, until, as according to some legends (collected by Alain Daniélou), they arrive at a place where Shiva has his seat. A meeting takes place. In this version, Ariadne meets Shiva in simple humanized form sitting on an old iron bed in a hut. She gets there by taxi. This reflects a true account from my own experience at Meherabad, Maharashtra, India. The mode of "Travelling Ariadne" differs from the crudeness of the "Creation Story." The mood is that of a Romance, a *Nostalgie*. Alain Daniélou, *Gods of Love and Ecstasy: The Traditions of Shiva and Dionysus*, Vermont, Inner Traditions, 1992. (The original was published in French by Libraire Fayard in 1979.)

2 Sappho, *Ribaldry of Greece*, ed. and trans. Jack Lindsay, London, Bestseller Library, Paul Elek Ltd, 1961, p. 19.

3 Mount Kailash – mount of everlasting destruction, the seat of Shiva and Parvati. Meru is also known as Mount Kailash.

# INDEX

# eBooks
## from Taylor & Francis
Helping you to choose the right eBooks for your Library

Add to your library's digital collection today with Taylor & Francis eBooks. We have over 50,000 eBooks in the Humanities, Social Sciences, Behavioural Sciences, Built Environment and Law, from leading imprints, including Routledge, Focal Press and Psychology Press.

**Choose from a range of subject packages or create your own!**

**Benefits for you**
- Free MARC records
- COUNTER-compliant usage statistics
- Flexible purchase and pricing options
- All titles DRM-free.

**Benefits for your user**
- Off-site, anytime access via Athens or referring URL
- Print or copy pages or chapters
- Full content search
- Bookmark, highlight and annotate text
- Access to thousands of pages of quality research at the click of a button.

**Free Trials Available**
We offer free trials to qualifying academic, corporate and government customers.

# eCollections
Choose from over 30 subject eCollections, including:

| | |
|---|---|
| Archaeology | Language Learning |
| Architecture | Law |
| Asian Studies | Literature |
| Business & Management | Media & Communication |
| Classical Studies | Middle East Studies |
| Construction | Music |
| Creative & Media Arts | Philosophy |
| Criminology & Criminal Justice | Planning |
| Economics | Politics |
| Education | Psychology & Mental Health |
| Energy | Religion |
| Engineering | Security |
| English Language & Linguistics | Social Work |
| Environment & Sustainability | Sociology |
| Geography | Sport |
| Health Studies | Theatre & Performance |
| History | Tourism, Hospitality & Events |

For more information, pricing enquiries or to order a free trial, please contact your local sales team: www.tandfebooks.com/page/sales

**www.tandfebooks.com**